STEPHEN KING
THE STAND

American Nightmares

THE STAND: AMERICAN NIGHTMARES. Contains material originally published in magazine form as THE STAND: AMERICAN NIGHTMARES #1-5. First printing 2009. ISBN# 978-0-7851-3621-7. Published by MARVEL PUBLISHING, INC., a subsidiary of MARVEL ENTERTAINMENT, INC. OFFICE OF PUBLICATION: 417 5th Avenue, New York, NY 10016. © 2009 Stephen King. All rights reserved. $24.99 per copy in the U.S. (GST #R127032852); Canadian Agreement #40668537. All characters featured in this publication and the distinctive names and likenesses thereof, and all related indicia are trademarks of Stephen King. Published by arrangement with The Doubleday Broadway Publishing Group, a division of Random House, Inc. This publication is produced under license from The Doubleday Broadway Publishing Group and Stephen King. No similarity between any of the names, characters, persons, and/or institutions in this book with those of any living or dead person or institution is intended, and any such similarity which may exist is purely coincidental. **Printed in the U.S.A.** ALAN FINE, EVP - Office Of The Chief Executive Marvel Entertainment, Inc. & CMO Marvel Characters B.V.; DAN BUCKLEY, Chief Executive Officer and Publisher - Print, Animation & Digital Media; JIM SOKOLOWSKI, Chief Operating Officer; DAVID GABRIEL, SVP of Publishing Sales & Circulation; DAVID BOGART, SVP of Business Affairs & Talent Management; MICHAEL PASCIULLO, VP Merchandising & Communications; JIM O'KEEFE, VP of Operations & Logistics; DAN CARR, Executive Director of Publishing Technology; JUSTIN F. GABRIE, Director of Publishing & Editorial Operations; SUSAN CRESPI, Editorial Operations Manager; ALEX MORALES, Publishing Operations Manager; STAN LEE, Chairman Emeritus. For information regarding advertising in Marvel Comics or on Marvel.com, please contact Mitch Dane, Advertising Director, at mdane@marvel.com. For Marvel subscription inquiries, please call 800-217-9158. **Manufactured between 9/28/09 and 10/28/09 by WORLD COLOR PRESS INC., VERSAILLES, KY, USA.**

10 9 8 7 6 5 4 3 2 1

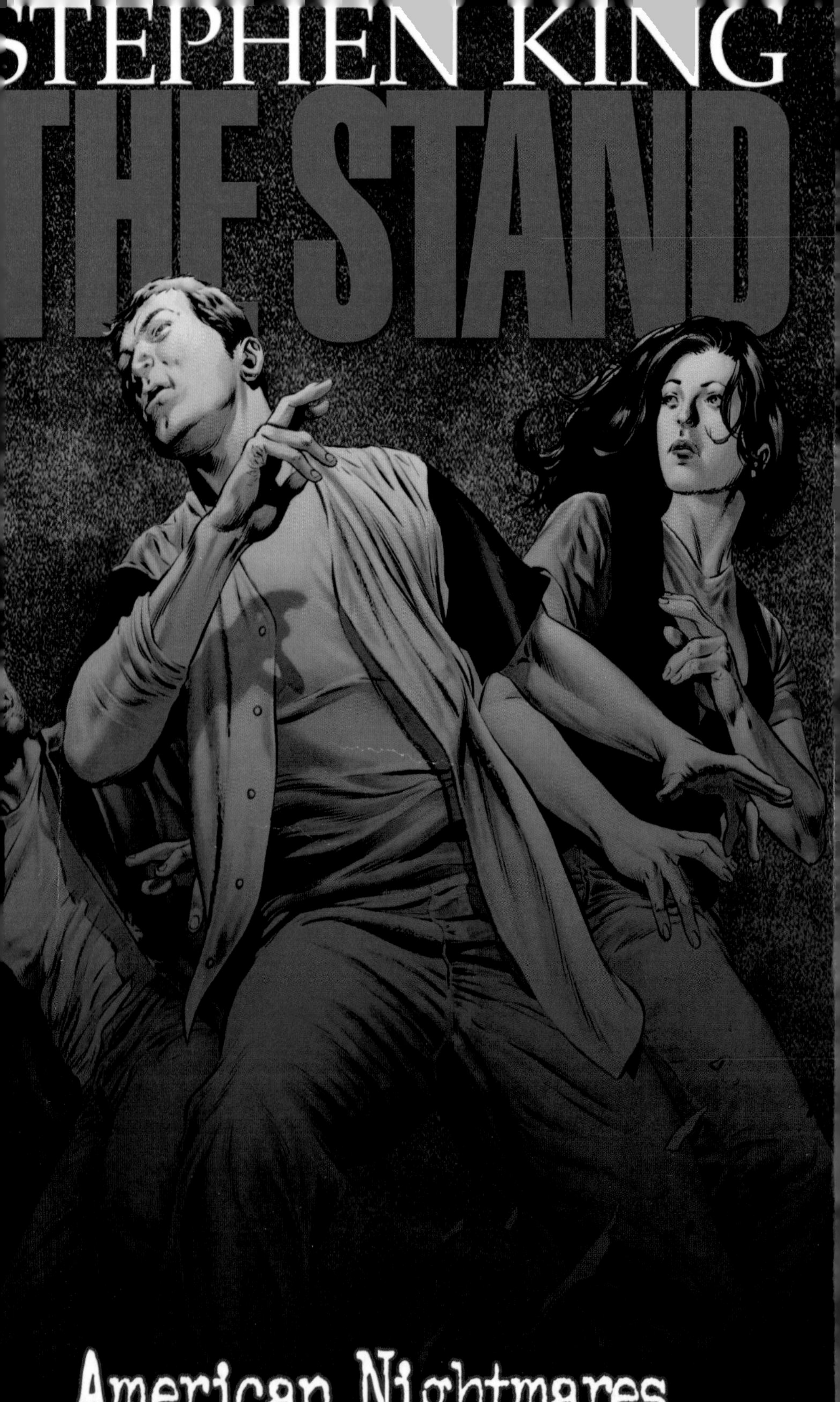
STEPHEN KING
THE STAND
American Nightmares

Creative Director and Executive Director:
STEPHEN KING

Script:
ROBERTO AGUIRRE-SACASA

Art:
MIKE PERKINS

Color Art:
LAURA MARTIN

Lettering:
VC'S RUS WOOTON

Assistant Editor:
MICHAEL HORWITZ

Associate Editor:
NATHAN COSBY

Consulting Editor:
BILL ROSEMANN

Senior Editor:
RALPH MACCHIO

Front Cover Art:
MIKE PERKINS & LAURA MARTIN

Back Cover Art:
LEE BERMEJO & LAURA MARTIN

Collection Editor: **MARK D. BEAZLEY**

Assistant Editors: **JOHN DENNING & ALEX STARBUCK**

Editor, Special Projects: **JENNIFER GRÜNWALD**

Senior Editor, Special Projects: **JEFF YOUNGQUIST**

Senior Vice President of Publishing Sales: **DAVID GABRIEL**

Senior Vice President of Strategic Development: **RUWAN JAYATILLEKE**

Book Designer: **SPRING HOTELING**

Editor in Chief: **JOE QUESADA**

Publisher: **DAN BUCKLEY**

Special Thanks to
Chuck Verrill, Marsha DeFilippo, , Brian Stark, Jim Nausedas,
Jim McCann, Arune Singh, Chris Allo, Lauren Sankovitch & Jeff Suter

For more information on THE STAND comics, visit marvel.com/comics/the_stand

To find Marvel Comics at a local comic shop, call 1-888-COMICBOOK

INTRODUCTION

As we see to our horror in AMERICAN NIGHTMARES, the effects of the superflu, Captain Trips, have devastated mankind. Only small pockets of humanity remain as our continued existence hangs by a thread. What could be more depressing than the contemplation of not just our personal demise, but the extinction of all that we have built—of civilization itself?

Throughout this graphic novelization, we're exploring the lives of those fortunate (unfortunate?) enough to have survived. Stephen King's incredible grasp of characterization has never been more in evidence as when he zeroes in on our protagonists, including Stu Redman, Rita Blakemoor, Nick Andros, Larry Underwood and Frannie Goldsmith. These are individuals struggling to deal with an unprecedented status quo change and King makes their struggles achingly real. Through various means—humor, denial, blind acceptance or hope, they each try to cling to something that will give them the strength to continue living. And in their survival trials we see our own daily tribulations writ large.

However, what if there was a character introduced who welcomed Armageddon, who actually reveled in the near total chaos the world had become? No, I'm not referring to the Walkin' Dude, Randall Flagg. Rather, I'm speaking of Donald Merwin Elbert, known since grade school as the Trashcan Man. I've had few discussions of The Stand wherein Elbert's name came up and the grins didn't become infectious. What I think we secretly admire about this guy is that he has used the collapse of society to unleash the darkest part of himself, the pyromaniac, and give full vent to his twisted urges.

And he's having a great time doing it! Young Donald started setting fires in people's trashcans in the fourth grade and never quit. Now, there's a whole unguarded world out there full of oil refineries and gas tanks just waiting to go up in an endless blaze of glory! There are fires to be set that will blacken whole forests and prairies, burning out of control for weeks on end. Trashcan Man has his life's work before him and conditions couldn't be more ideal for its completion. While the tatters of humanity are wandering around in shock, wondering if they'll see another day, Trashy has unswerving purpose in his eyes as he sets fire to all those things that rightly need burning in this brave new world. He knows what he's about and what he's got to do. And brother, he loves his job! Within these pages, Roberto Aquirre Sacasa, Mike Perkins and Laura Martin bring him to stunning visual life. He's a King creation you'll never forget.

So, next time you ponder the end of civilization and feel depressed, remember the lesson of Trashcan Man: Even the apocalypse can be a blast. It's all in how you perceive it. Burn, baby, burn!

Ralph Macchio
September 2009

PREVIOUSLY

Someone at the Project Blue government facility in the Californian desert made a mistake. And now, the deadly flu-like virus "Captain Trips," which has a mortality rate in excess of 99 percent, has decimated most of the country's population.

The thus-far-uninfected are tasked with surviving in a world they no longer understand... Among the living:

Nick Andros, the newly-crowned, deaf-mute deputy of Shoyo, Arkansas, who guards a jail full of dying criminals—the same men who once beat him to a pump...

Larry Underwood, who fled L.A. for the safety of his mother's arms in New York City—and then had to comfort her as she succumbed to the flu ravaging her frail body...

Frannie Goldsmith, whose unexpected pregnancy drove a deeper wedge between her and her estranged mother Carla—before Captain Trips claimed the lives of Carla and Frannie's beloved father, Peter...

And Stuart Redman, who has spent the last few weeks locked in a cell in the CDC, dreaming of escape—and of a faceless boogeyman who seems to be growing more and more powerful...

Welcome to the End of the World!

chapter ONE

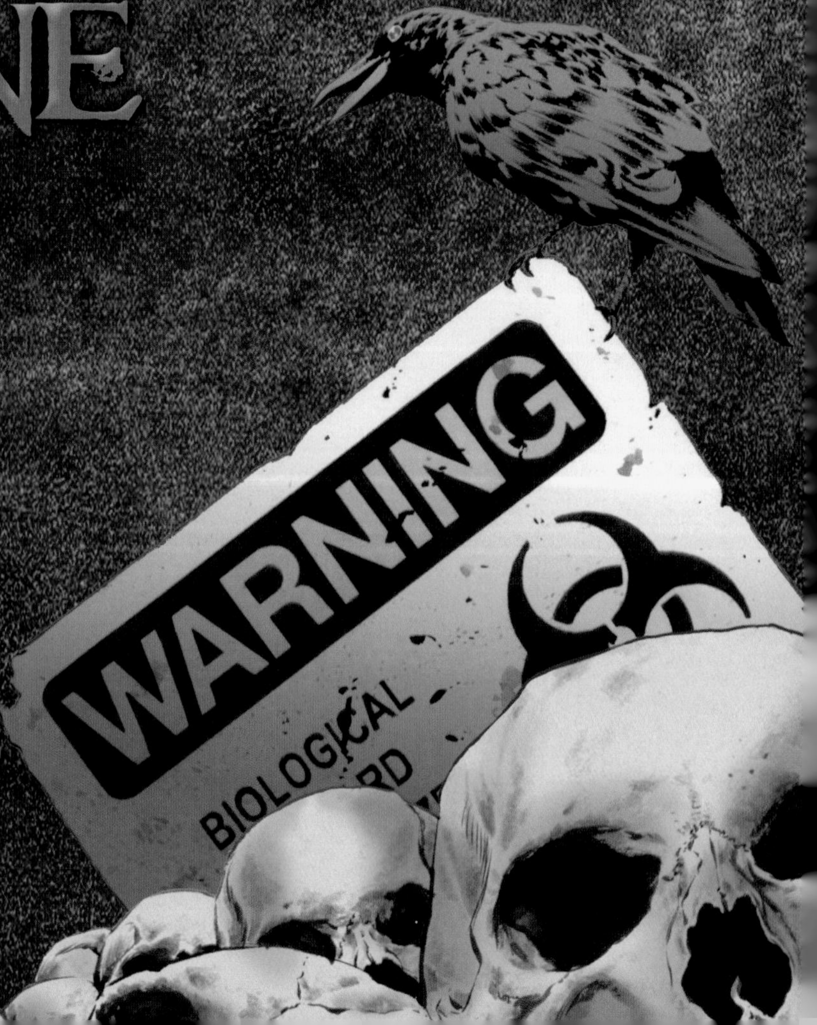
WARNING
BIOLOGICAL

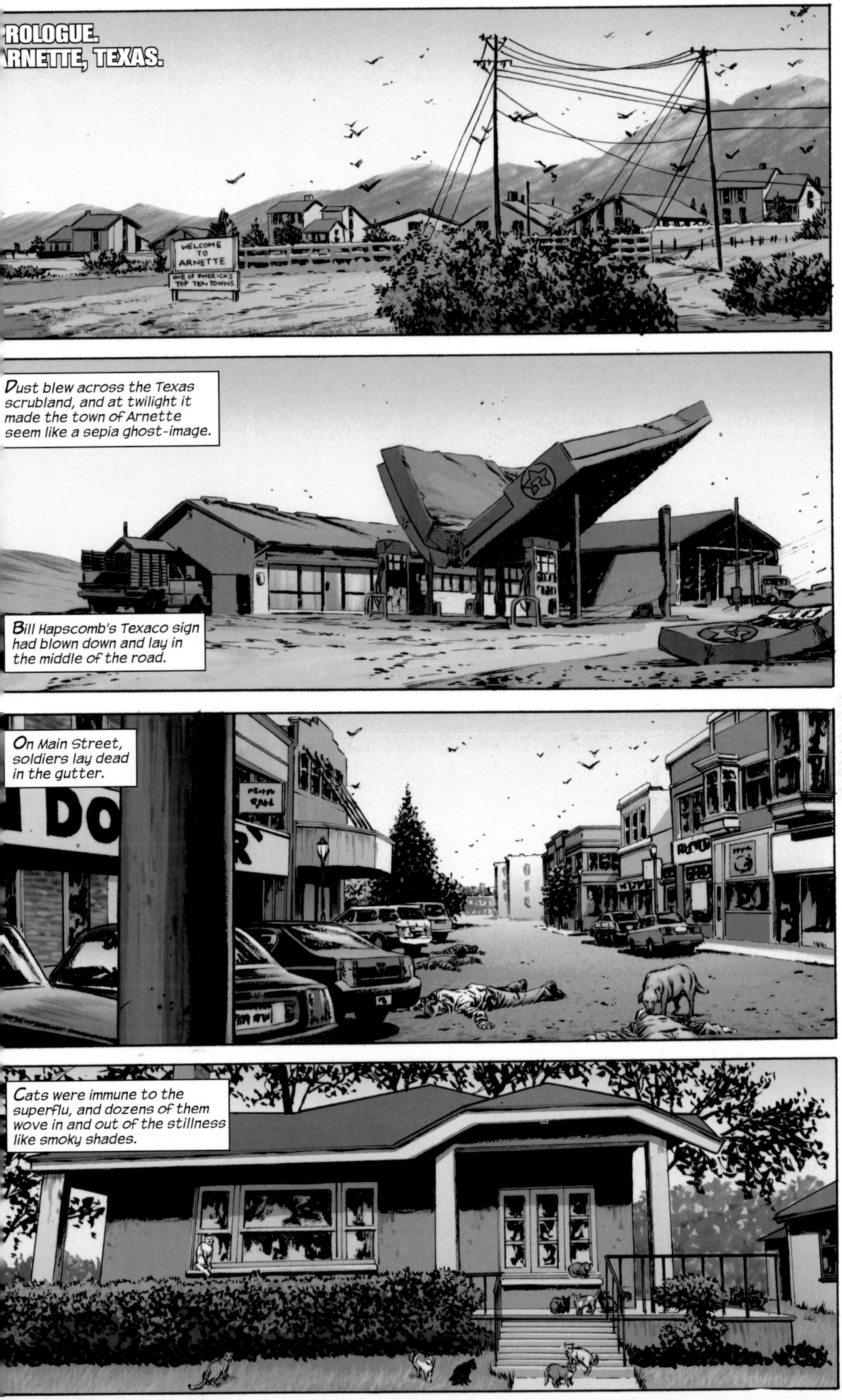
ROLOGUE.
RNETTE, TEXAS.
WELCOME TO ARNETTE
ONE OF AMERICA'S TOP TEN TOWNS
Dust blew across the Texas scrubland, and at twilight it made the town of Arnette seem like a sepia ghost-image.
Bill Hapscomb's Texaco sign had blown down and lay in the middle of the road.
On Main Street, soldiers lay dead in the gutter.
Cats were immune to the superflu, and dozens of them wove in and out of the stillness like smoky shades.

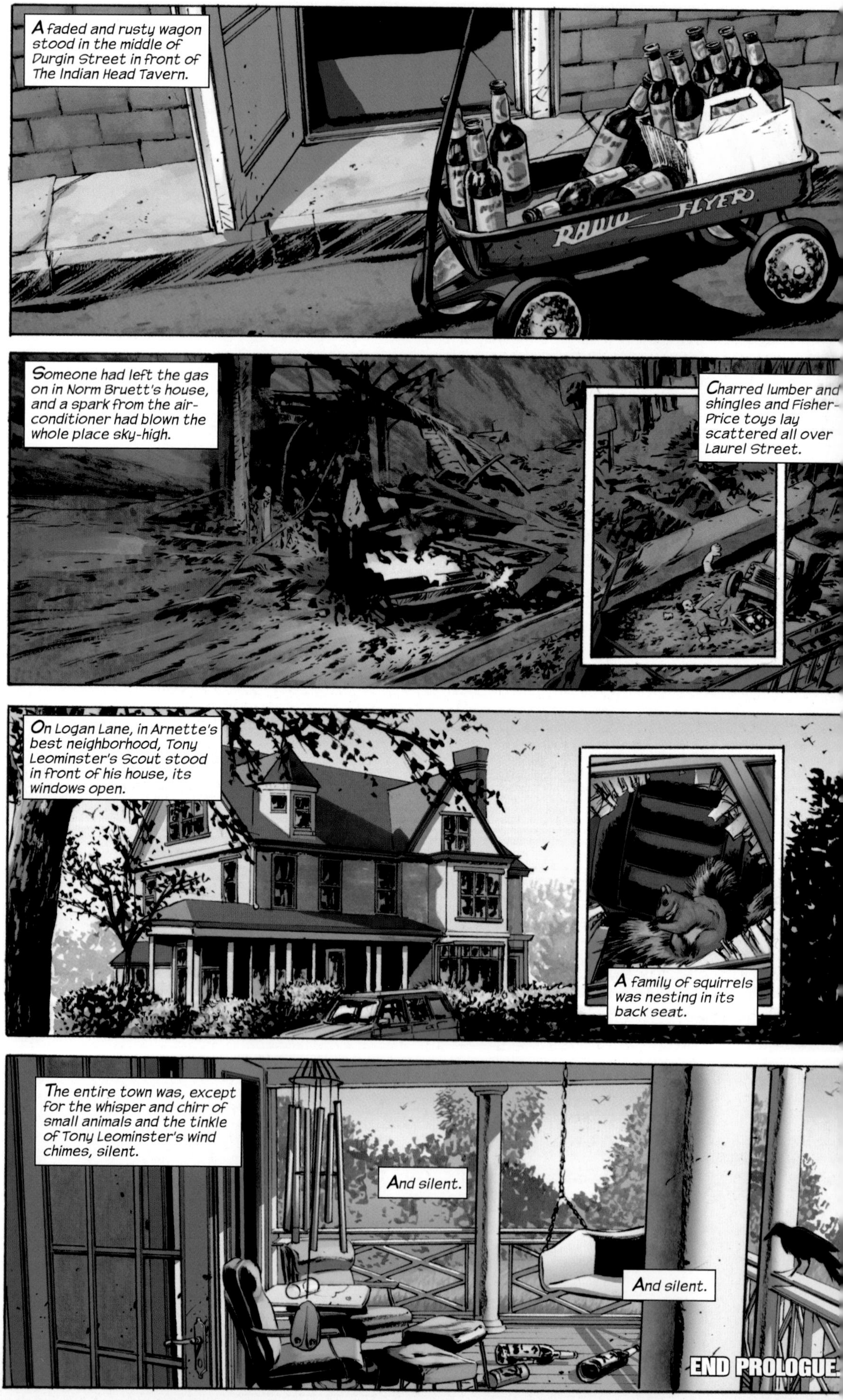

A faded and rusty wagon stood in the middle of Durgin Street in front of The Indian Head Tavern.
RADIO FLYER
Someone had left the gas on in Norm Bruett's house, and a spark from the air-conditioner had blown the whole place sky-high.
Charred lumber and shingles and Fisher-Price toys lay scattered all over Laurel Street.
On Logan Lane, in Arnette's best neighborhood, Tony Leominster's Scout stood in front of his house, its windows open.
A family of squirrels was nesting in its back seat.
The entire town was, except for the whisper and chirr of small animals and the tinkle of Tony Leominster's wind chimes, silent.
And silent.
And silent.
END PROLOGUE.

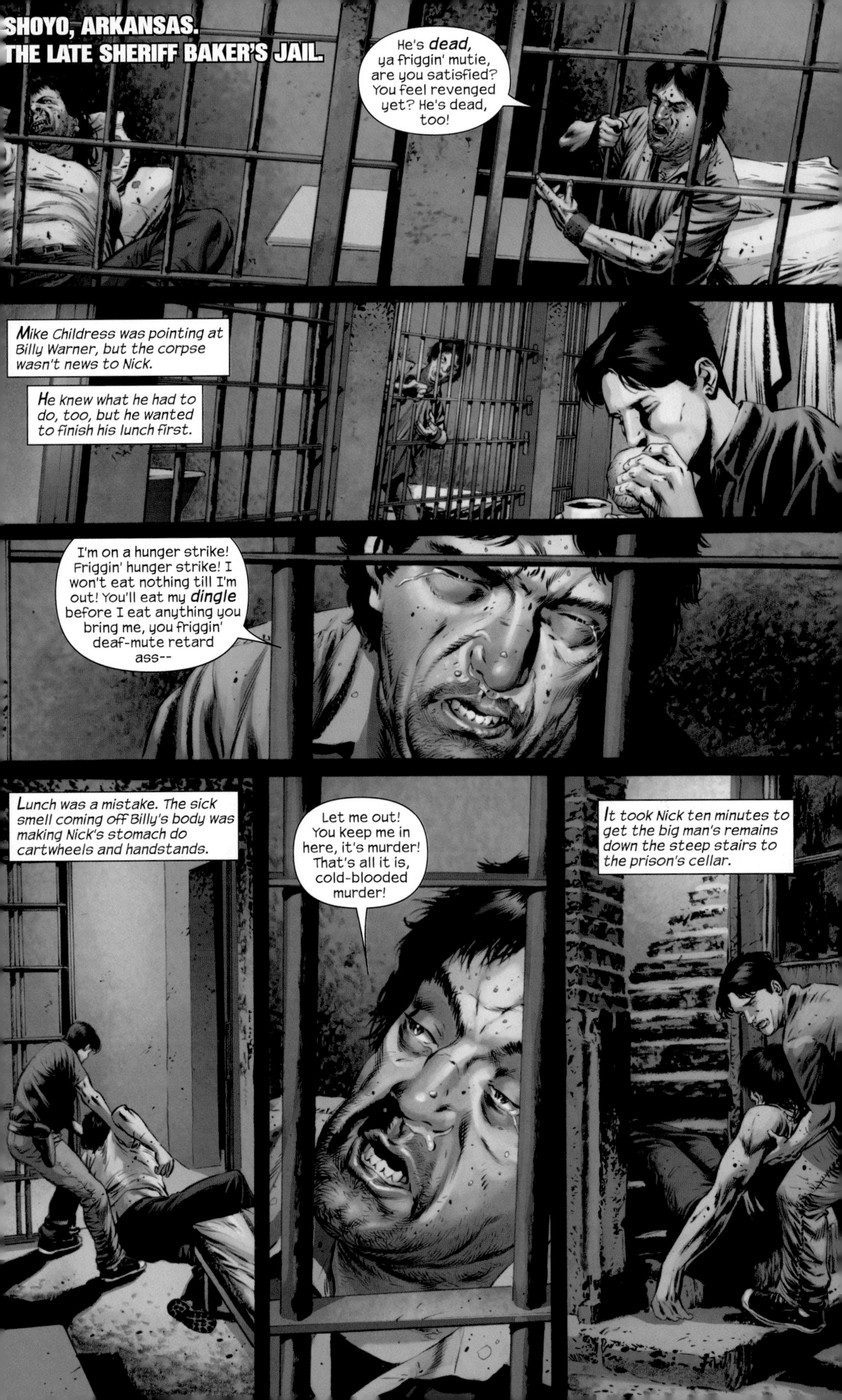
SHOYO, ARKANSAS.
THE LATE SHERIFF BAKER'S JAIL.
He's dead, ya friggin' mutie, are you satisfied? You feel revenged yet? He's dead, too!
Mike Childress was pointing at Billy Warner, but the corpse wasn't news to Nick.
He knew what he had to do, too, but he wanted to finish his lunch first.
I'm on a hunger strike! Friggin' hunger strike! I won't eat nothing till I'm out! You'll eat my dingle before I eat anything you bring me, you friggin' deaf-mute retard ass--
Lunch was a mistake. The sick smell coming off Billy's body was making Nick's stomach do cartwheels and handstands.
Let me out! You keep me in here, it's murder! That's all it is, cold-blooded murder!
It took Nick ten minutes to get the big man's remains down the steep stairs to the prison's cellar.

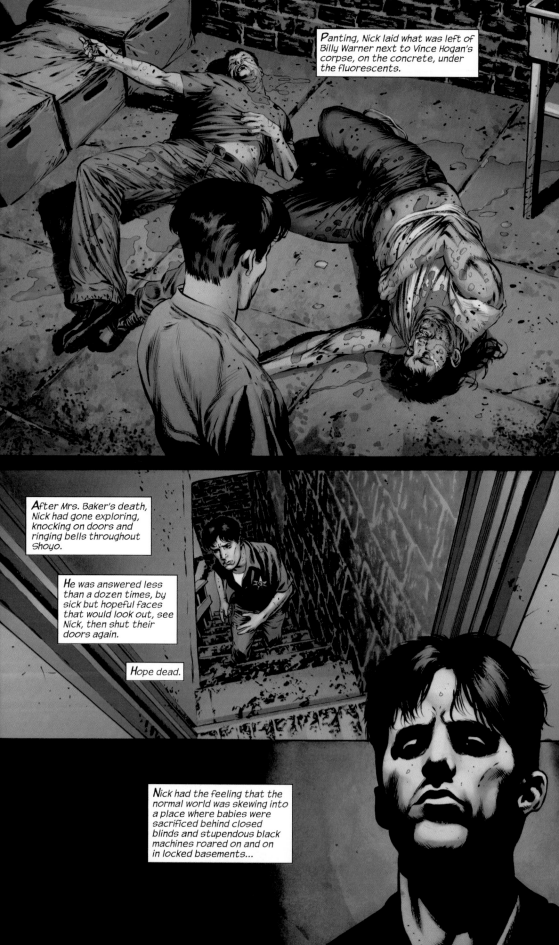

Panting, Nick laid what was left of Billy Warner next to Vince Hogan's corpse, on the concrete, under the fluorescents.

After Mrs. Baker's death, Nick had gone exploring, knocking on doors and ringing bells throughout Shoyo.

He was answered less than a dozen times, by sick but hopeful faces that would look out, see Nick, then shut their doors again.

Hope dead.

Nick had the feeling that the normal world was skewing into a place where babies were sacrificed behind closed blinds and stupendous black machines roared on and on in locked basements...

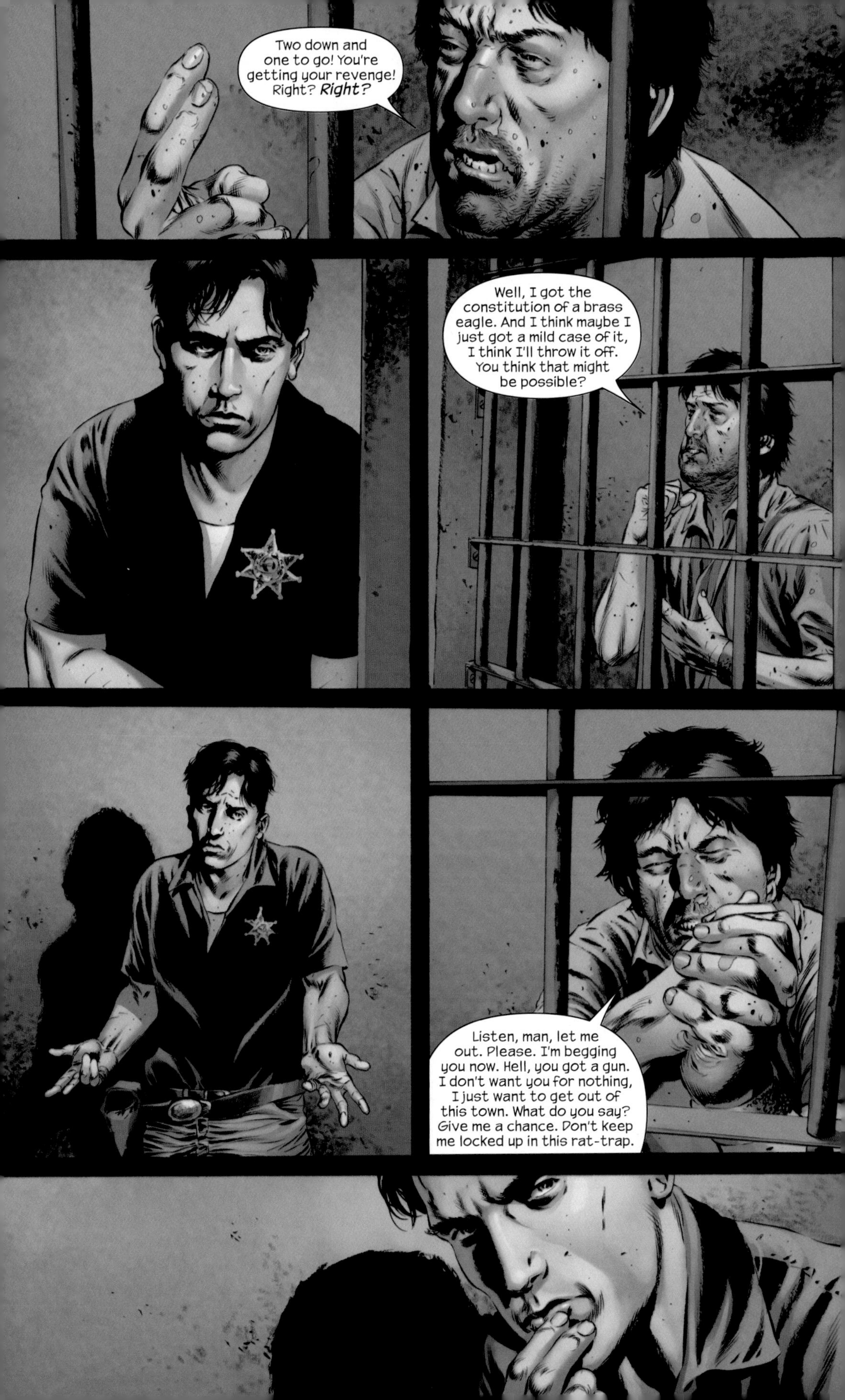

Two down and one to go! You're getting your revenge! Right? *Right?*
Well, I got the constitution of a brass eagle. And I think maybe I just got a mild case of it, I think I'll throw it off. You think that might be possible?
Listen, man, let me out. Please. I'm begging you now. Hell, you got a gun. I don't want you for nothing, I just want to get out of this town. What do you say? Give me a chance. Don't keep me locked up in this rat-trap.

My God...

All this? *All this?*

I'm sorry we beat up on you, it was Ray's idea, me and Vince tried to stop him but he gets drinkin' and he gets crazy and--

≈cough≈

≈cough≈

I'm getting the hell out of here. You're wise, you'll do the same thing, mutie. This is like the black death or something.

Nick Andros never saw Mike Childress again...

...but his heart felt lighter immediately, having freed the sick man, and that night, he would lie down on his cot and fall asleep almost at once.

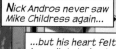

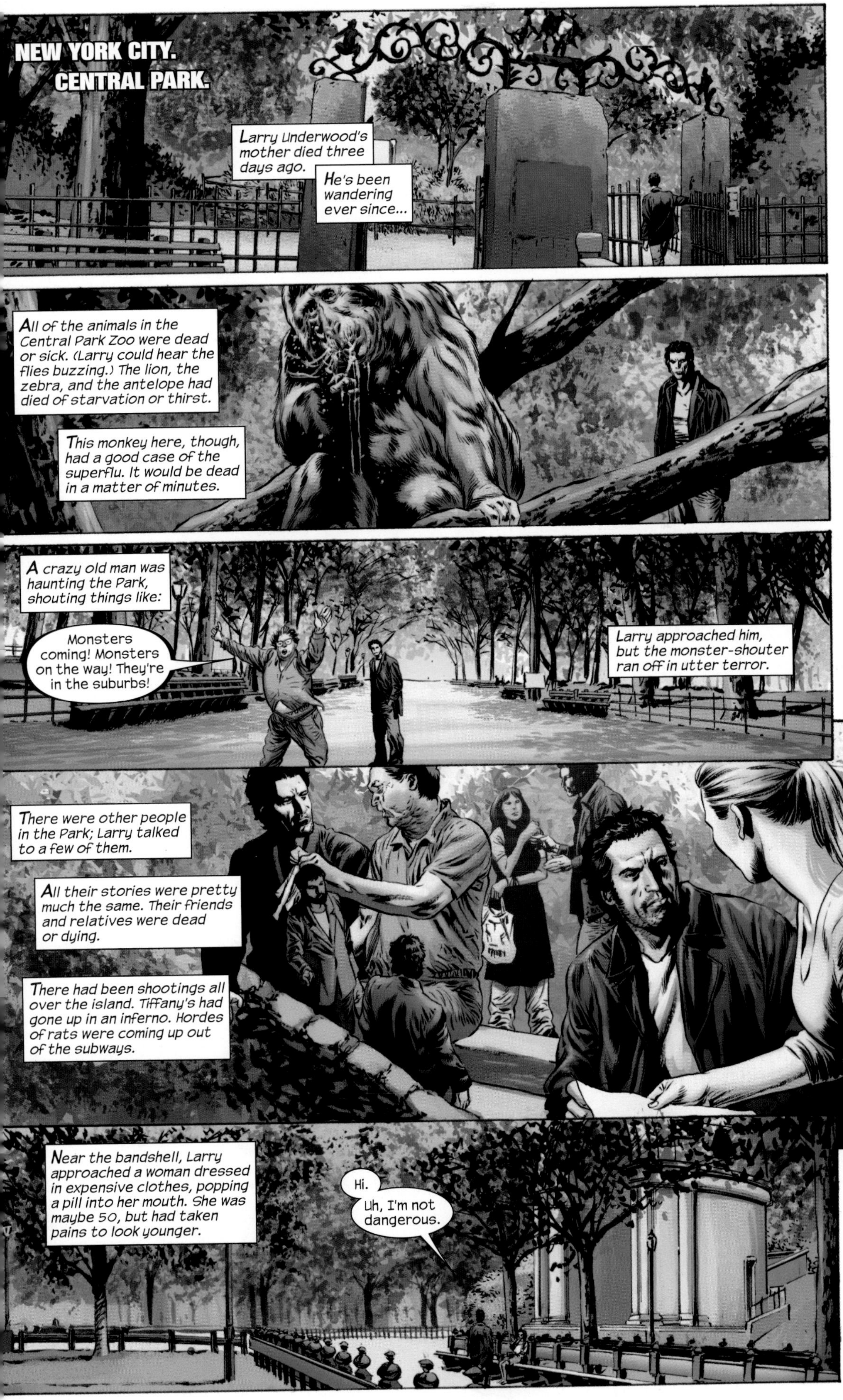
NEW YORK CITY.
CENTRAL PARK.
Larry Underwood's mother died three days ago.
He's been wandering ever since...
All of the animals in the Central Park Zoo were dead or sick. (Larry could hear the flies buzzing.) The lion, the zebra, and the antelope had died of starvation or thirst.
This monkey here, though, had a good case of the superflu. It would be dead in a matter of minutes.
A crazy old man was haunting the Park, shouting things like:
Monsters coming! Monsters on the way! They're in the suburbs!
Larry approached him, but the monster-shouter ran off in utter terror.
There were other people in the Park; Larry talked to a few of them.
All their stories were pretty much the same. Their friends and relatives were dead or dying.
There had been shootings all over the island. Tiffany's had gone up in an inferno. Hordes of rats were coming up out of the subways.
Near the bandshell, Larry approached a woman dressed in expensive clothes, popping a pill into her mouth. She was maybe 50, but had taken pains to look younger.
Hi.
Uh, I'm not dangerous.

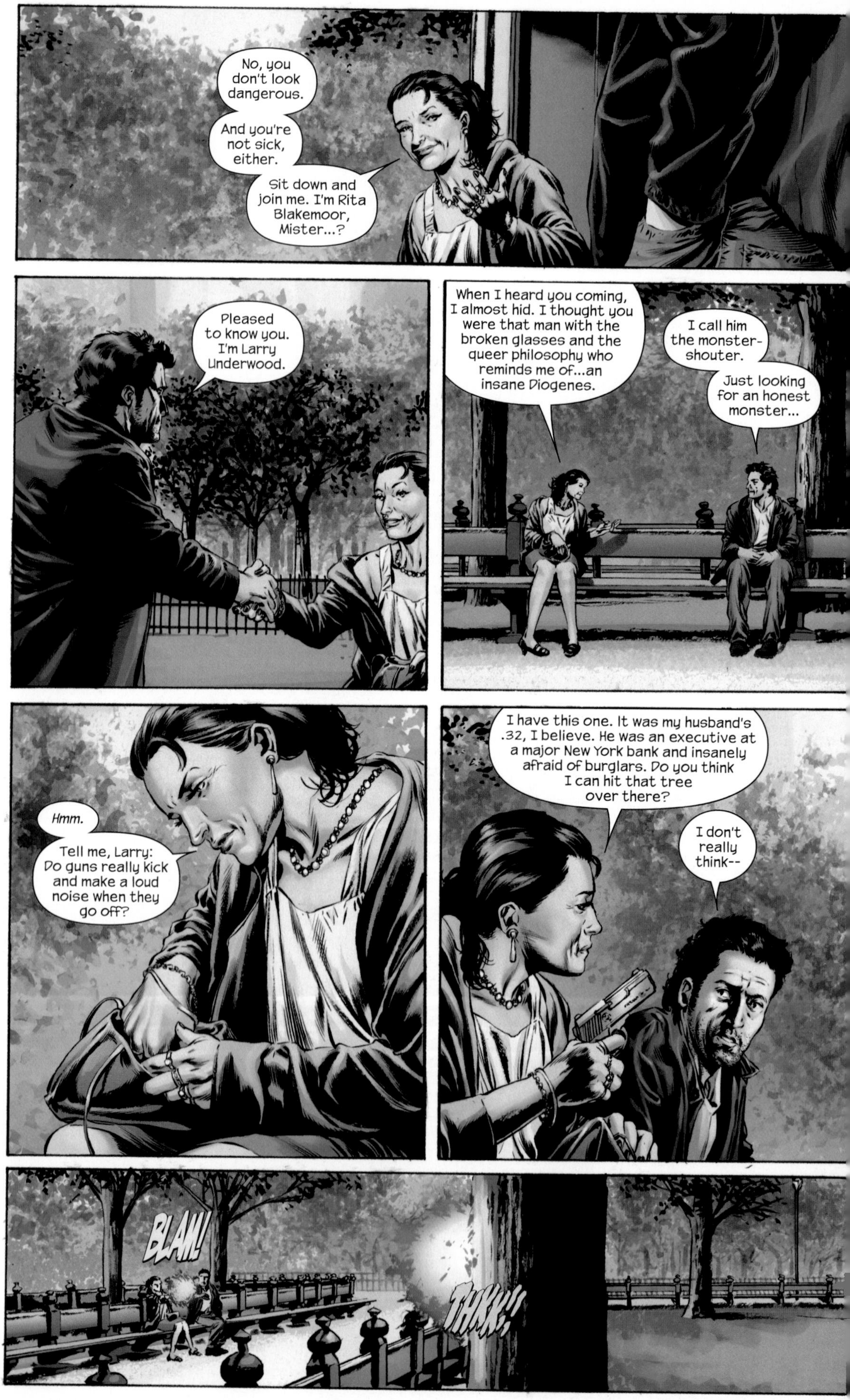
No, you don't look dangerous.
And you're not sick, either.
Sit down and join me. I'm Rita Blakemoor, Mister...?
Pleased to know you. I'm Larry Underwood.
When I heard you coming, I almost hid. I thought you were that man with the broken glasses and the queer philosophy who reminds me of...an insane Diogenes.
I call him the monster-shouter.
Just looking for an honest monster...
Hmm.
Tell me, Larry: Do guns really kick and make a loud noise when they go off?
I have this one. It was my husband's .32, I believe. He was an executive at a major New York bank and insanely afraid of burglars. Do you think I can hit that tree over there?
I don't really think--
BLAM!
THKK!!

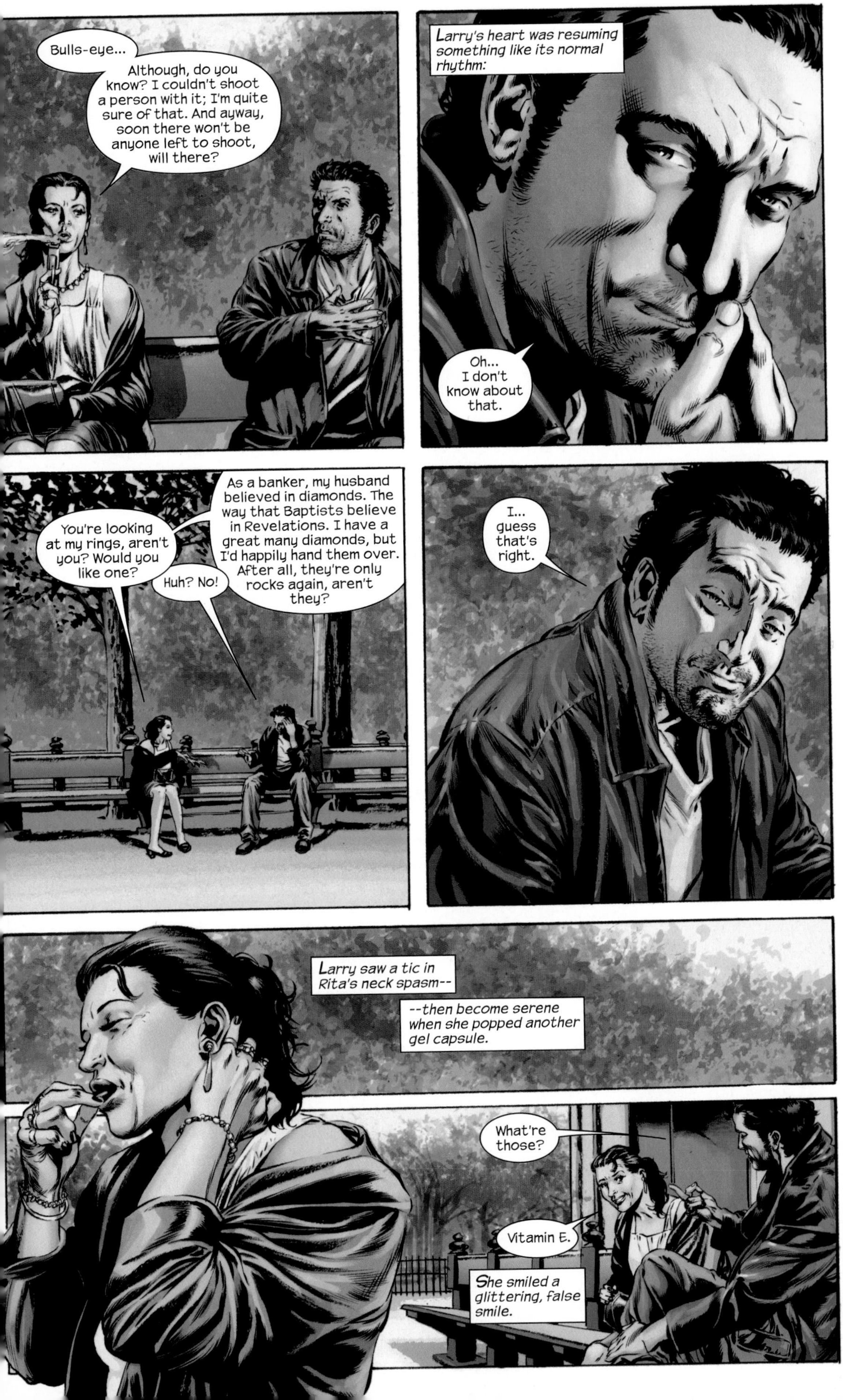
Bulls-eye...
Although, do you know? I couldn't shoot a person with it; I'm quite sure of that. And ayway, soon there won't be anyone left to shoot, will there?
Larry's heart was resuming something like its normal rhythm:
Oh... I don't know about that.
You're looking at my rings, aren't you? Would you like one?
Huh? No!
As a banker, my husband believed in diamonds. The way that Baptists believe in Revelations. I have a great many diamonds, but I'd happily hand them over. After all, they're only rocks again, aren't they?
I... guess that's right.
Larry saw a tic in Rita's neck spasm--
--then become serene when she popped another gel capsule.
What're those?
Vitamin E.
She smiled a glittering, false smile.

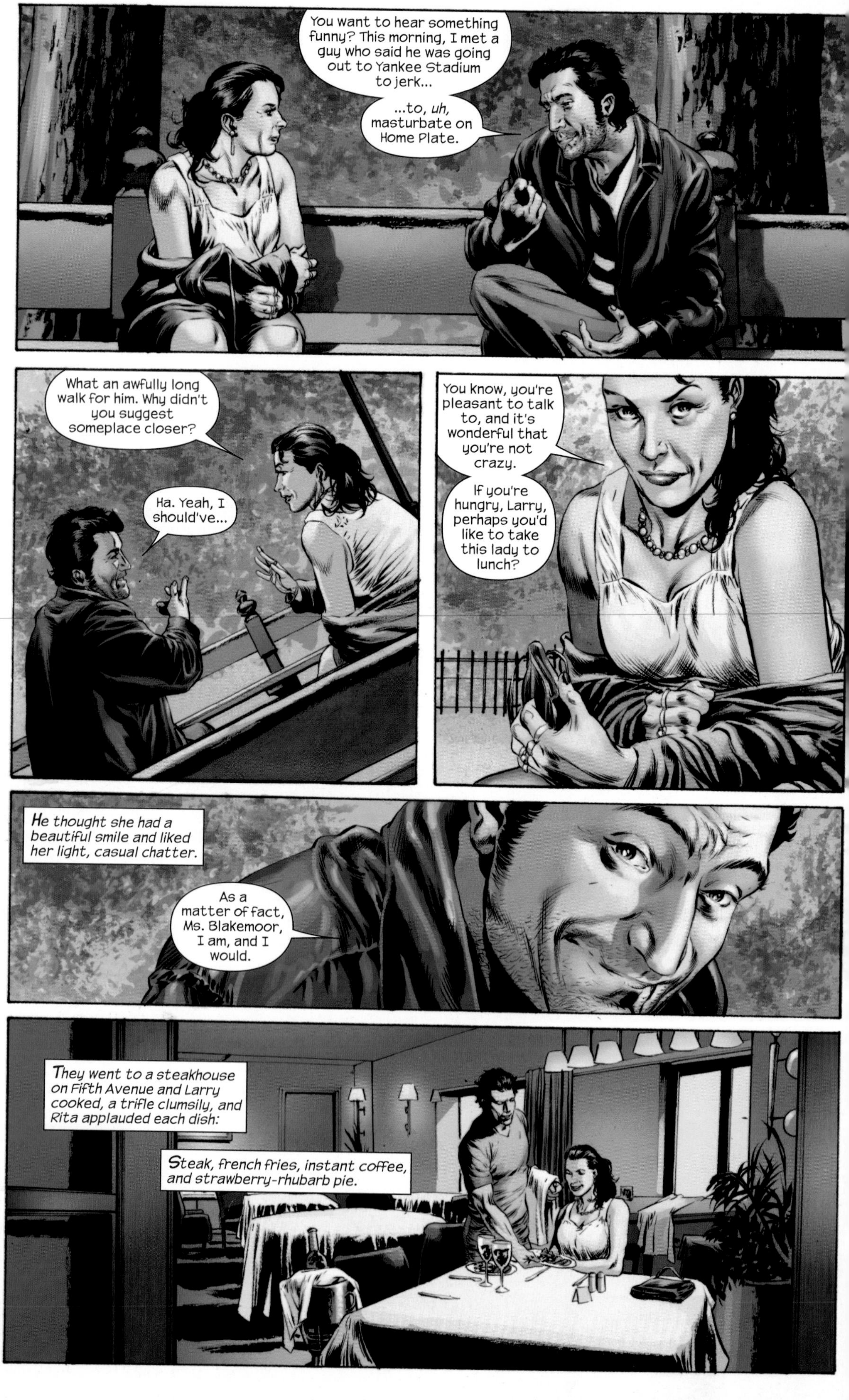
You want to hear something funny? This morning, I met a guy who said he was going out to Yankee Stadium to jerk...
...to, *uh*, masturbate on Home Plate.
What an awfully long walk for him. Why didn't you suggest someplace closer?
Ha. Yeah, I should've...
You know, you're pleasant to talk to, and it's wonderful that you're not crazy.
If you're hungry, Larry, perhaps you'd like to take this lady to lunch?
He thought she had a beautiful smile and liked her light, casual chatter.
As a matter of fact, Ms. Blakemoor, I am, and I would.
They went to a steakhouse on Fifth Avenue and Larry cooked, a trifle clumsily, and Rita applauded each dish:
Steak, french fries, instant coffee, and strawberry-rhubarb pie.

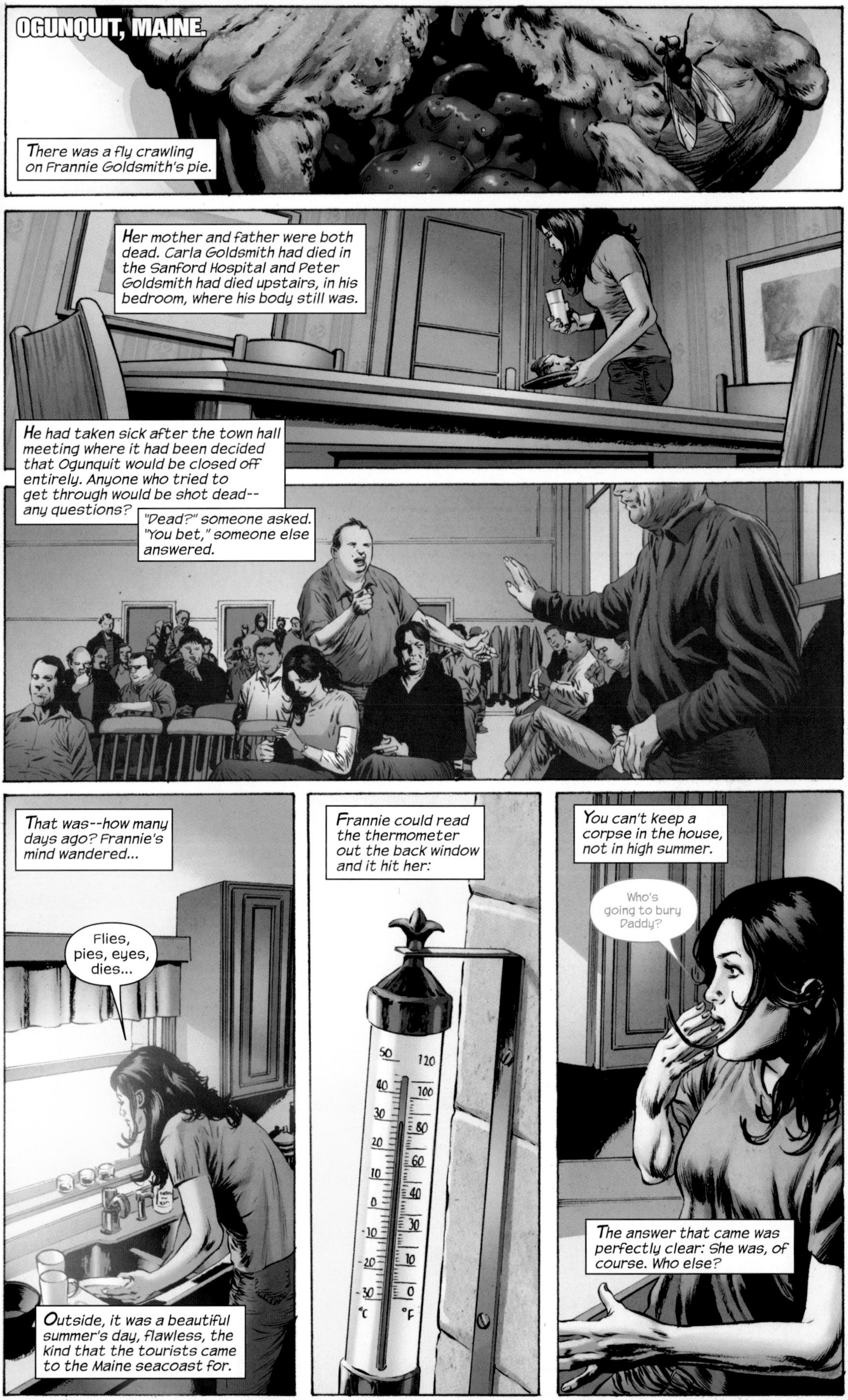

OGUNQUIT, MAINE.
There was a fly crawling on Frannie Goldsmith's pie.
Her mother and father were both dead. Carla Goldsmith had died in the Sanford Hospital and Peter Goldsmith had died upstairs, in his bedroom, where his body still was.
He had taken sick after the town hall meeting where it had been decided that Ogunquit would be closed off entirely. Anyone who tried to get through would be shot dead--any questions?
"Dead?" someone asked. "You bet," someone else answered.
That was--how many days ago? Frannie's mind wandered...
Flies, pies, eyes, dies...
Outside, it was a beautiful summer's day, flawless, the kind that the tourists came to the Maine seacoast for.
Frannie could read the thermometer out the back window and it hit her:
You can't keep a corpse in the house, not in high summer.
Who's going to bury Daddy?
The answer that came was perfectly clear: She was, of course. Who else?

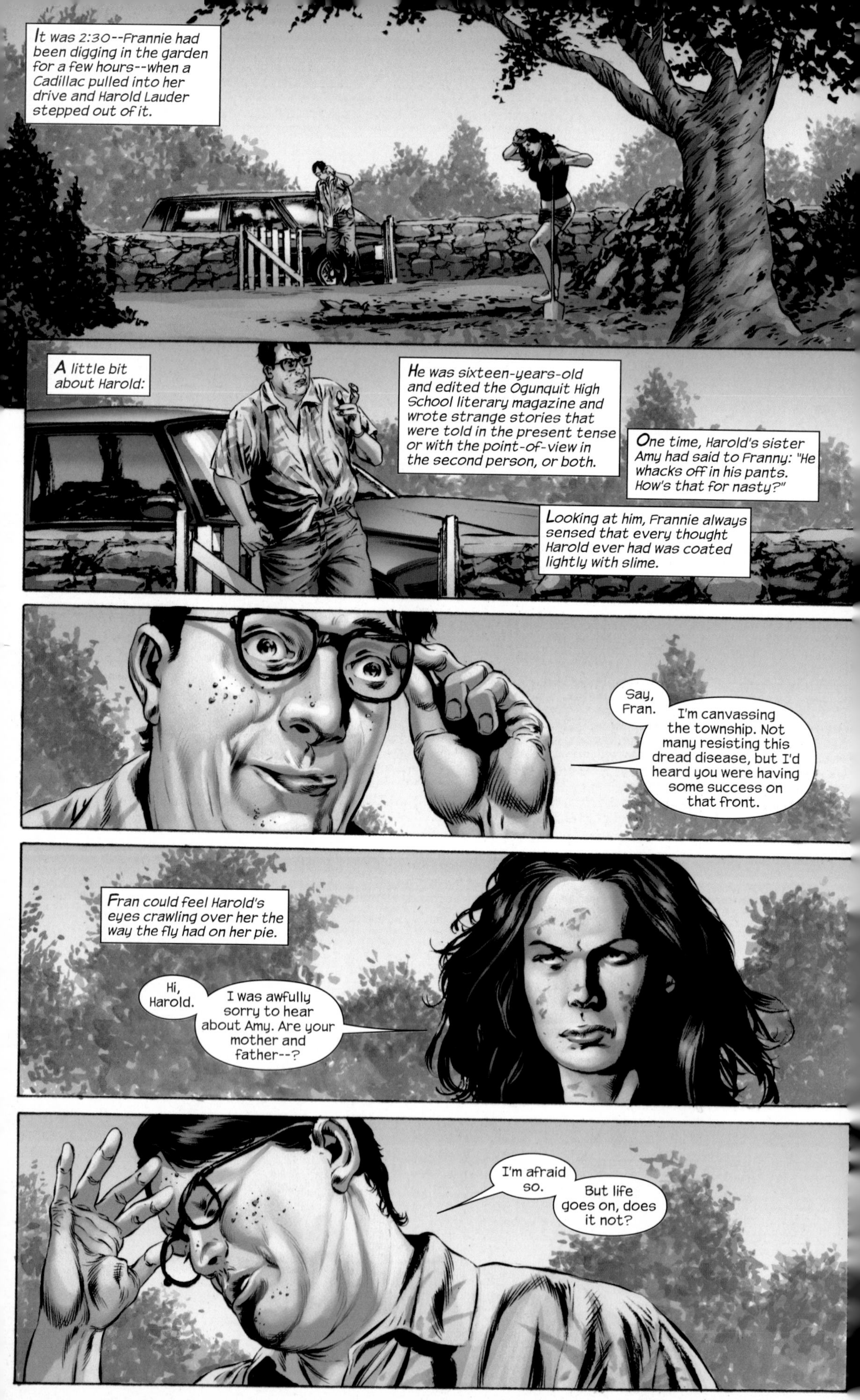
It was 2:30--Frannie had been digging in the garden for a few hours--when a Cadillac pulled into her drive and Harold Lauder stepped out of it.
A little bit about Harold:
He was sixteen-years-old and edited the Ogunquit High School literary magazine and wrote strange stories that were told in the present tense or with the point-of-view in the second person, or both.
One time, Harold's sister Amy had said to Franny: "He whacks off in his pants. How's that for nasty?"
Looking at him, Frannie always sensed that every thought Harold ever had was coated lightly with slime.
Say, Fran.
I'm canvassing the township. Not many resisting this dread disease, but I'd heard you were having some success on that front.
Fran could feel Harold's eyes crawling over her the way the fly had on her pie.
Hi, Harold.
I was awfully sorry to hear about Amy. Are your mother and father--?
I'm afraid so.
But life goes on, does it not?

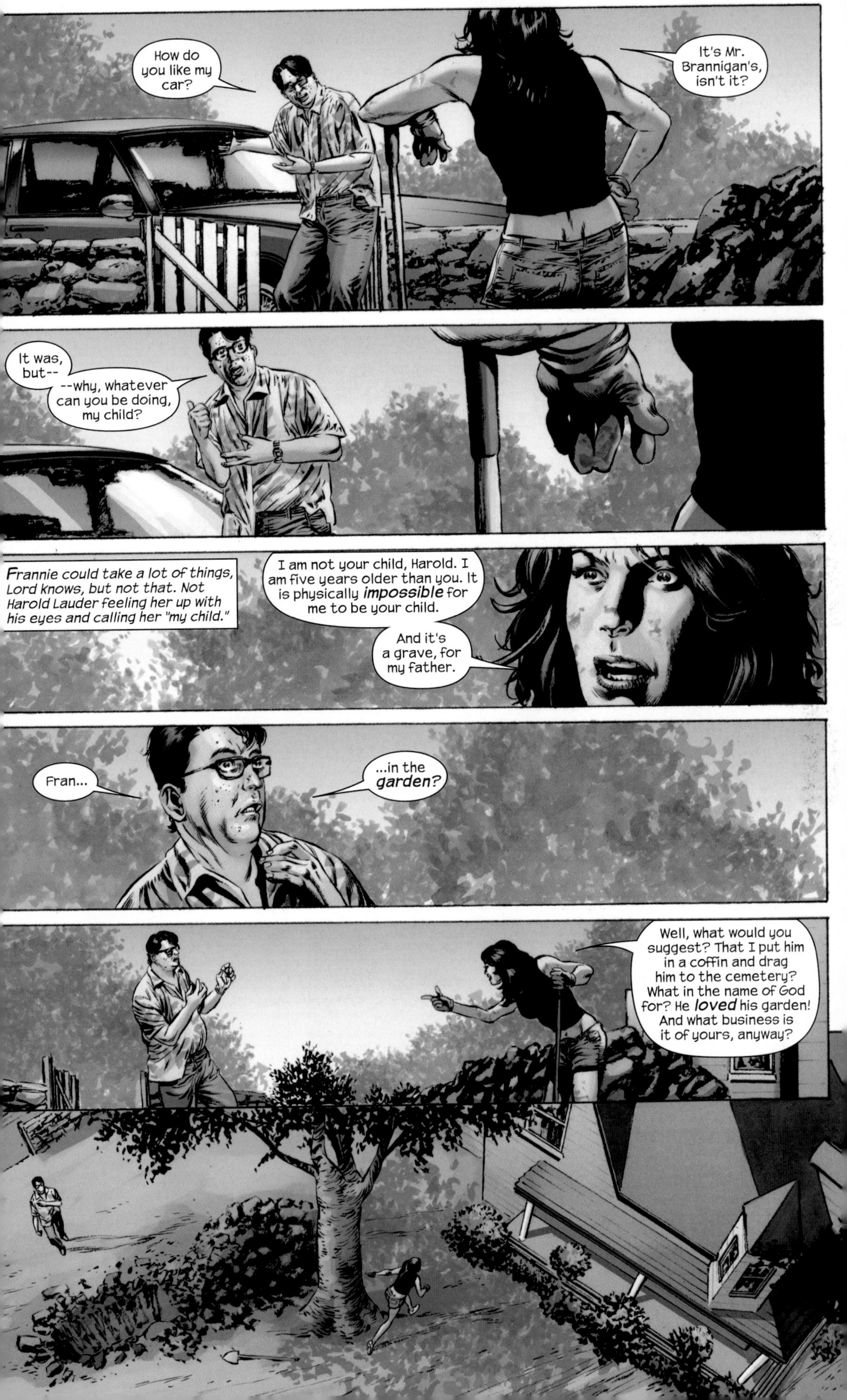
How do you like my car?
It's Mr. Brannigan's, isn't it?
It was, but--
--why, whatever can you be doing, my child?
Frannie could take a lot of things, Lord knows, but not that. Not Harold Lauder feeling her up with his eyes and calling her "my child."
I am not your child, Harold. I am five years older than you. It is physically impossible for me to be your child.
And it's a grave, for my father.
Fran...
...in the garden?
Well, what would you suggest? That I put him in a coffin and drag him to the cemetery? What in the name of God for? He loved his garden! And what business is it of yours, anyway?

A few moments later, the voice came from outside the screen door, low and hesitant.

Fran?

I've been driving around in that Cadillac on my learner's permit all day...I feel like an impostor or an actor in a play...there have been moments today when I've been sure I was mad...

She suddenly felt bad for Harold (who had probably never had a date in his life). He was trying hard to be a good guy, which for him must have been like speaking a foreign language.

You're not crazy, Harold. *We're* not crazy. What's that line? I'll be in your dream if you'll be in mine?

No, someone will come. After this disease, whatever it is, burns itself out. Someone in authority...

Fran...it was the people in authority who *did* this.

But--it's just some funny strain of the flu, Harold.

No, Mother Nature doesn't work that way, sorry. Some bacteriologist in some government installation somewhere announced one day, "Look what I made. It kills almost everybody. Isn't it great?" And then somebody spilled it.

Look, I'm going to get out of Ogunquit. If I stay much longer, I really *will* go crazy. Why don't you come with me? I don't know where, not yet, but somewhere.

... When you think of a place, come ask me again.

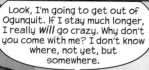

All right, I will!

What are you gonna do in the meantime?

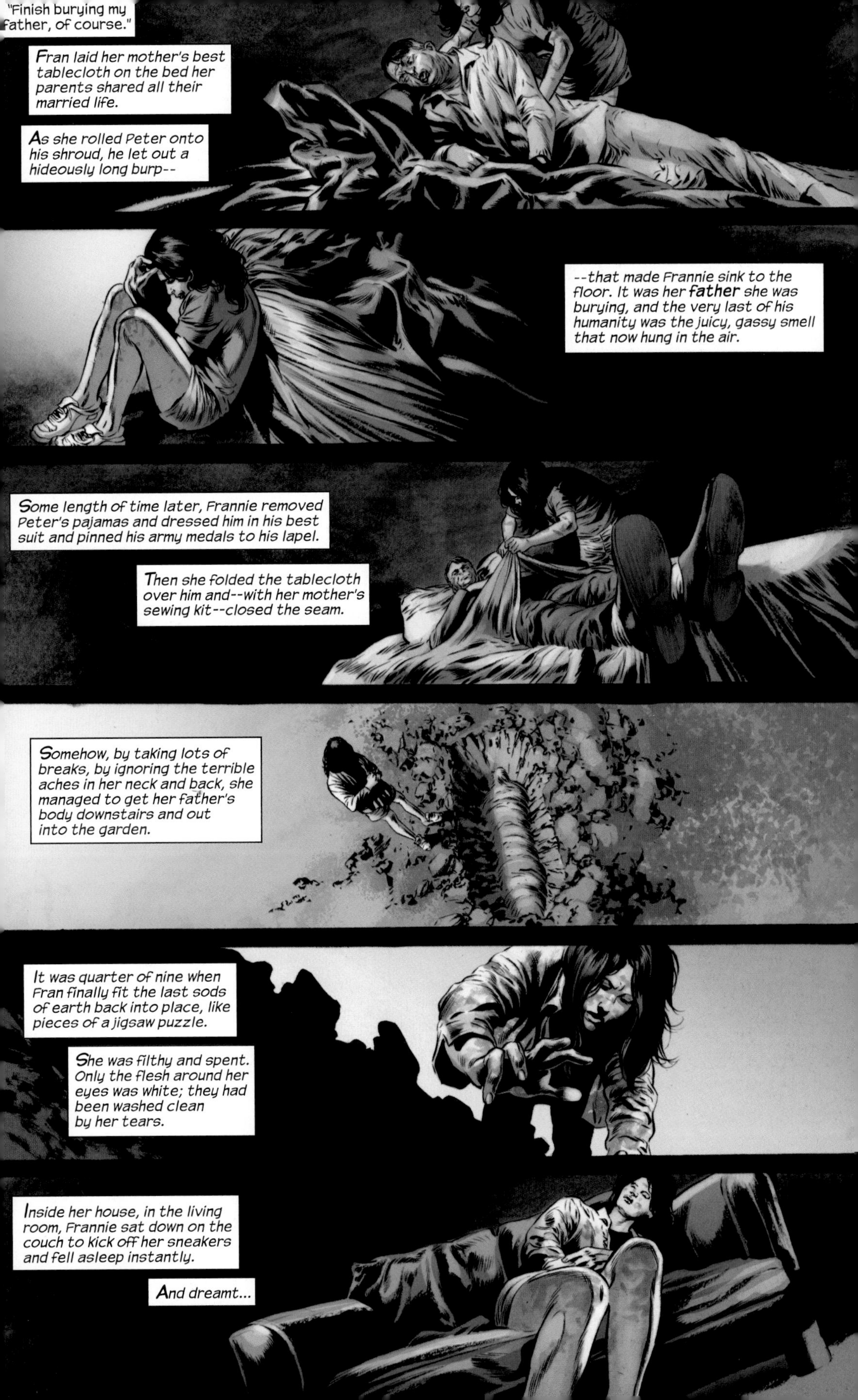
"Finish burying my father, of course."
Fran laid her mother's best tablecloth on the bed her parents shared all their married life.
As she rolled Peter onto his shroud, he let out a hideously long burp--
--that made Frannie sink to the floor. It was her father she was burying, and the very last of his humanity was the juicy, gassy smell that now hung in the air.
Some length of time later, Frannie removed Peter's pajamas and dressed him in his best suit and pinned his army medals to his lapel.
Then she folded the tablecloth over him and--with her mother's sewing kit--closed the seam.
Somehow, by taking lots of breaks, by ignoring the terrible aches in her neck and back, she managed to get her father's body downstairs and out into the garden.
It was quarter of nine when Fran finally fit the last sods of earth back into place, like pieces of a jigsaw puzzle.
She was filthy and spent. Only the flesh around her eyes was white; they had been washed clean by her tears.
Inside her house, in the living room, Frannie sat down on the couch to kick off her sneakers and fell asleep instantly.
And dreamt...

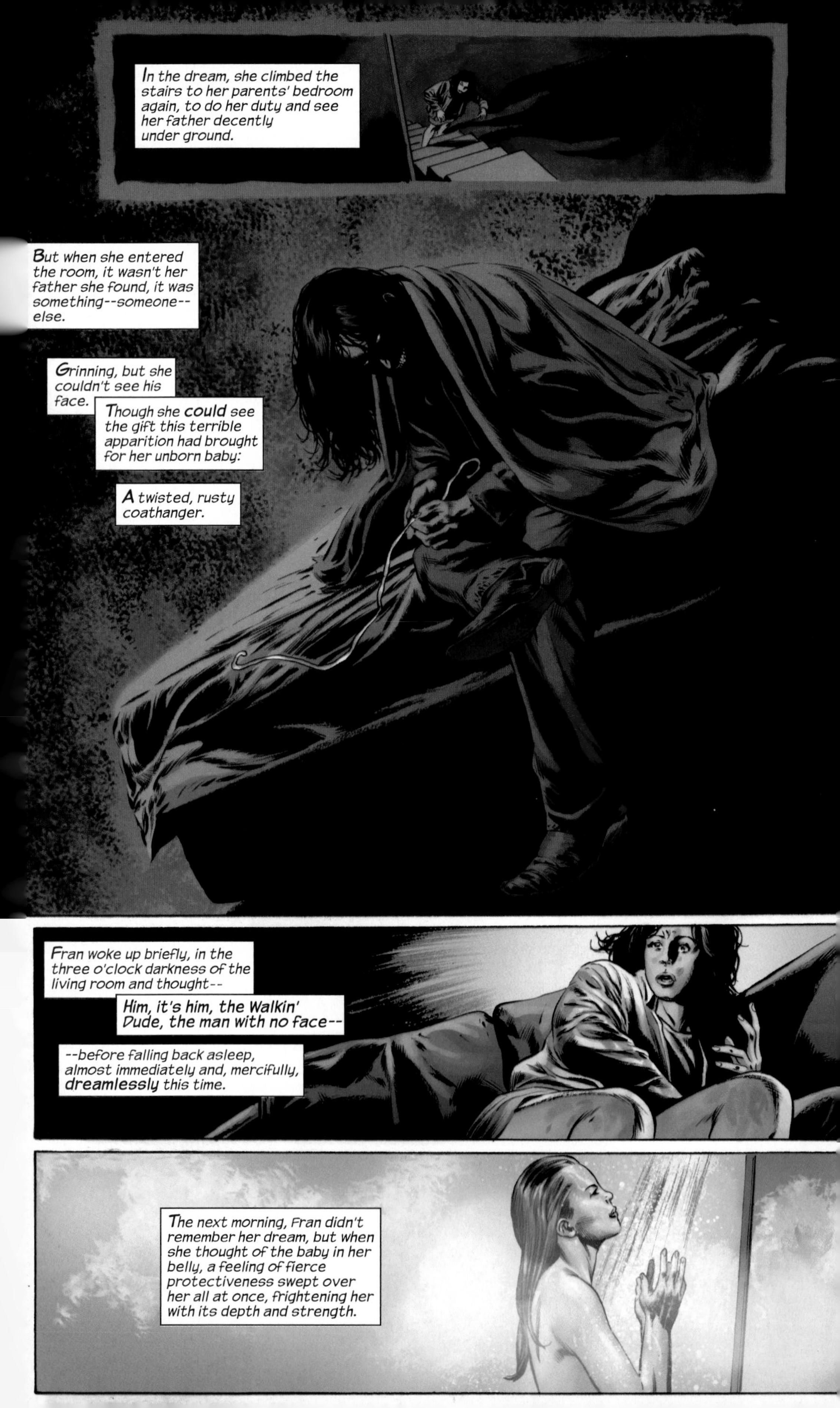

In the dream, she climbed the stairs to her parents' bedroom again, to do her duty and see her father decently under ground.
But when she entered the room, it wasn't her father she found, it was something--someone--else.
Grinning, but she couldn't see his face.
Though she **could** see the gift this terrible apparition had brought for her unborn baby:
A twisted, rusty coathanger.
Fran woke up briefly, in the three o'clock darkness of the living room and thought--
Him, it's him, the Walkin' Dude, the man with no face--
--before falling back asleep, almost immediately and, mercifully, **dreamlessly** this time.
The next morning, Fran didn't remember her dream, but when she thought of the baby in her belly, a feeling of fierce protectiveness swept over her all at once, frightening her with its depth and strength.

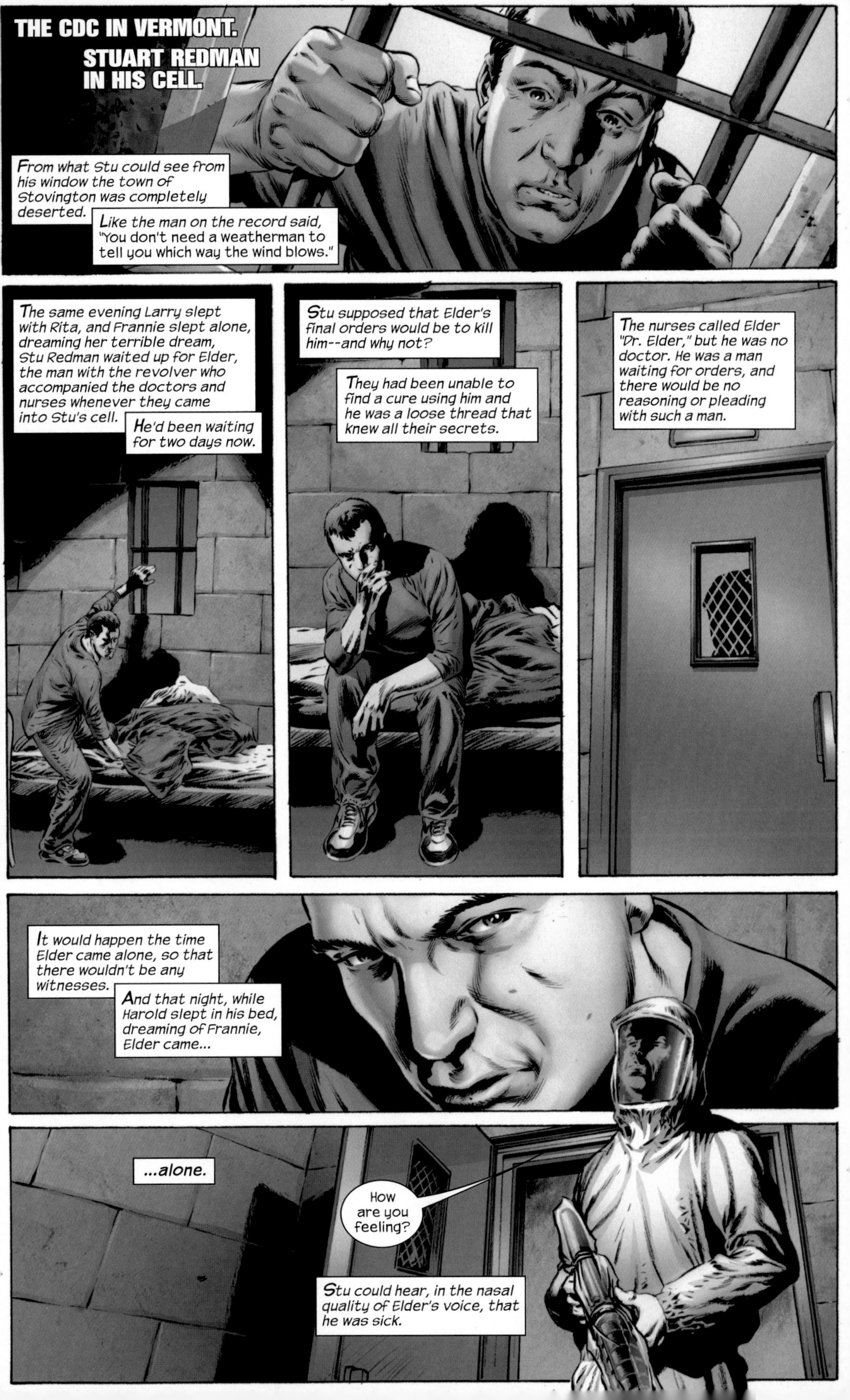
THE CDC IN VERMONT.
STUART REDMAN IN HIS CELL.
From what Stu could see from his window the town of Stovington was completely deserted.
Like the man on the record said, "You don't need a weatherman to tell you which way the wind blows."
The same evening Larry slept with Rita, and Frannie slept alone, dreaming her terrible dream, Stu Redman waited up for Elder, the man with the revolver who accompanied the doctors and nurses whenever they came into Stu's cell.
He'd been waiting for two days now.
Stu supposed that Elder's final orders would be to kill him--and why not?
They had been unable to find a cure using him and he was a loose thread that knew all their secrets.
The nurses called Elder "Dr. Elder," but he was no doctor. He was a man waiting for orders, and there would be no reasoning or pleading with such a man.
It would happen the time Elder came alone, so that there wouldn't be any witnesses.
And that night, while Harold slept in his bed, dreaming of Frannie, Elder came...
...alone.
How are you feeling?
Stu could hear, in the nasal quality of Elder's voice, that he was sick.

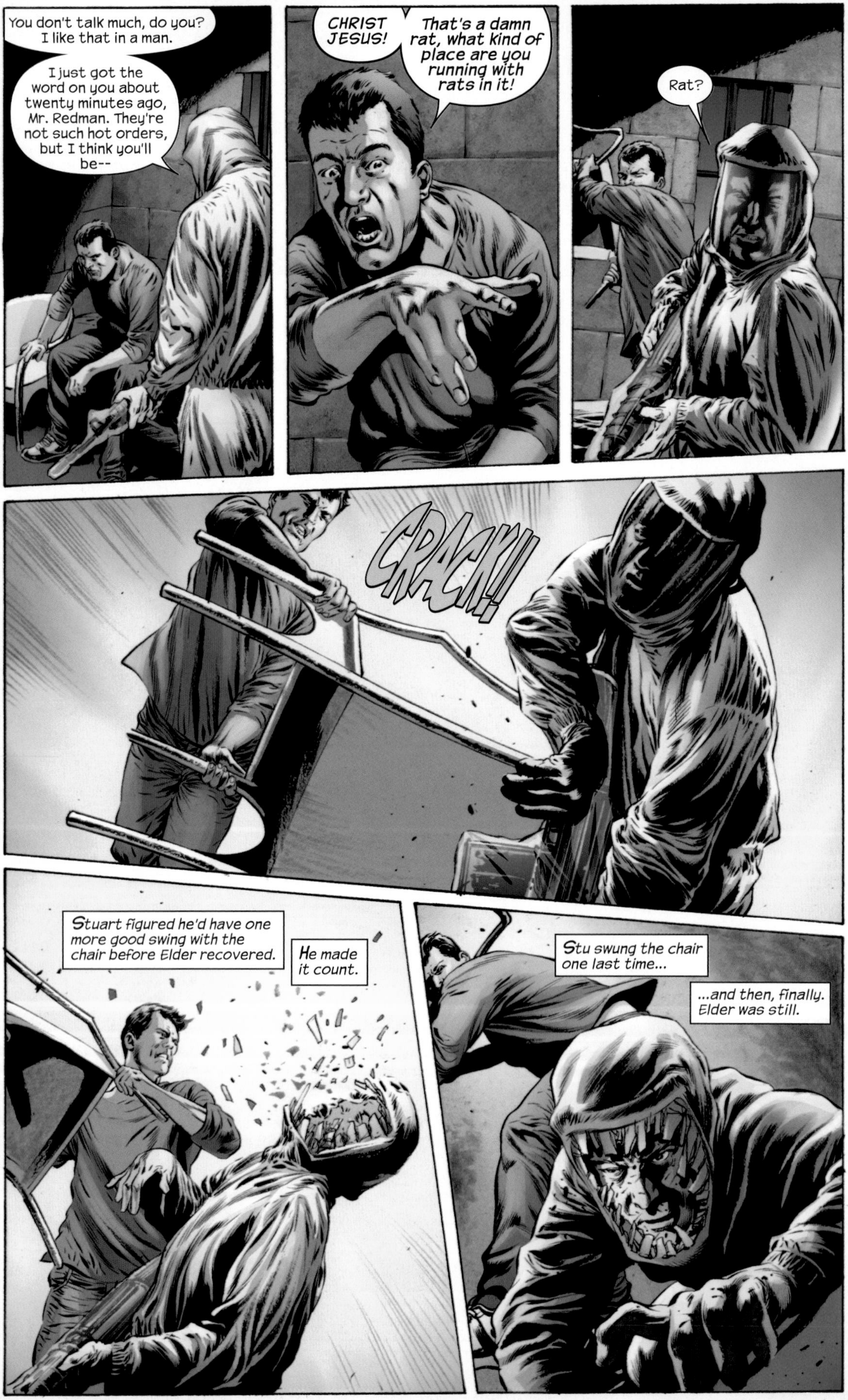
You don't talk much, do you? I like that in a man.
I just got the word on you about twenty minutes ago, Mr. Redman. They're not such hot orders, but I think you'll be--
CHRIST JESUS!
That's a damn rat, what kind of place are you running with rats in it!
Rat?
CRACK!!
Stuart figured he'd have one more good swing with the chair before Elder recovered.
He made it count.
Stu swung the chair one last time...
...and then, finally. Elder was still.

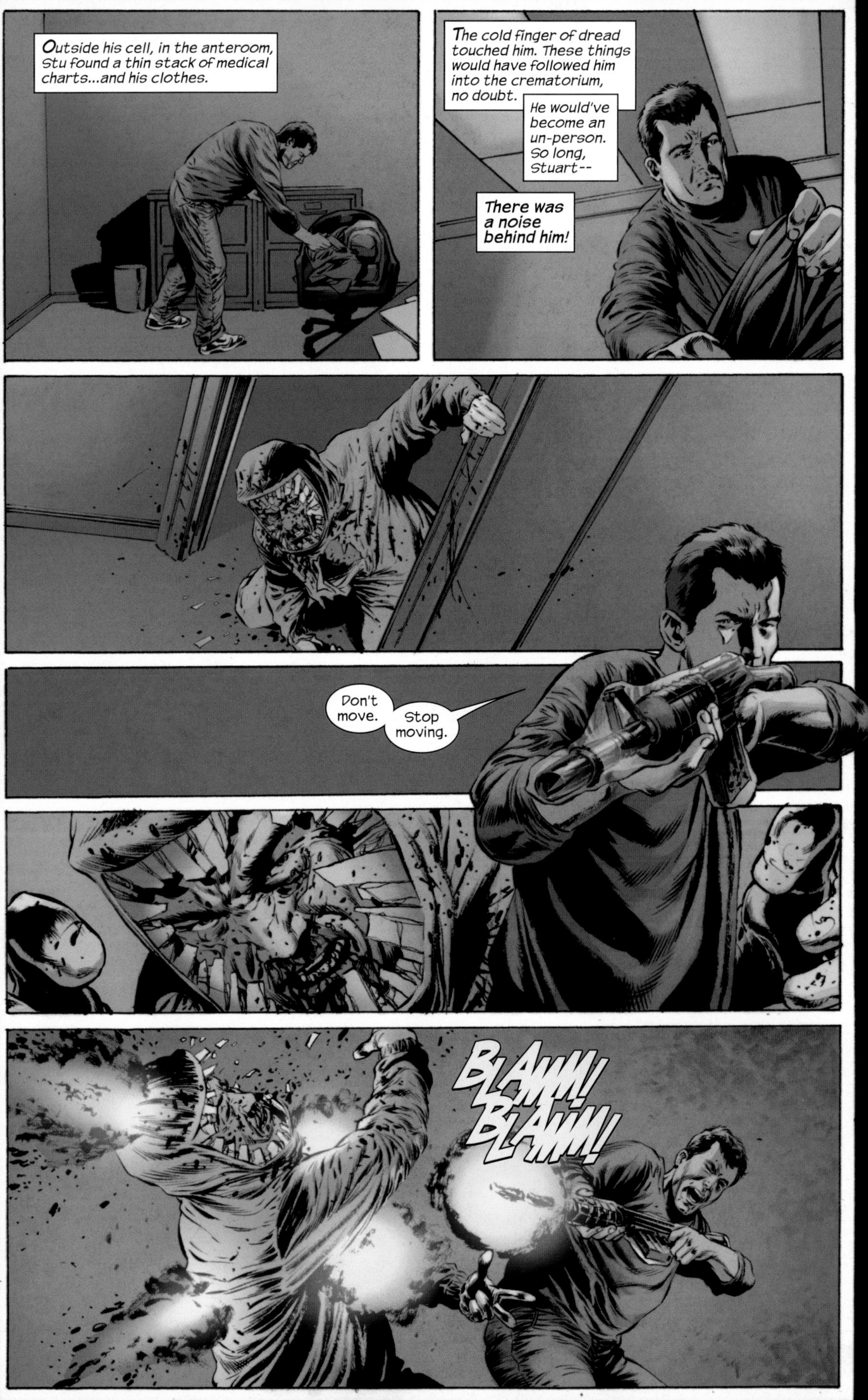

Outside his cell, in the anteroom, Stu found a thin stack of medical charts...and his clothes.
The cold finger of dread touched him. These things would have followed him into the crematorium, no doubt.
He would've become an un-person. So long, Stuart--
There was a noise behind him!
Don't move.
Stop moving.
BLAMM! BLAMM!

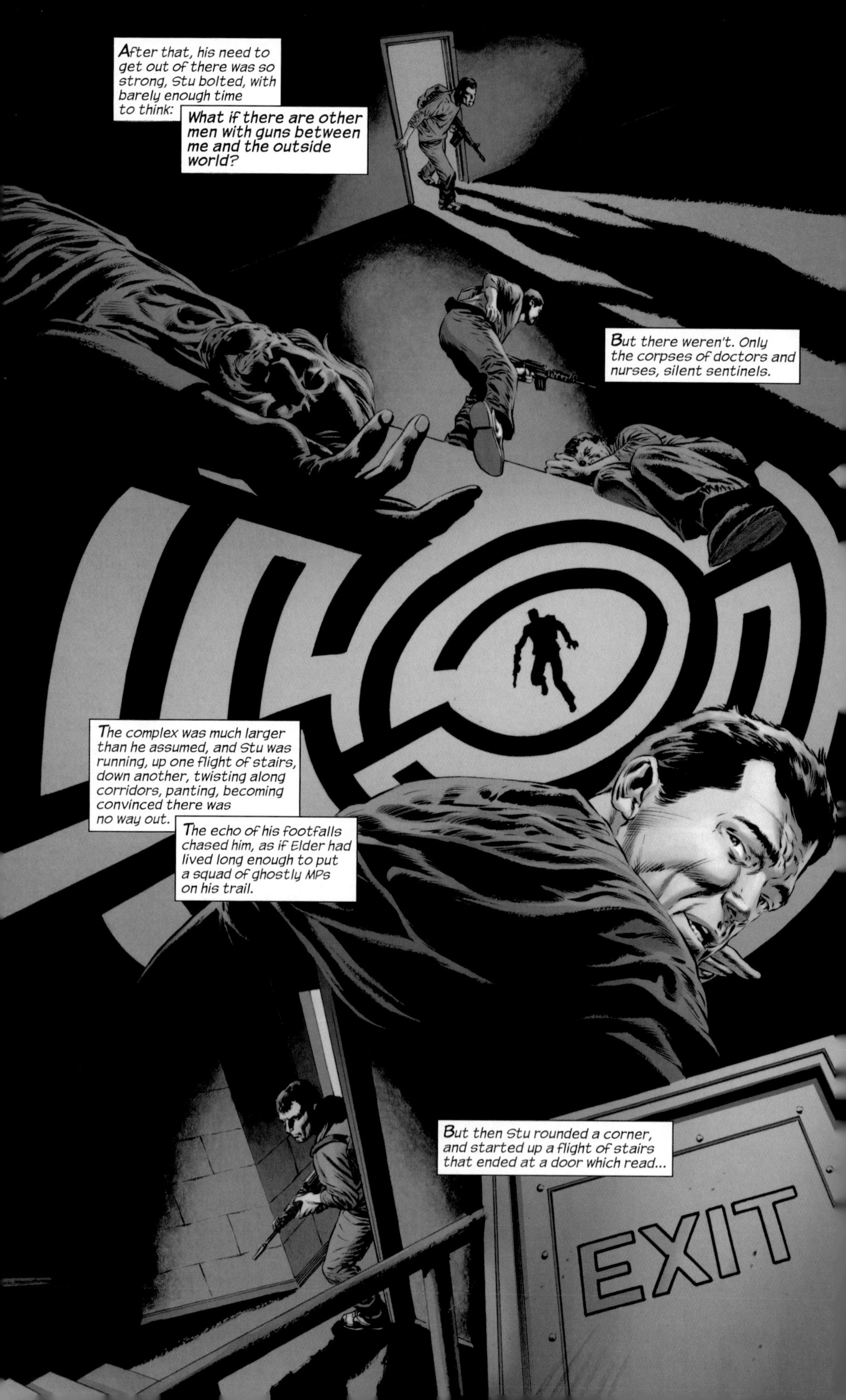
After that, his need to get out of there was so strong, Stu bolted, with barely enough time to think:
What if there are other men with guns between me and the outside world?
But there weren't. Only the corpses of doctors and nurses, silent sentinels.
The complex was much larger than he assumed, and Stu was running, up one flight of stairs, down another, twisting along corridors, panting, becoming convinced there was no way out.
The echo of his footfalls chased him, as if Elder had lived long enough to put a squad of ghostly MPs on his trail.
But then Stu rounded a corner, and started up a flight of stairs that ended at a door which read...
EXIT

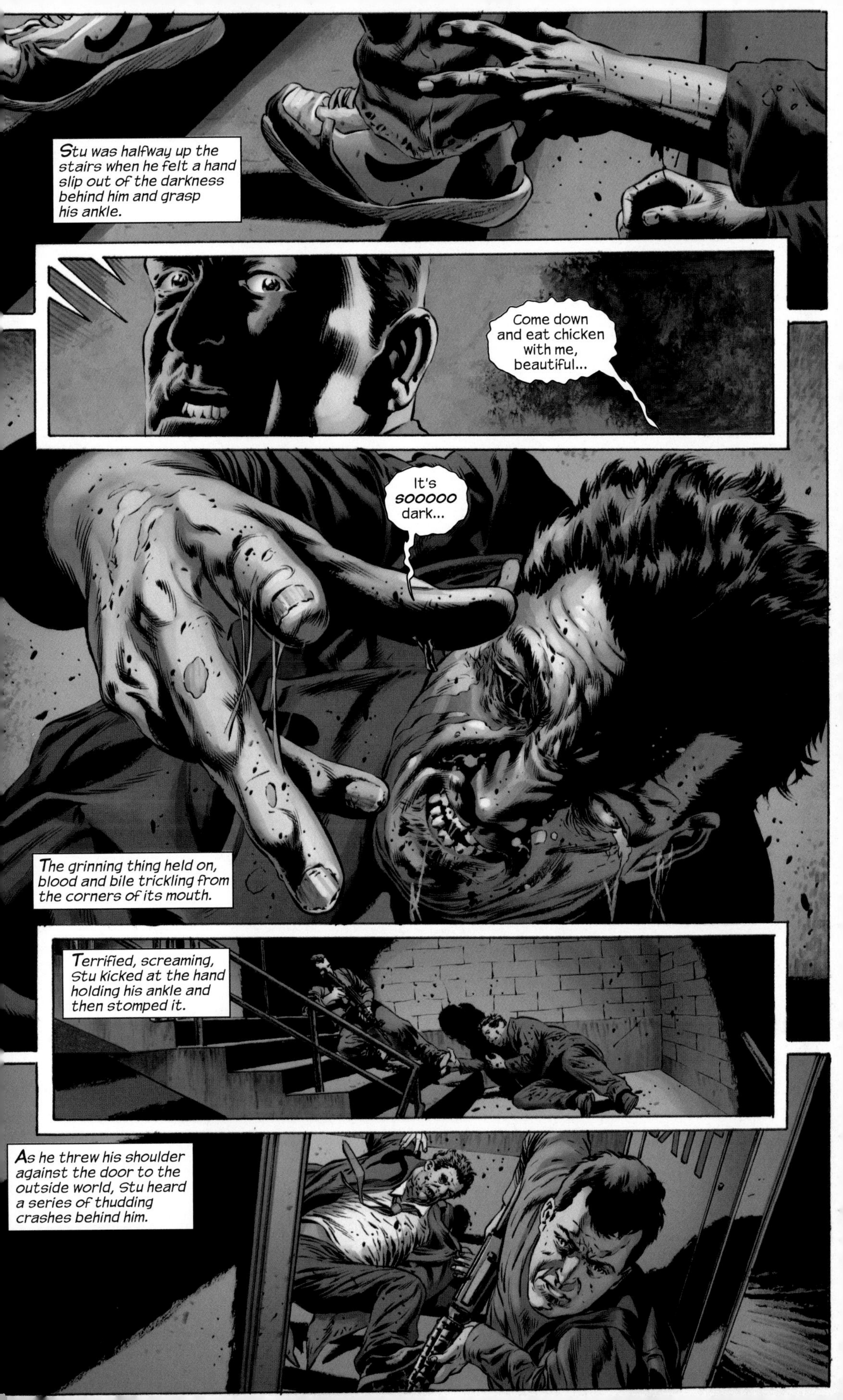
Stu was halfway up the stairs when he felt a hand slip out of the darkness behind him and grasp his ankle.
Come down and eat chicken with me, beautiful...
It's soooooo dark...
The grinning thing held on, blood and bile trickling from the corners of its mouth.
Terrified, screaming, Stu kicked at the hand holding his ankle and then stomped it.
As he threw his shoulder against the door to the outside world, Stu heard a series of thudding crashes behind him.

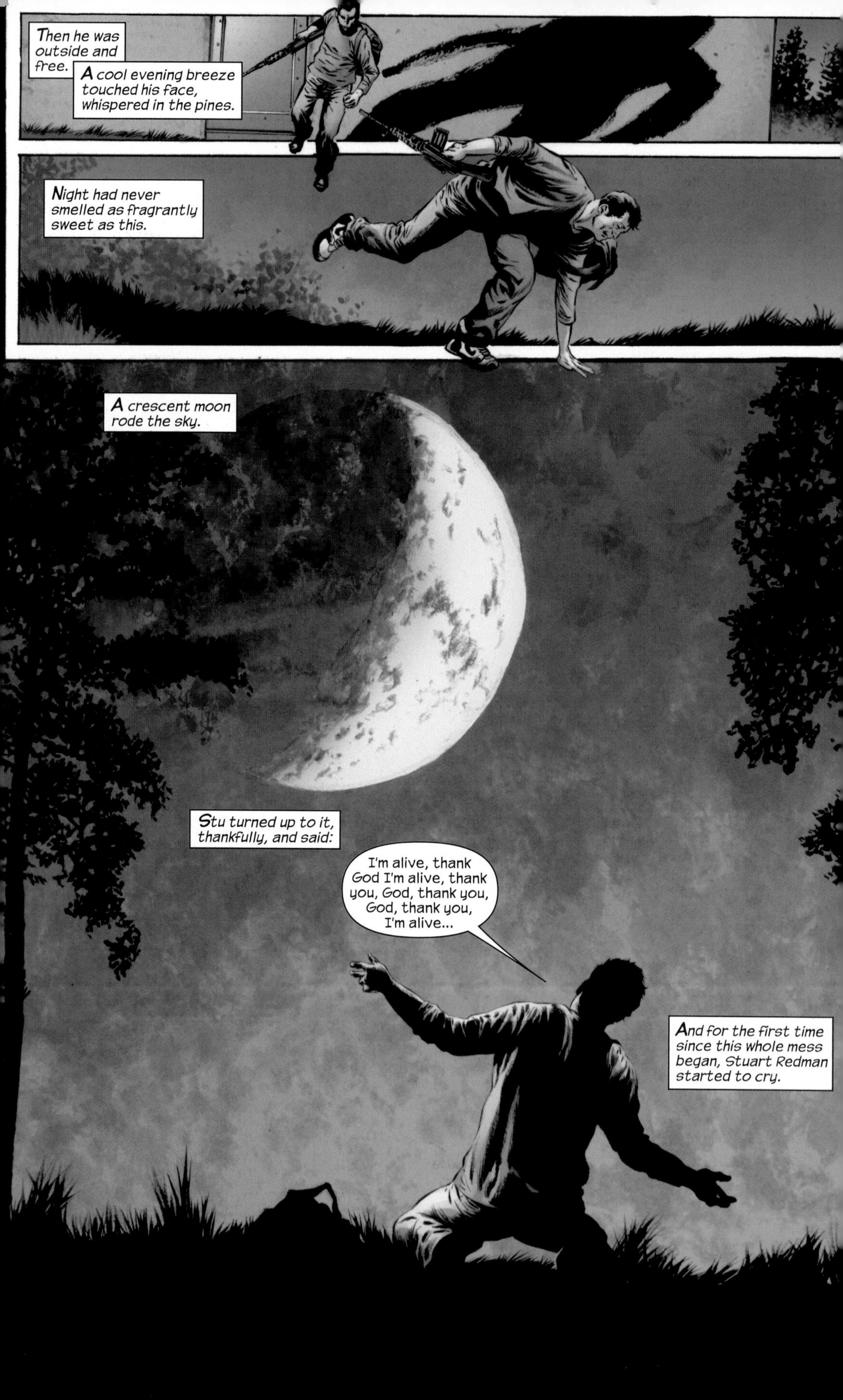

Then he was outside and free.
A cool evening breeze touched his face, whispered in the pines.
Night had never smelled as fragrantly sweet as this.
A crescent moon rode the sky.
Stu turned up to it, thankfully, and said:
I'm alive, thank God I'm alive, thank you, God, thank you, God, thank you, I'm alive...
And for the first time since this whole mess began, Stuart Redman started to cry.

chapter TWO

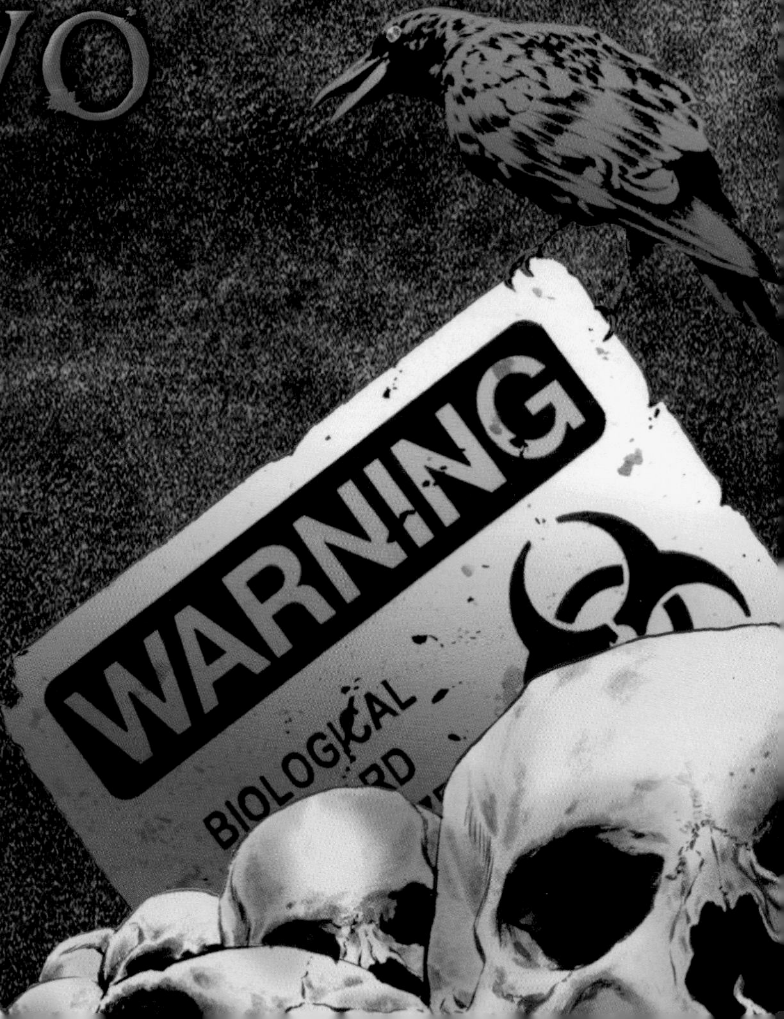
WARNING
BIOLOGICAL

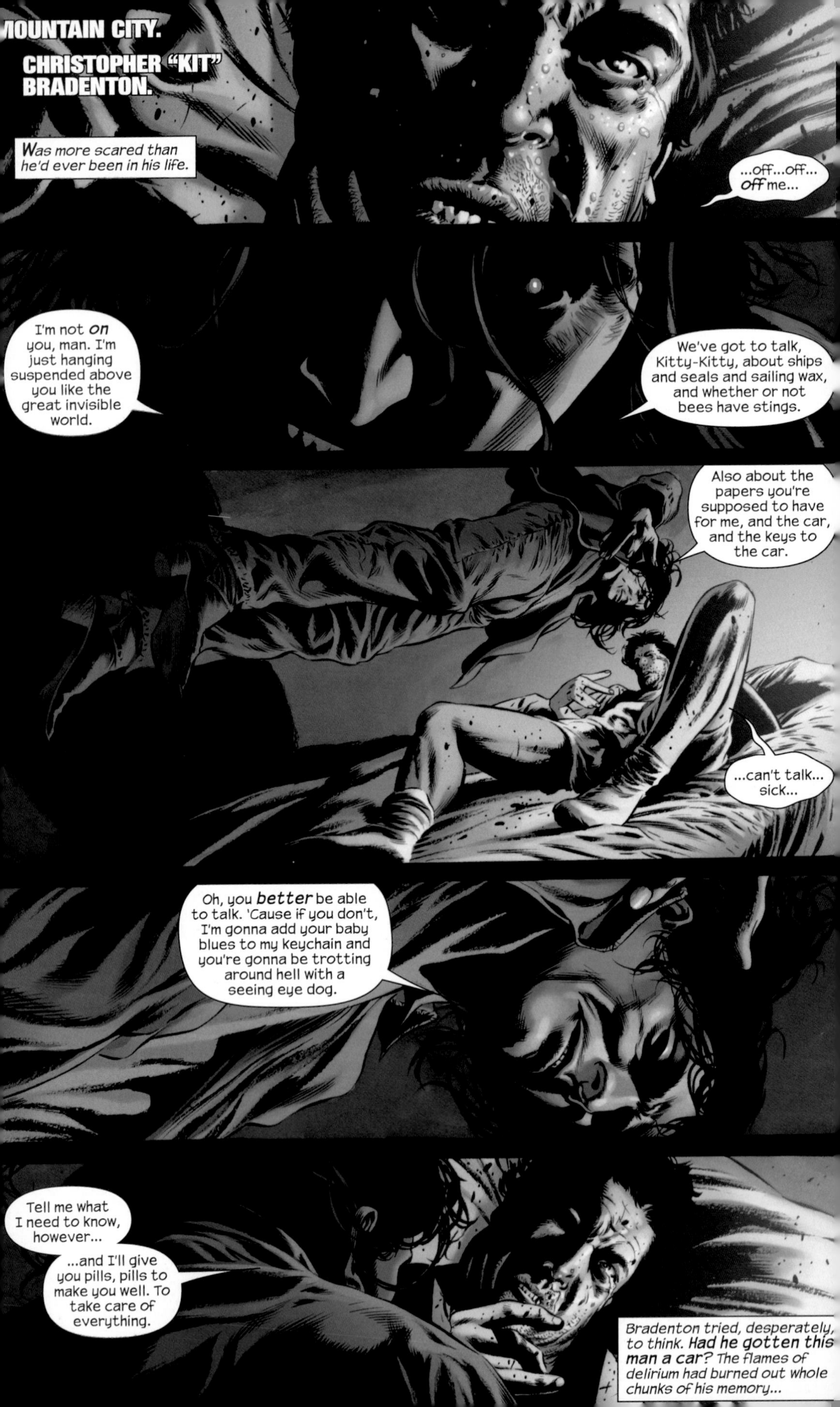

MOUNTAIN CITY.
CHRISTOPHER "KIT" BRADENTON.
Was more scared than he'd ever been in his life.
...off...off... off me...
I'm not on you, man. I'm just hanging suspended above you like the great invisible world.
We've got to talk, Kitty-Kitty, about ships and seals and sailing wax, and whether or not bees have stings.
Also about the papers you're supposed to have for me, and the car, and the keys to the car.
...can't talk... sick...
Oh, you better be able to talk. 'Cause if you don't, I'm gonna add your baby blues to my keychain and you're gonna be trotting around hell with a seeing eye dog.
Tell me what I need to know, however...
...and I'll give you pills, pills to make you well. To take care of everything.
Bradenton tried, desperately, to think. Had he gotten this man a car? The flames of delirium had burned out whole chunks of his memory...

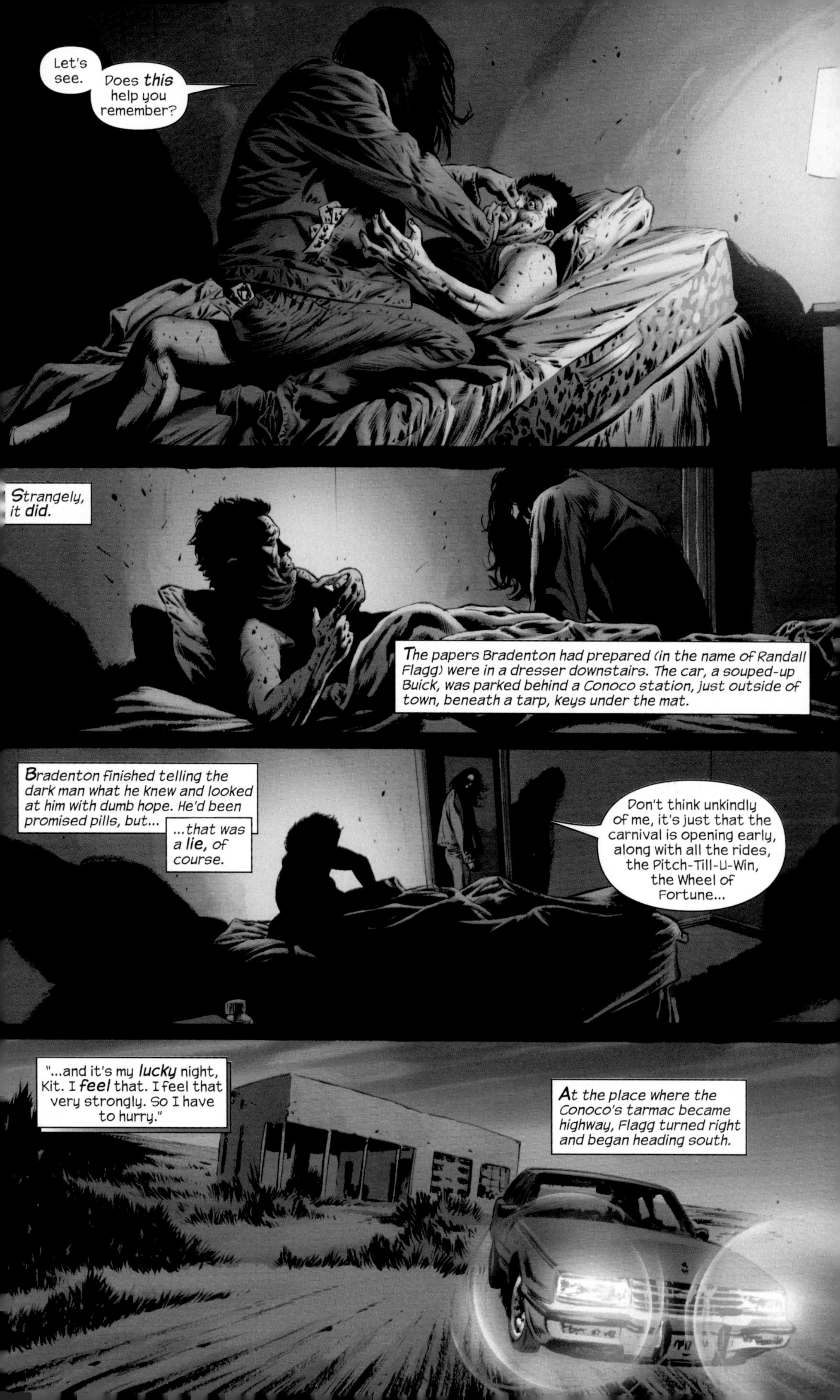
Let's see.
Does this help you remember?
Strangely, it did.
The papers Bradenton had prepared (in the name of Randall Flagg) were in a dresser downstairs. The car, a souped-up Buick, was parked behind a Conoco station, just outside of town, beneath a tarp, keys under the mat.
Bradenton finished telling the dark man what he knew and looked at him with dumb hope. He'd been promised pills, but...
...that was a lie, of course.
Don't think unkindly of me, it's just that the carnival is opening early, along with all the rides, the Pitch-Till-U-Win, the Wheel of Fortune...
"...and it's my lucky night, Kit. I feel that. I feel that very strongly. So I have to hurry."
At the place where the Conoco's tarmac became highway, Flagg turned right and began heading south.

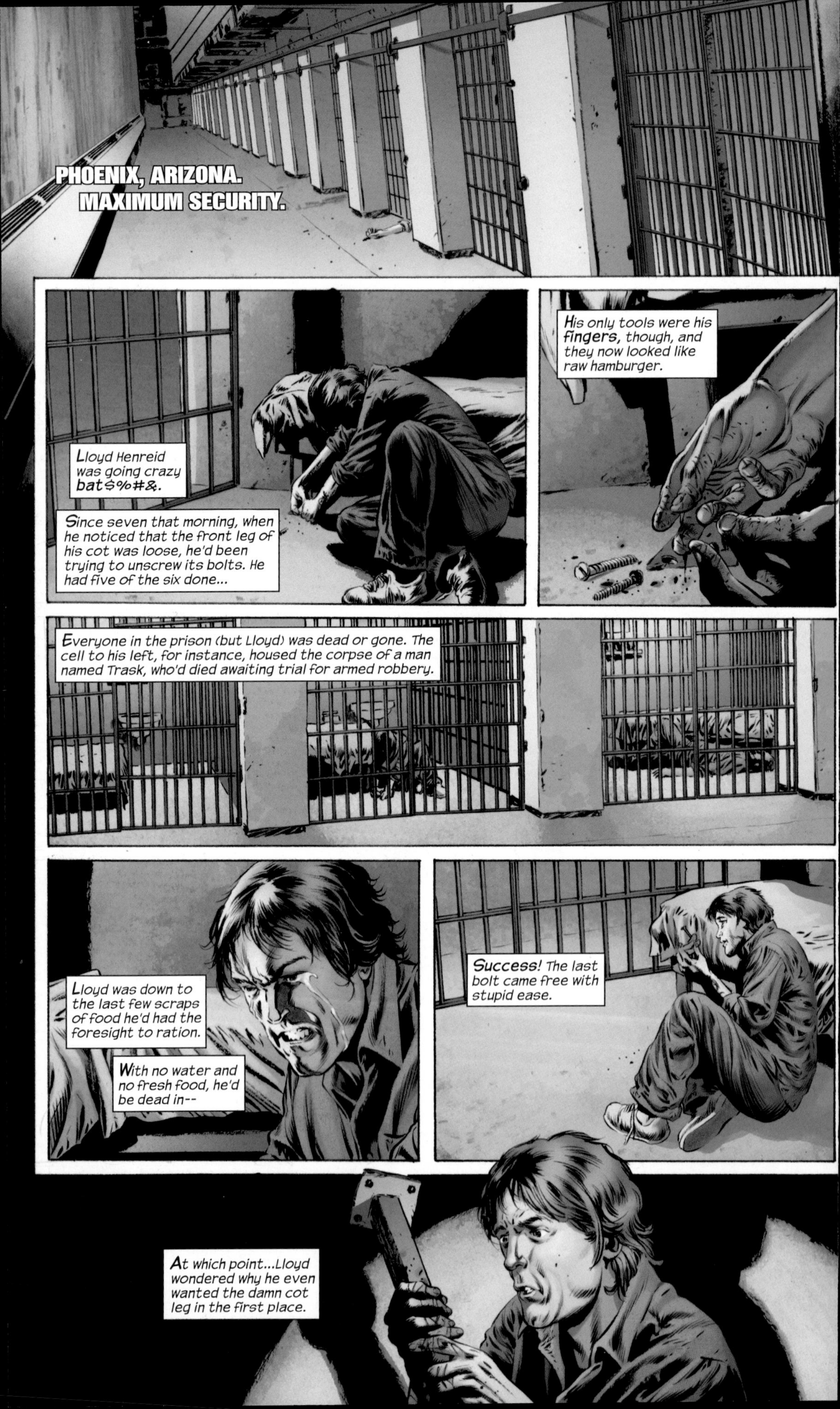
PHOENIX, ARIZONA. MAXIMUM SECURITY.
Lloyd Henreid was going crazy bat$%#&.
Since seven that morning, when he noticed that the front leg of his cot was loose, he'd been trying to unscrew its bolts. He had five of the six done...
His only tools were his fingers, though, and they now looked like raw hamburger.
Everyone in the prison (but Lloyd) was dead or gone. The cell to his left, for instance, housed the corpse of a man named Trask, who'd died awaiting trial for armed robbery.
Lloyd was down to the last few scraps of food he'd had the foresight to ration.
With no water and no fresh food, he'd be dead in--
Success! The last bolt came free with stupid ease.
At which point...Lloyd wondered why he even wanted the damn cot leg in the first place.

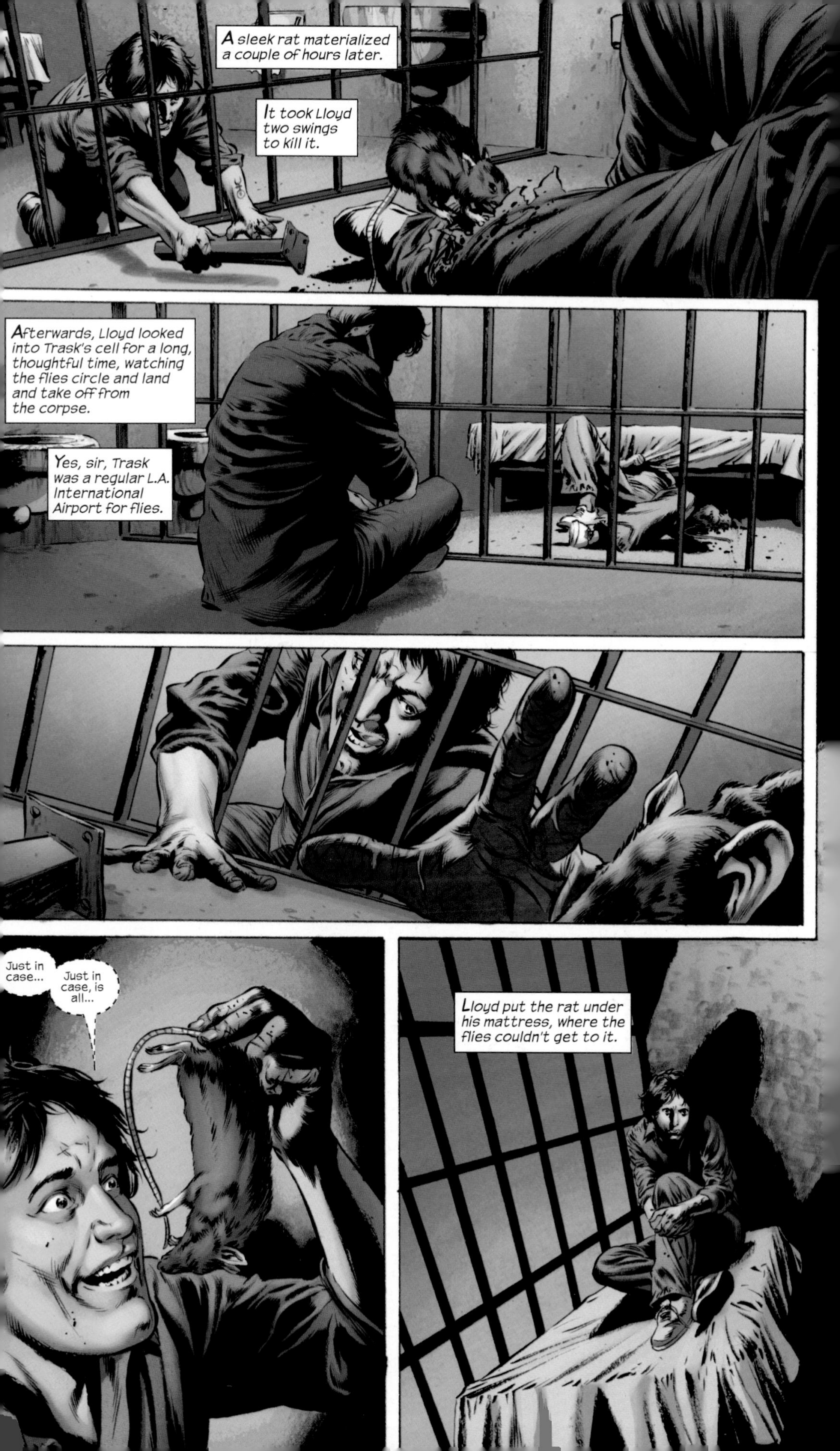
A sleek rat materialized a couple of hours later.
It took Lloyd two swings to kill it.
Afterwards, Lloyd looked into Trask's cell for a long, thoughtful time, watching the flies circle and land and take off from the corpse.
Yes, sir, Trask was a regular L.A. International Airport for flies.
Just in case...
Just in case, is all...
Lloyd put the rat under his mattress, where the flies couldn't get to it.

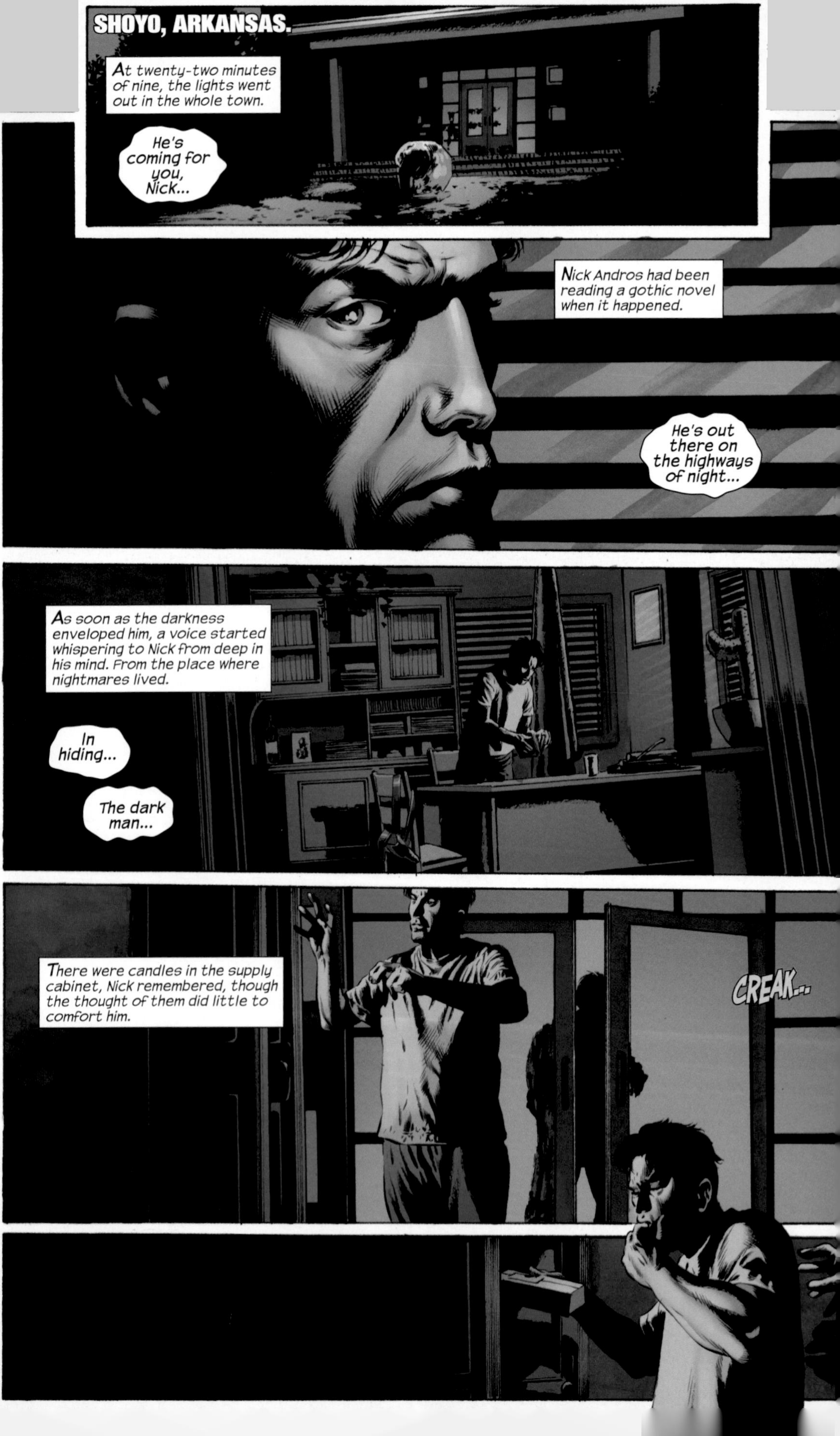

SHOYO, ARKANSAS.
At twenty-two minutes of nine, the lights went out in the whole town.
He's coming for you, Nick...
Nick Andros had been reading a gothic novel when it happened.
He's out there on the highways of night...
As soon as the darkness enveloped him, a voice started whispering to Nick from deep in his mind. From the place where nightmares lived.
In hiding...
The dark man...
There were candles in the supply cabinet, Nick remembered, though the thought of them did little to comfort him.
CREAK...

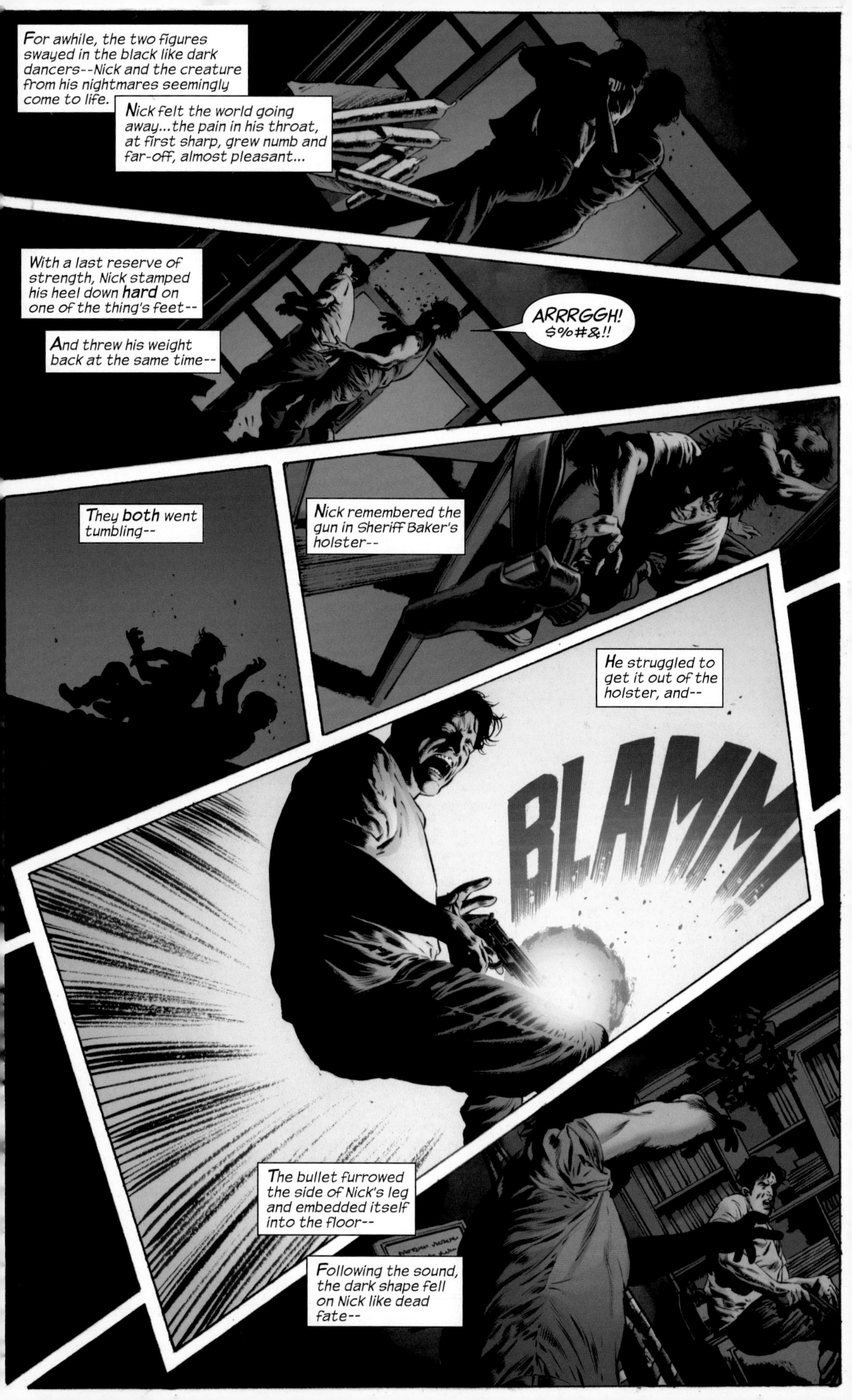
For awhile, the two figures swayed in the black like dark dancers--Nick and the creature from his nightmares seemingly come to life.
Nick felt the world going away...the pain in his throat, at first sharp, grew numb and far-off, almost pleasant...
With a last reserve of strength, Nick stamped his heel down hard on one of the thing's feet--
And threw his weight back at the same time--
ARRRGGH! $%#&!!
They both went tumbling--
Nick remembered the gun in Sheriff Baker's holster--
He struggled to get it out of the holster, and--
BLAMM!
The bullet furrowed the side of Nick's leg and embedded itself into the floor--
Following the sound, the dark shape fell on Nick like dead fate--

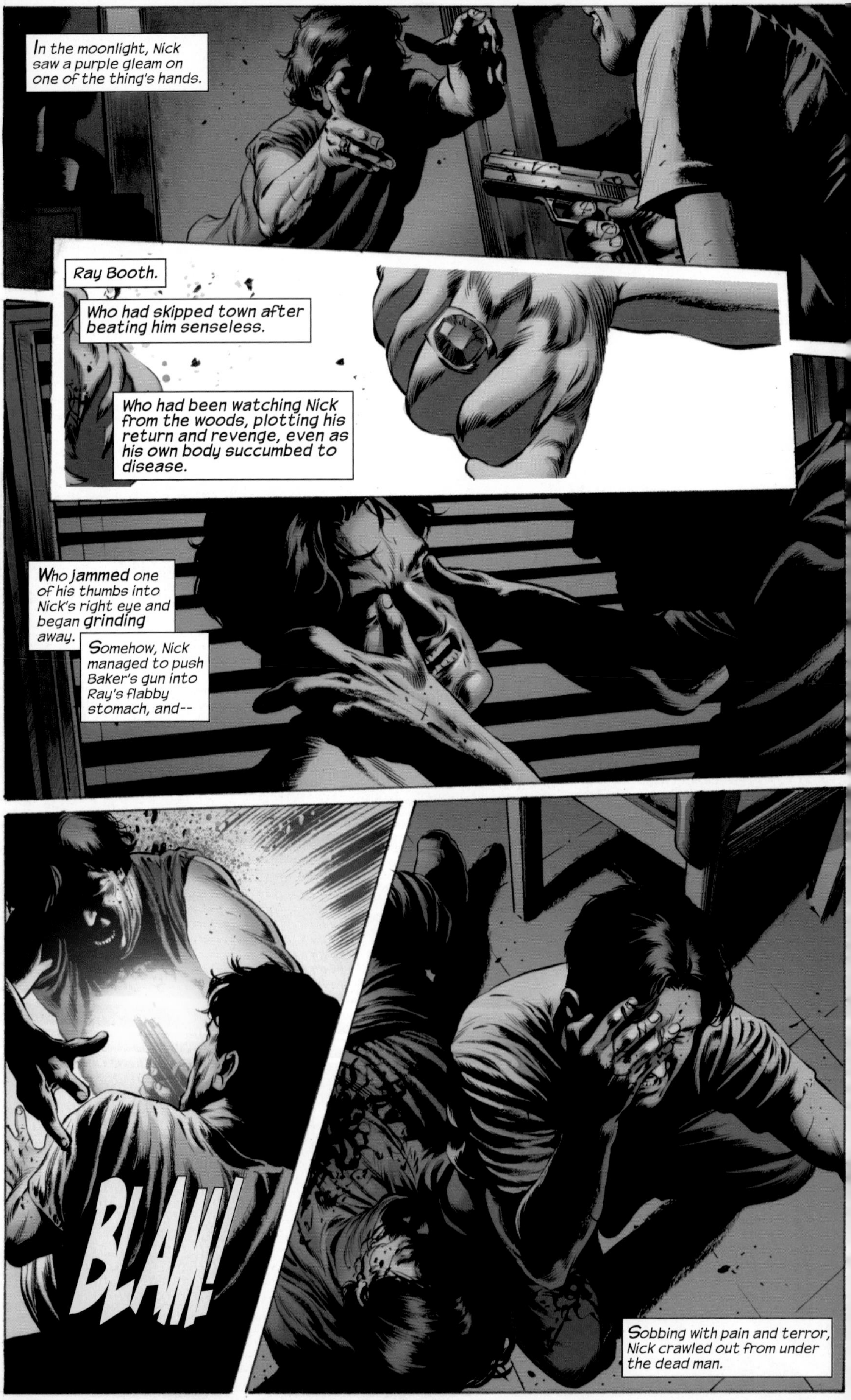
In the moonlight, Nick saw a purple gleam on one of the thing's hands.
Ray Booth.
Who had skipped town after beating him senseless.
Who had been watching Nick from the woods, plotting his return and revenge, even as his own body succumbed to disease.
Who jammed one of his thumbs into Nick's right eye and began grinding away.
Somehow, Nick managed to push Baker's gun into Ray's flabby stomach, and--
BLAM!
Sobbing with pain and terror, Nick crawled out from under the dead man.

After awhile, Nick found and lit a candle.

Ray looked like a dead whale cast up on a beach.

Nick inspected himself in the small mirror Sheriff Baker had used to comb his hair...

He wasn't sure, but he thought he might be **one-eyed** now, as well as deaf and dumb.

Spent as he was, Nick started kicking Ray Booth's corpse, over and over, shrieking (in his mind) at the dead man: *Are you happy?*

You would've left me deaf, dumb, and blind in this land of the dead if you could've!

How do you like this now? Huh? You like this?

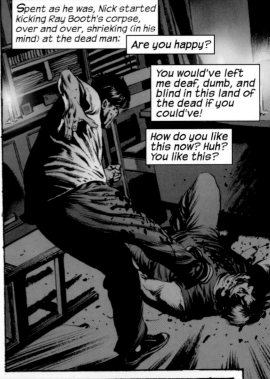

Outside the station, the dark held hard and fast.

Outside, all the lights of the world were going out.

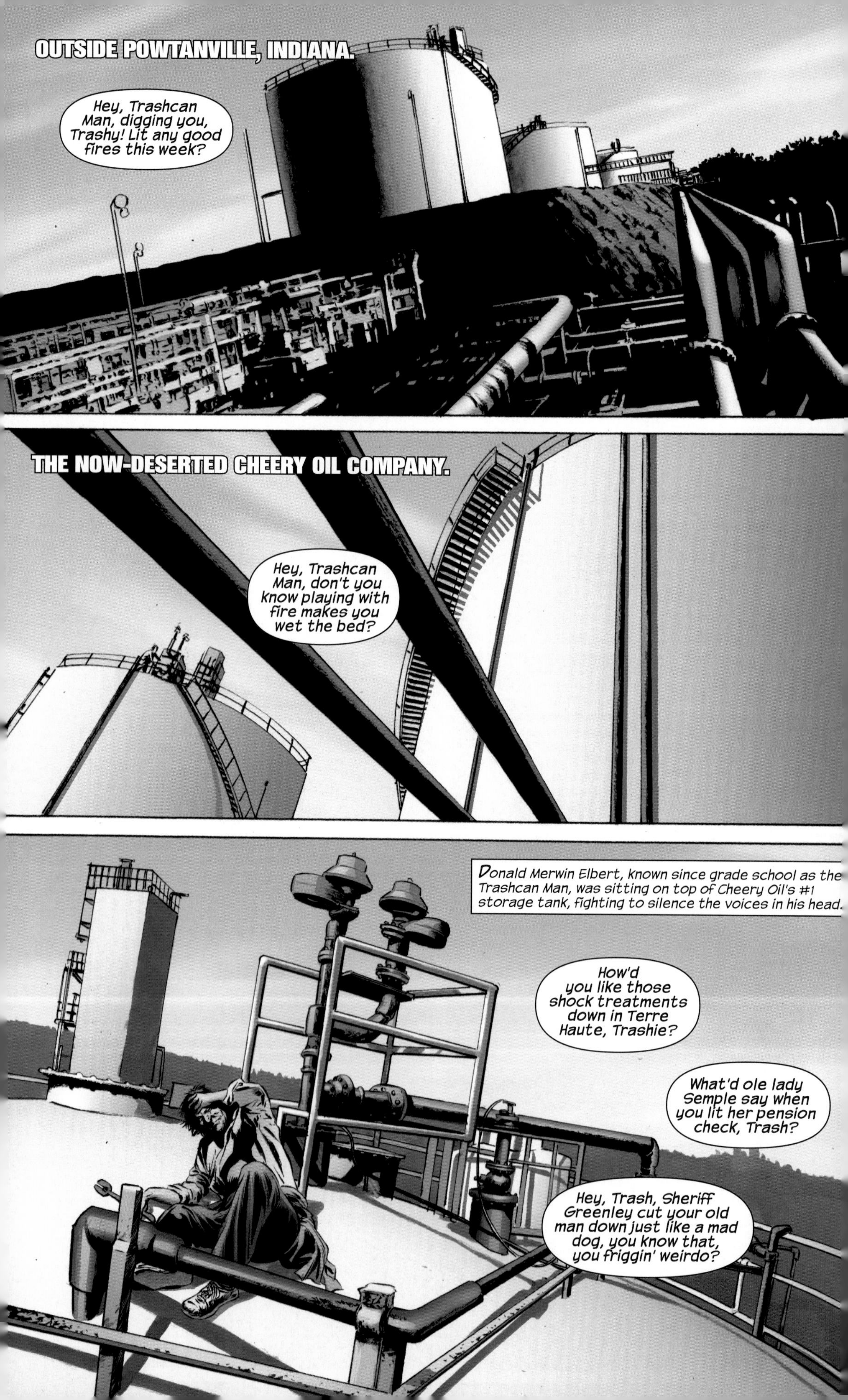
OUTSIDE POWTANVILLE, INDIANA.
Hey, Trashcan Man, digging you, Trashy! Lit any good fires this week?
THE NOW-DESERTED CHEERY OIL COMPANY.
Hey, Trashcan Man, don't you know playing with fire makes you wet the bed?
Donald Merwin Elbert, known since grade school as the Trashcan Man, was sitting on top of Cheery Oil's #1 storage tank, fighting to silence the voices in his head.
How'd you like those shock treatments down in Terre Haute, Trashie?
What'd ole lady Semple say when you lit her pension check, Trash?
Hey, Trash, Sheriff Greenley cut your old man down just like a mad dog, you know that, you friggin' weirdo?

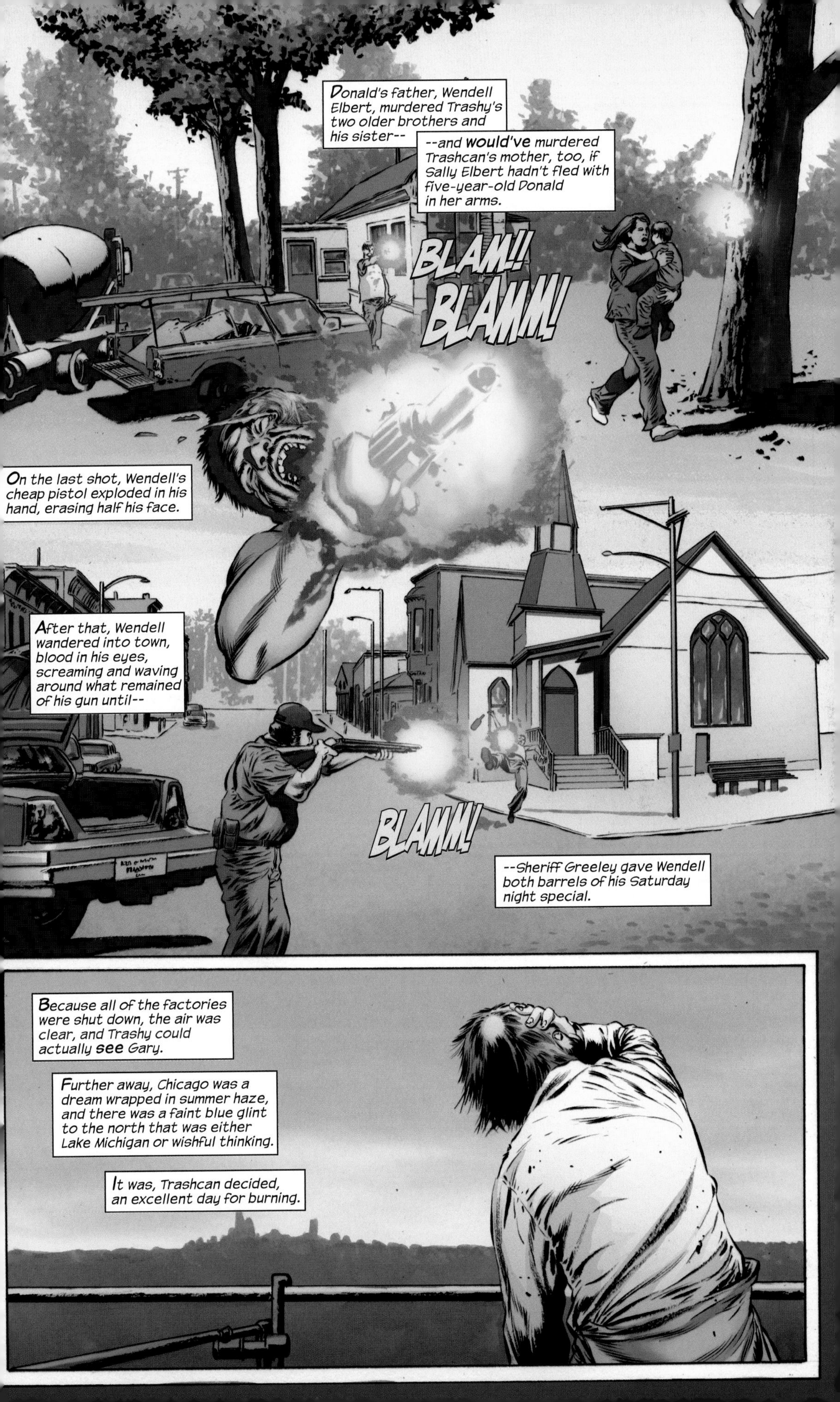

Donald's father, Wendell Elbert, murdered Trashy's two older brothers and his sister--
--and would've murdered Trashcan's mother, too, if Sally Elbert hadn't fled with five-year-old Donald in her arms.
BLAM!! BLAMM!
On the last shot, Wendell's cheap pistol exploded in his hand, erasing half his face.
After that, Wendell wandered into town, blood in his eyes, screaming and waving around what remained of his gun until--
BLAMM!
--Sheriff Greeley gave Wendell both barrels of his Saturday night special.
Because all of the factories were shut down, the air was clear, and Trashy could actually see Gary.
Further away, Chicago was a dream wrapped in summer haze, and there was a faint blue glint to the north that was either Lake Michigan or wishful thinking.
It was, Trashcan decided, an excellent day for burning.

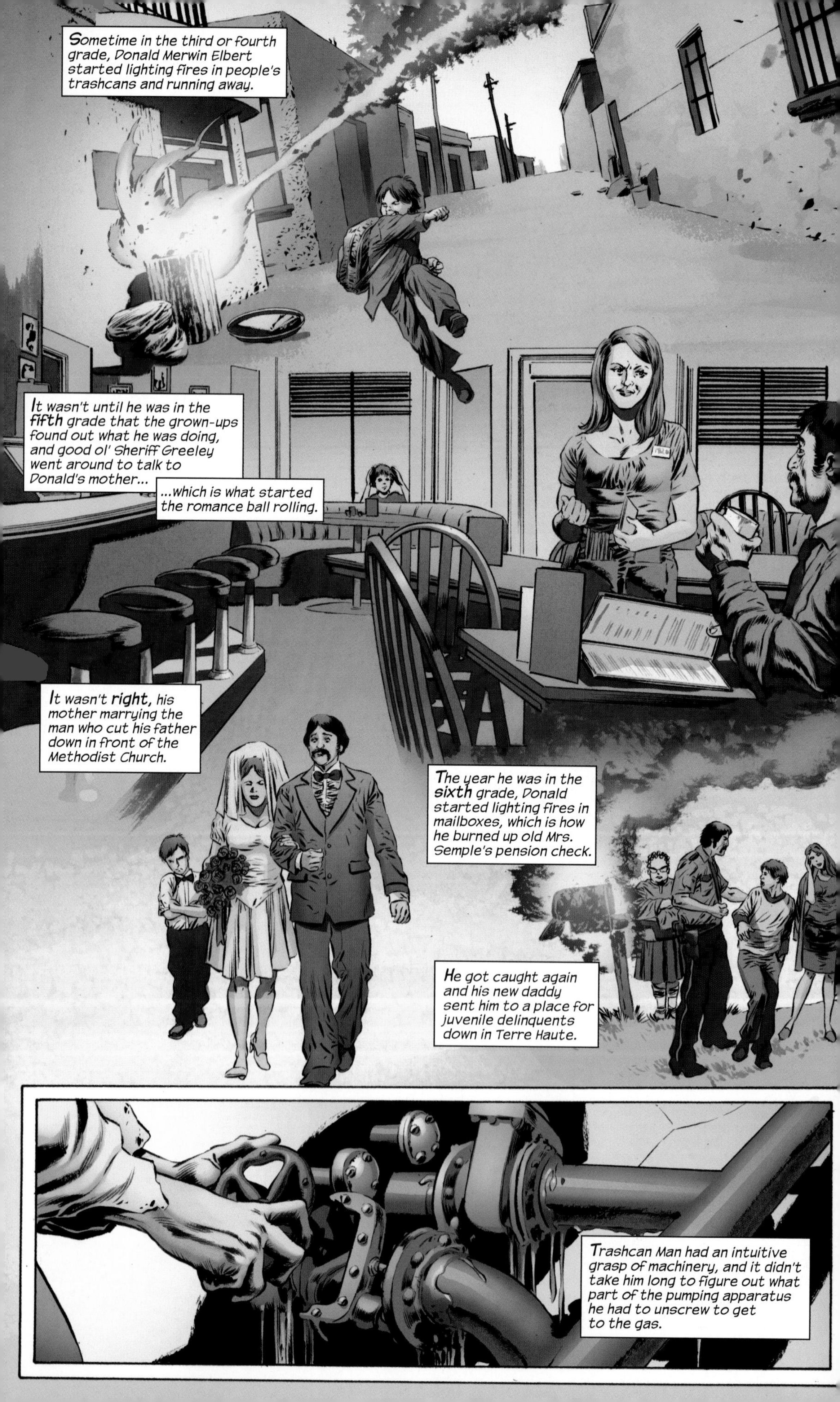

Sometime in the third or fourth grade, Donald Merwin Elbert started lighting fires in people's trashcans and running away.
It wasn't until he was in the **fifth** grade that the grown-ups found out what he was doing, and good ol' Sheriff Greeley went around to talk to Donald's mother...
...which is what started the romance ball rolling.
It wasn't **right**, his mother marrying the man who cut his father down in front of the Methodist Church.
The year he was in the **sixth** grade, Donald started lighting fires in mailboxes, which is how he burned up old Mrs. Semple's pension check.
He got caught again and his new daddy sent him to a place for juvenile delinquents down in Terre Haute.
Trashcan Man had an intuitive grasp of machinery, and it didn't take him long to figure out what part of the pumping apparatus he had to unscrew to get to the gas.

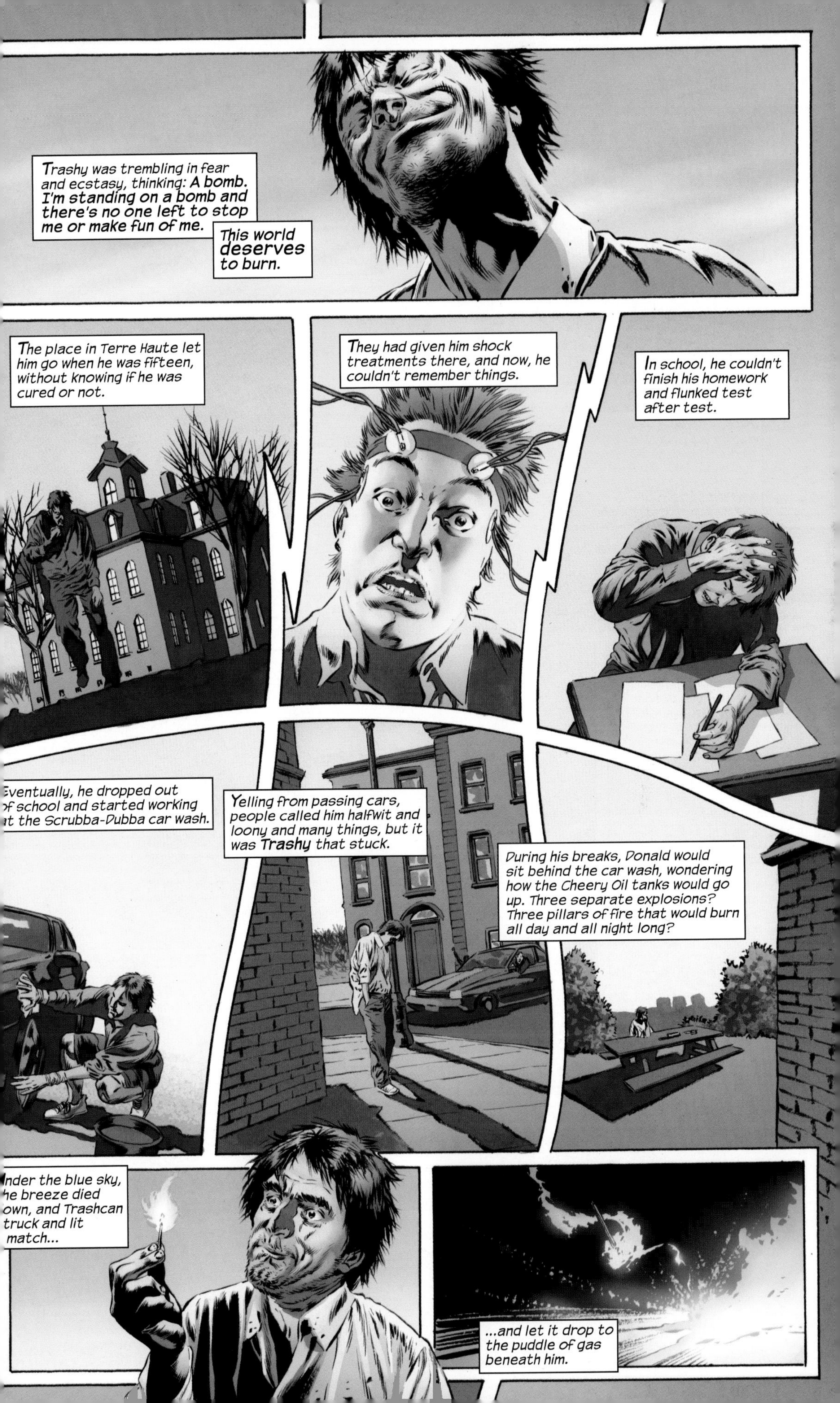

Trashy was trembling in fear and ecstasy, thinking: A bomb. I'm standing on a bomb and there's no one left to stop me or make fun of me.
This world deserves to burn.
The place in Terre Haute let him go when he was fifteen, without knowing if he was cured or not.
They had given him shock treatments there, and now, he couldn't remember things.
In school, he couldn't finish his homework and flunked test after test.
Eventually, he dropped out of school and started working at the Scrubba-Dubba car wash.
Yelling from passing cars, people called him halfwit and loony and many things, but it was Trashy that stuck.
During his breaks, Donald would sit behind the car wash, wondering how the Cheery Oil tanks would go up. Three separate explosions? Three pillars of fire that would burn all day and all night long?
nder the blue sky, he breeze died own, and Trashcan truck and lit match...
...and let it drop to the puddle of gas beneath him.

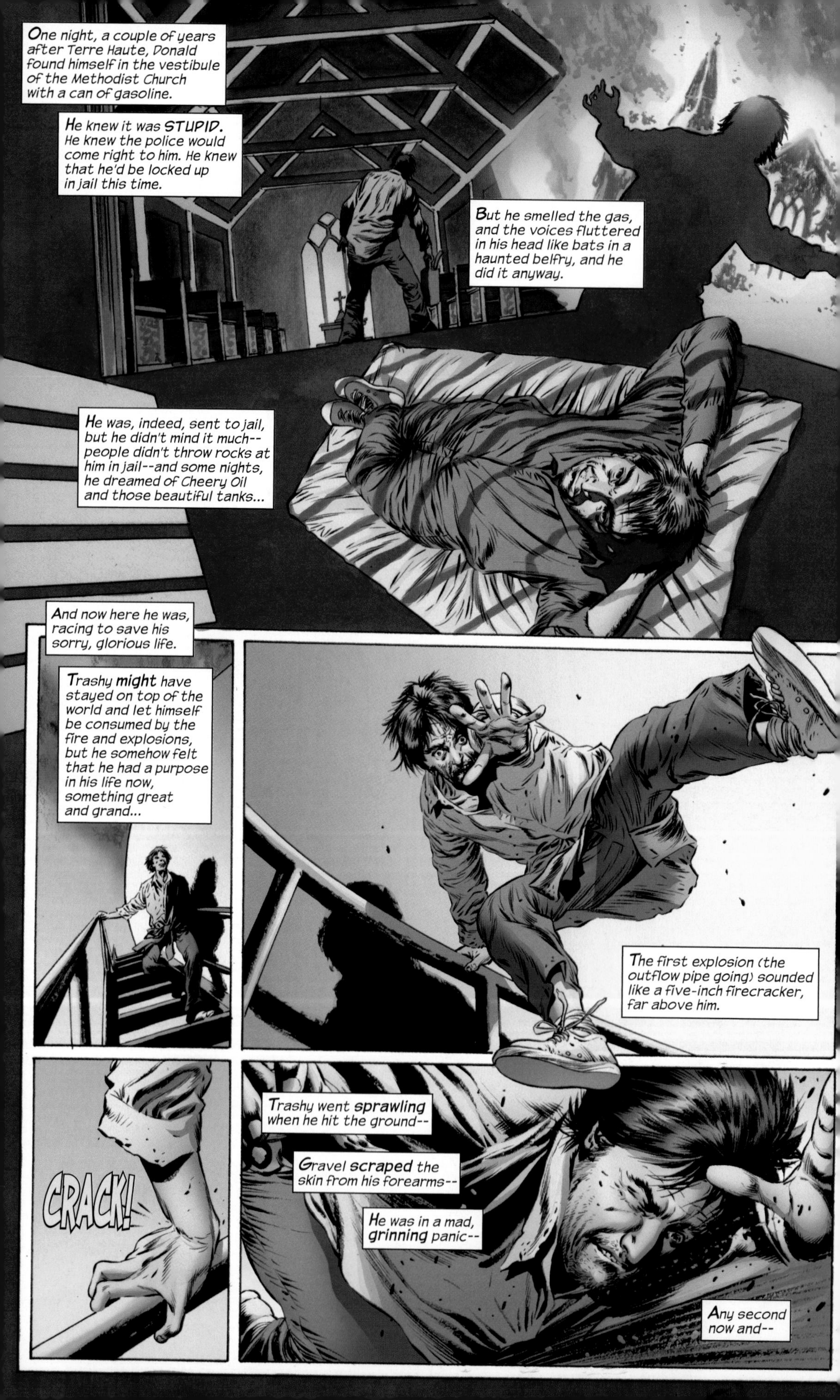
One night, a couple of years after Terre Haute, Donald found himself in the vestibule of the Methodist Church with a can of gasoline.
He knew it was STUPID. He knew the police would come right to him. He knew that he'd be locked up in jail this time.
But he smelled the gas, and the voices fluttered in his head like bats in a haunted belfry, and he did it anyway.
He was, indeed, sent to jail, but he didn't mind it much--people didn't throw rocks at him in jail--and some nights, he dreamed of Cheery Oil and those beautiful tanks...
And now here he was, racing to save his sorry, glorious life.
Trashy might have stayed on top of the world and let himself be consumed by the fire and explosions, but he somehow felt that he had a purpose in his life now, something great and grand...
The first explosion (the outflow pipe going) sounded like a five-inch firecracker, far above him.
CRACK!
Trashy went sprawling when he hit the ground--
Gravel scraped the skin from his forearms--
He was in a mad, grinning panic--
Any second now and--

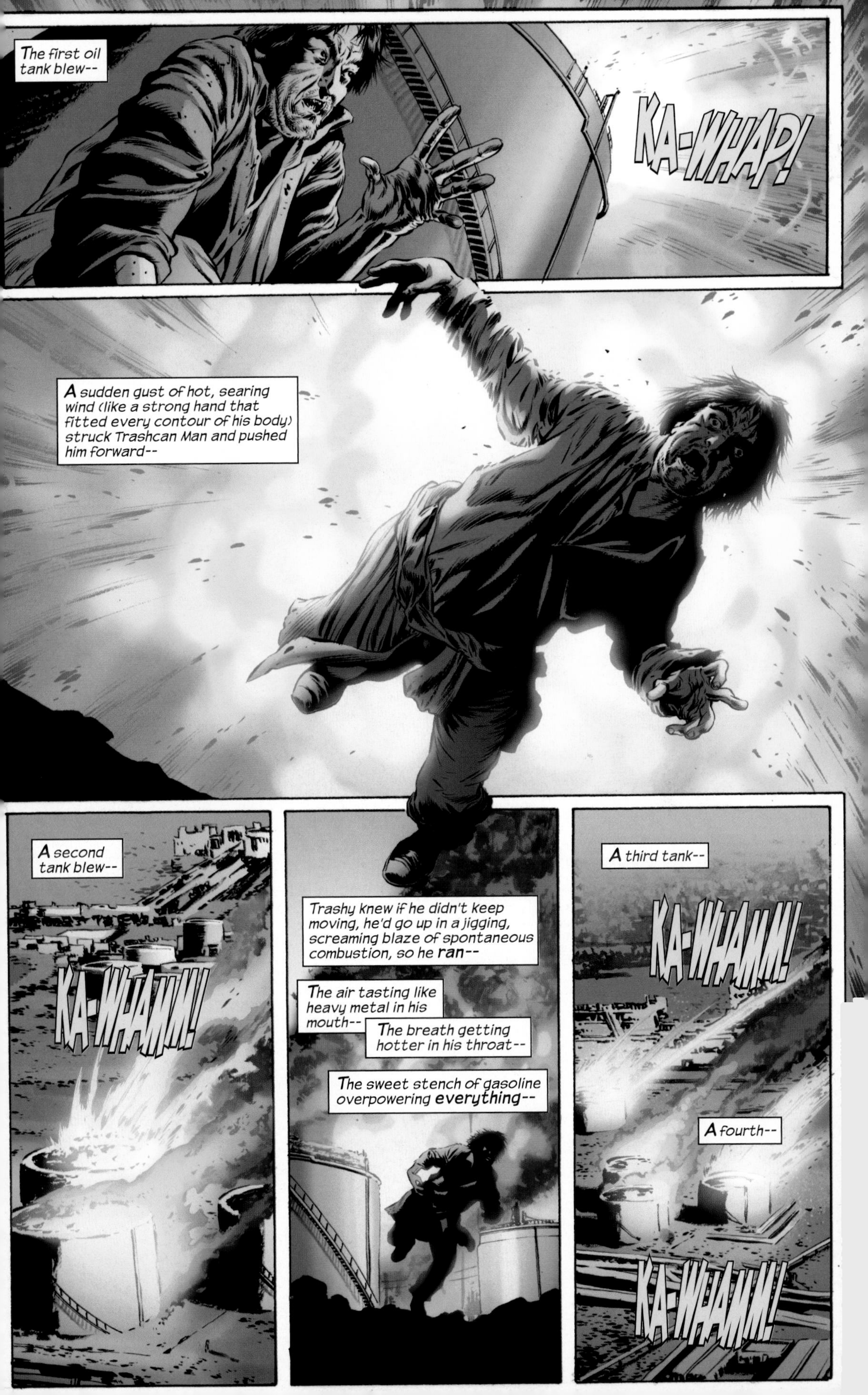
The first oil tank blew--
KA-WHAP!
A sudden gust of hot, searing wind (like a strong hand that fitted every contour of his body) struck Trashcan Man and pushed him forward--
A second tank blew--
KA-WHAMM!
Trashy knew if he didn't keep moving, he'd go up in a jigging, screaming blaze of spontaneous combustion, so he **ran**--
The air tasting like heavy metal in his mouth--
The breath getting hotter in his throat--
The sweet stench of gasoline overpowering **everything**--
A third tank--
KA-WHAMM!
A fourth--
KA-WHAMM!

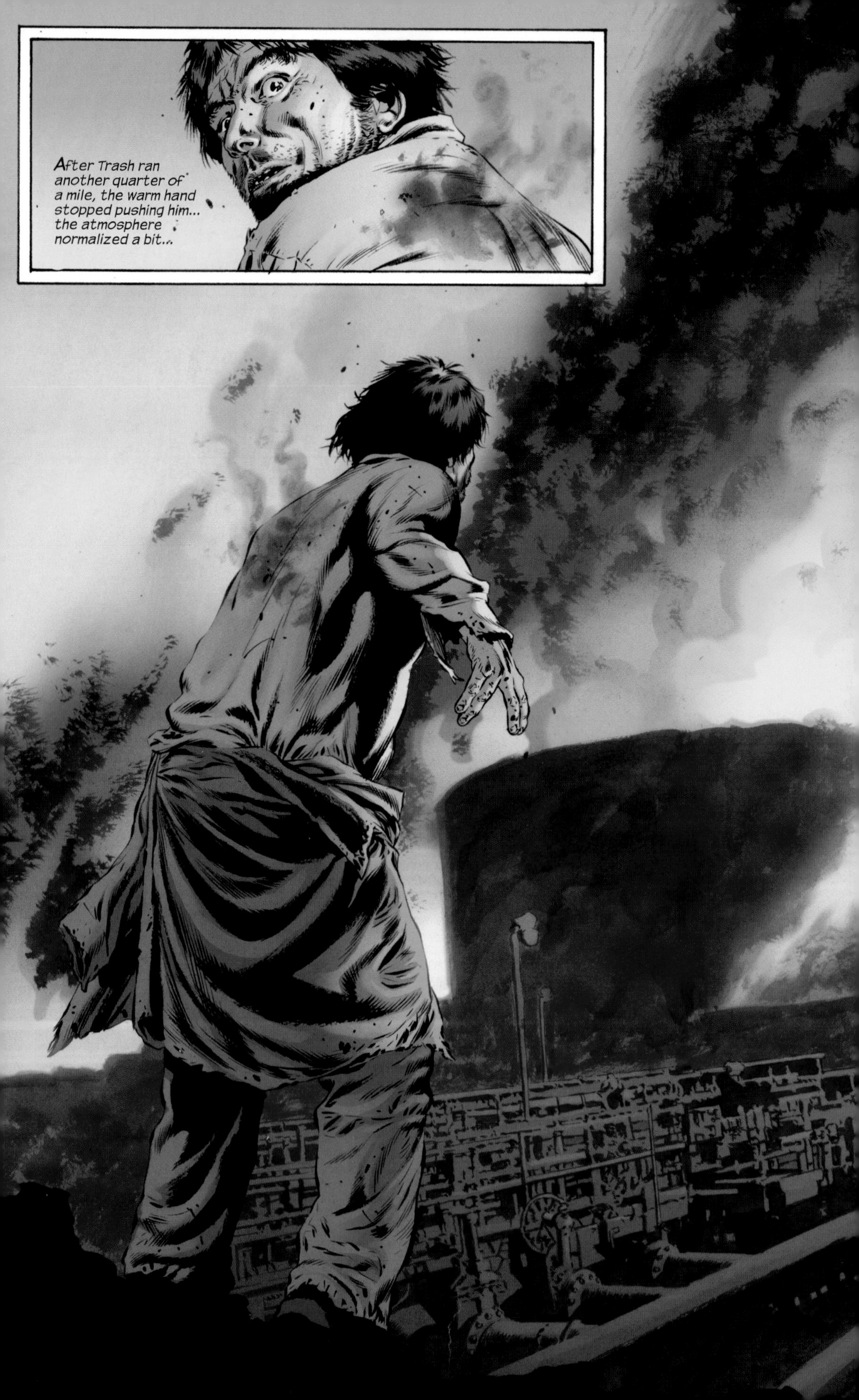
After Trash ran another quarter of a mile, the warm hand stopped pushing him... the atmosphere normalized a bit...

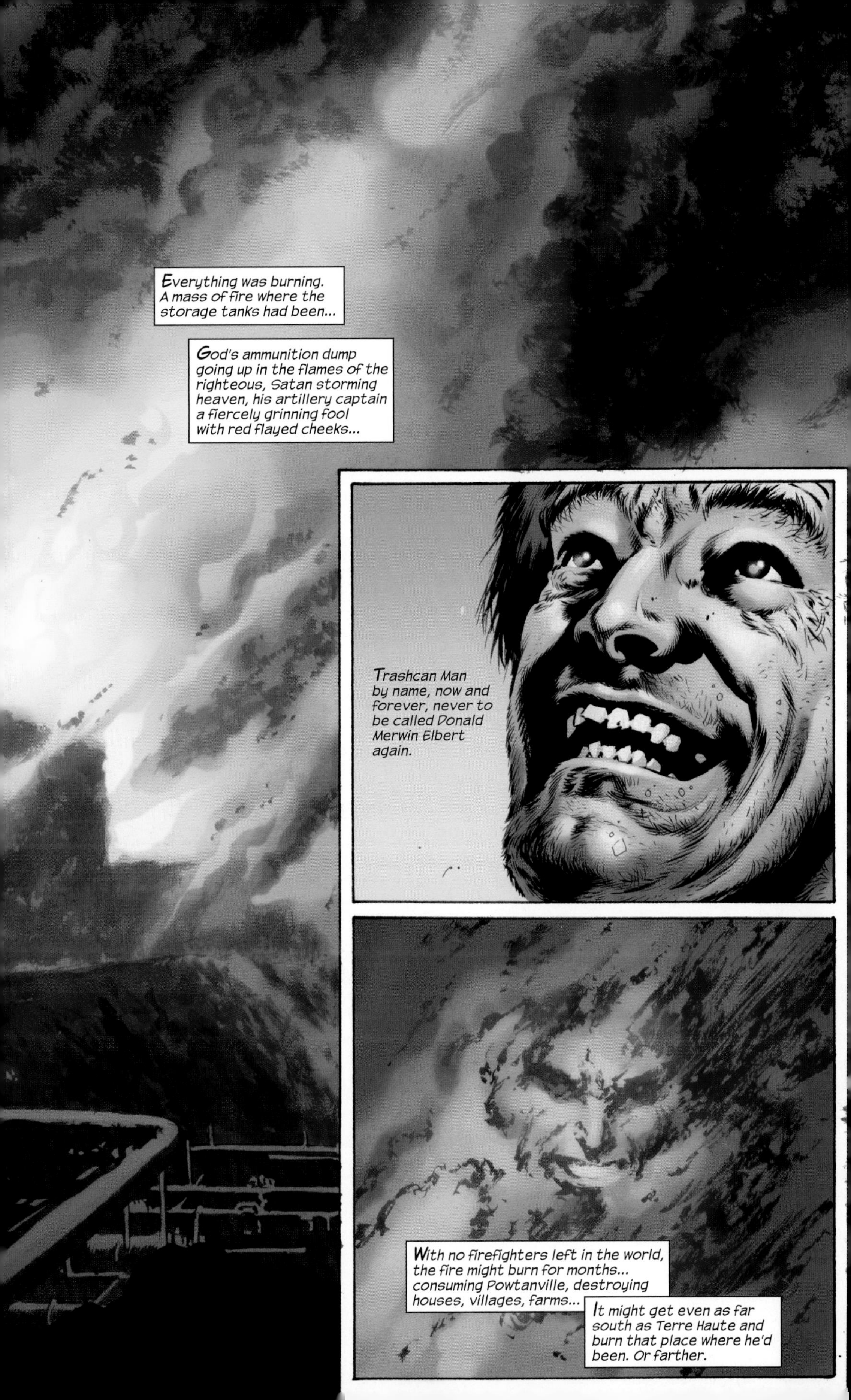
Everything was burning. A mass of fire where the storage tanks had been...
God's ammunition dump going up in the flames of the righteous, Satan storming heaven, his artillery captain a fiercely grinning fool with red flayed cheeks...
Trashcan Man by name, now and forever, never to be called Donald Merwin Elbert again.
With no firefighters left in the world, the fire might burn for months... consuming Powtanville, destroying houses, villages, farms...
It might get even as far south as Terre Haute and burn that place where he'd been. Or farther.

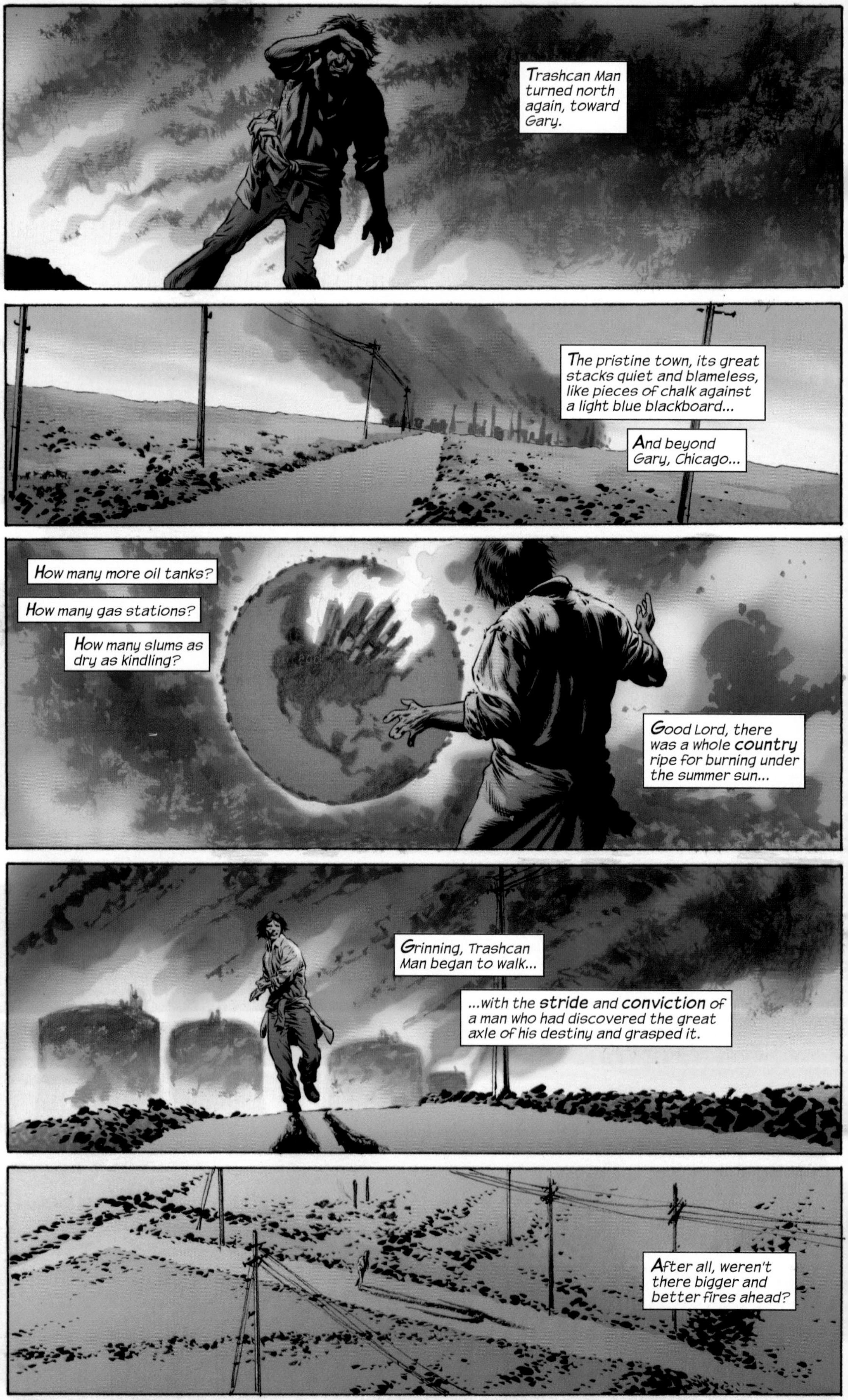
Trashcan Man turned north again, toward Gary.
The pristine town, its great stacks quiet and blameless, like pieces of chalk against a light blue blackboard...
And beyond Gary, Chicago...
How many more oil tanks?
How many gas stations?
How many slums as dry as kindling?
Good Lord, there was a whole country ripe for burning under the summer sun...
Grinning, Trashcan Man began to walk...
...with the stride and conviction of a man who had discovered the great axle of his destiny and grasped it.
After all, weren't there bigger and better fires ahead?

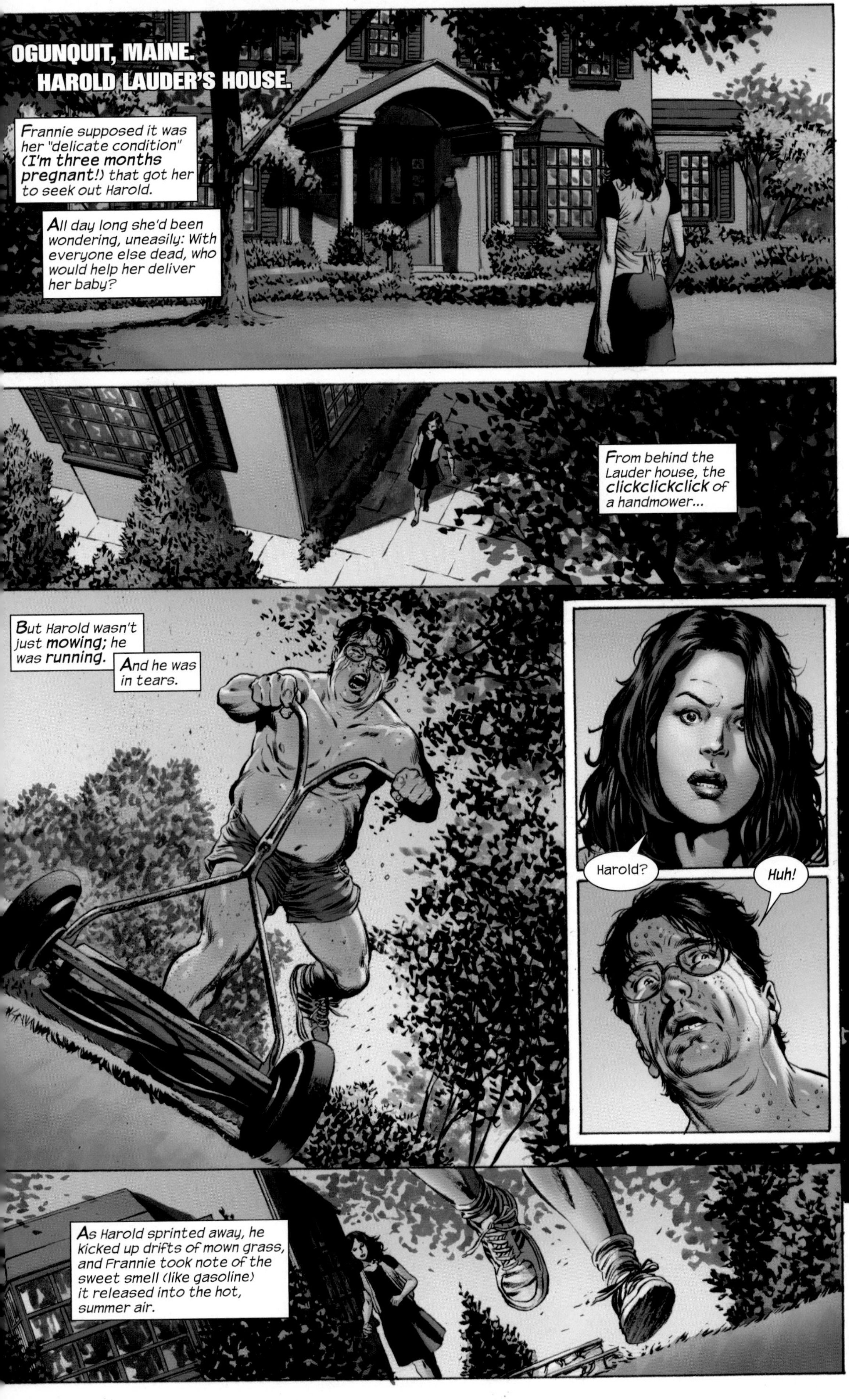
OGUNQUIT, MAINE.
HAROLD LAUDER'S HOUSE.
Frannie supposed it was her "delicate condition" (I'm three months pregnant!) that got her to seek out Harold.
All day long she'd been wondering, uneasily: With everyone else dead, who would help her deliver her baby?
From behind the Lauder house, the clickclickclick of a handmower...
But Harold wasn't just mowing; he was running.
And he was in tears.
Harold?
Huh!
As Harold sprinted away, he kicked up drifts of mown grass, and Frannie took note of the sweet smell (like gasoline) it released into the hot, summer air.

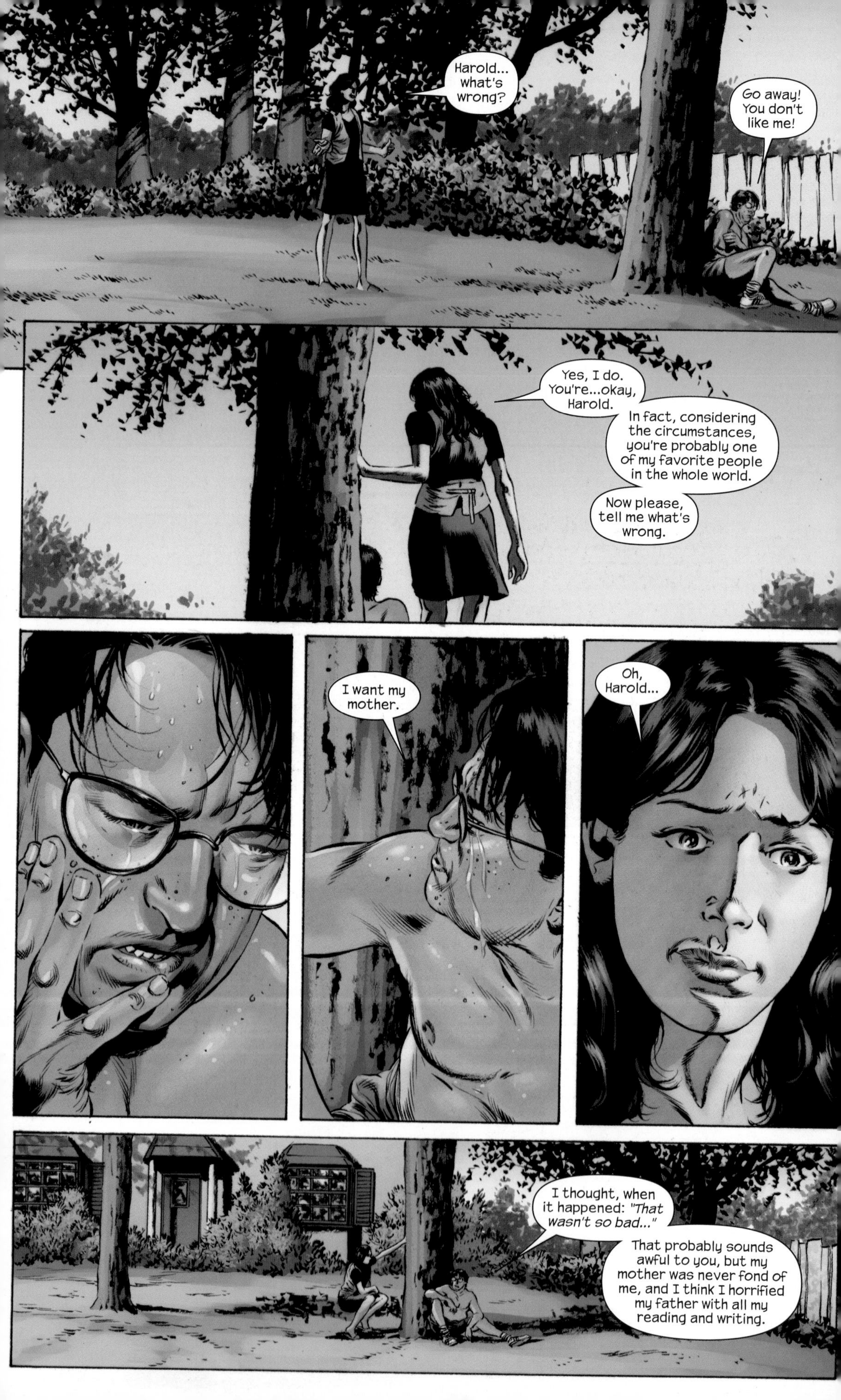
Harold... what's wrong?
Go away! You don't like me!
Yes, I do. You're...okay, Harold.
In fact, considering the circumstances, you're probably one of my favorite people in the whole world.
Now please, tell me what's wrong.
I want my mother.
Oh, Harold...
I thought, when it happened: "That wasn't so bad..."
That probably sounds awful to you, but my mother was never fond of me, and I think I horrified my father with all my reading and writing.

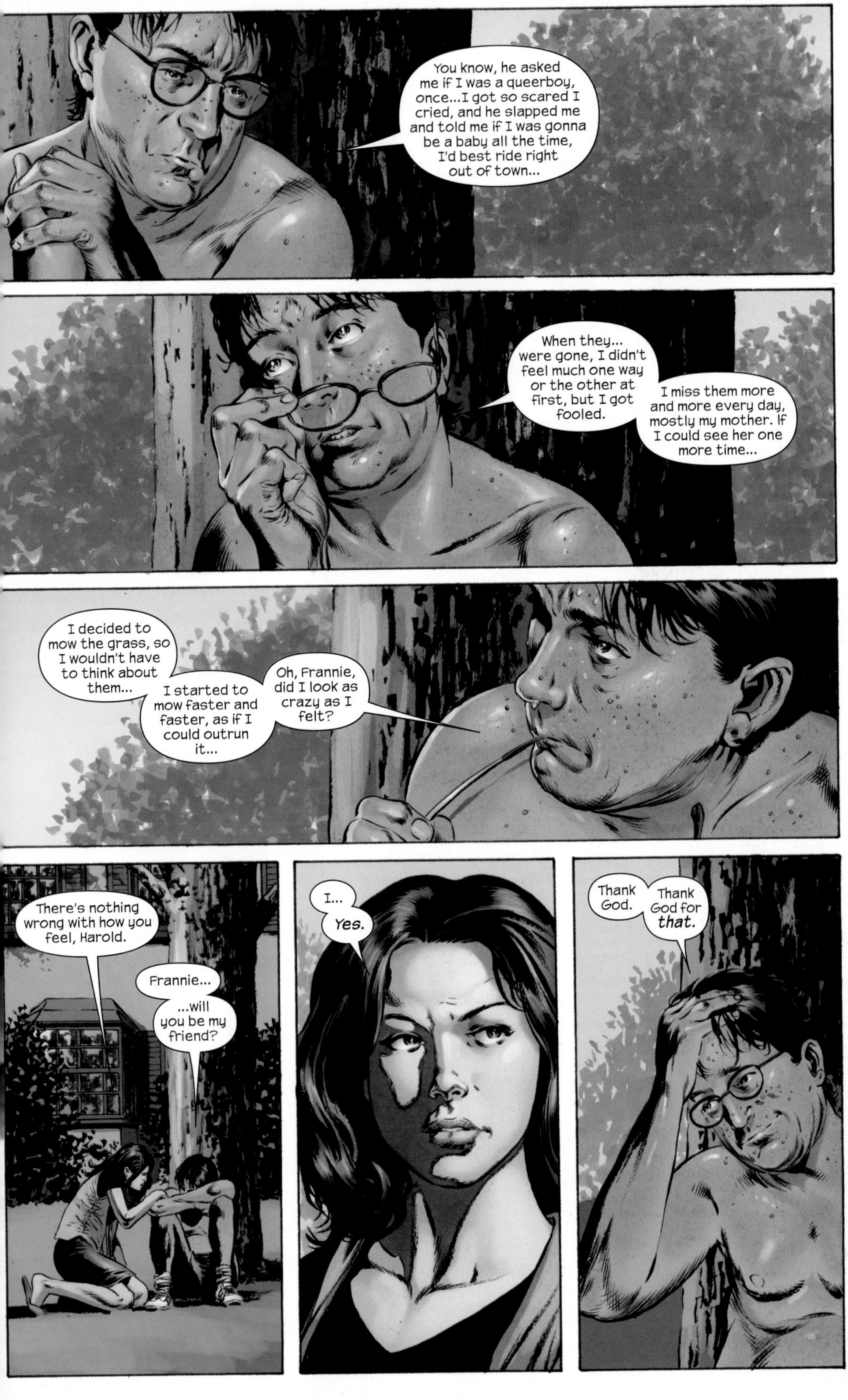
You know, he asked me if I was a queerboy, once...I got so scared I cried, and he slapped me and told me if I was gonna be a baby all the time, I'd best ride right out of town...
When they... were gone, I didn't feel much one way or the other at first, but I got fooled.
I miss them more and more every day, mostly my mother. If I could see her one more time...
I decided to mow the grass, so I wouldn't have to think about them...
I started to mow faster and faster, as if I could outrun it...
Oh, Frannie, did I look as crazy as I felt?
There's nothing wrong with how you feel, Harold.
Frannie...
...will you be my friend?
I...
Yes.
Thank God.
Thank God for *that.*

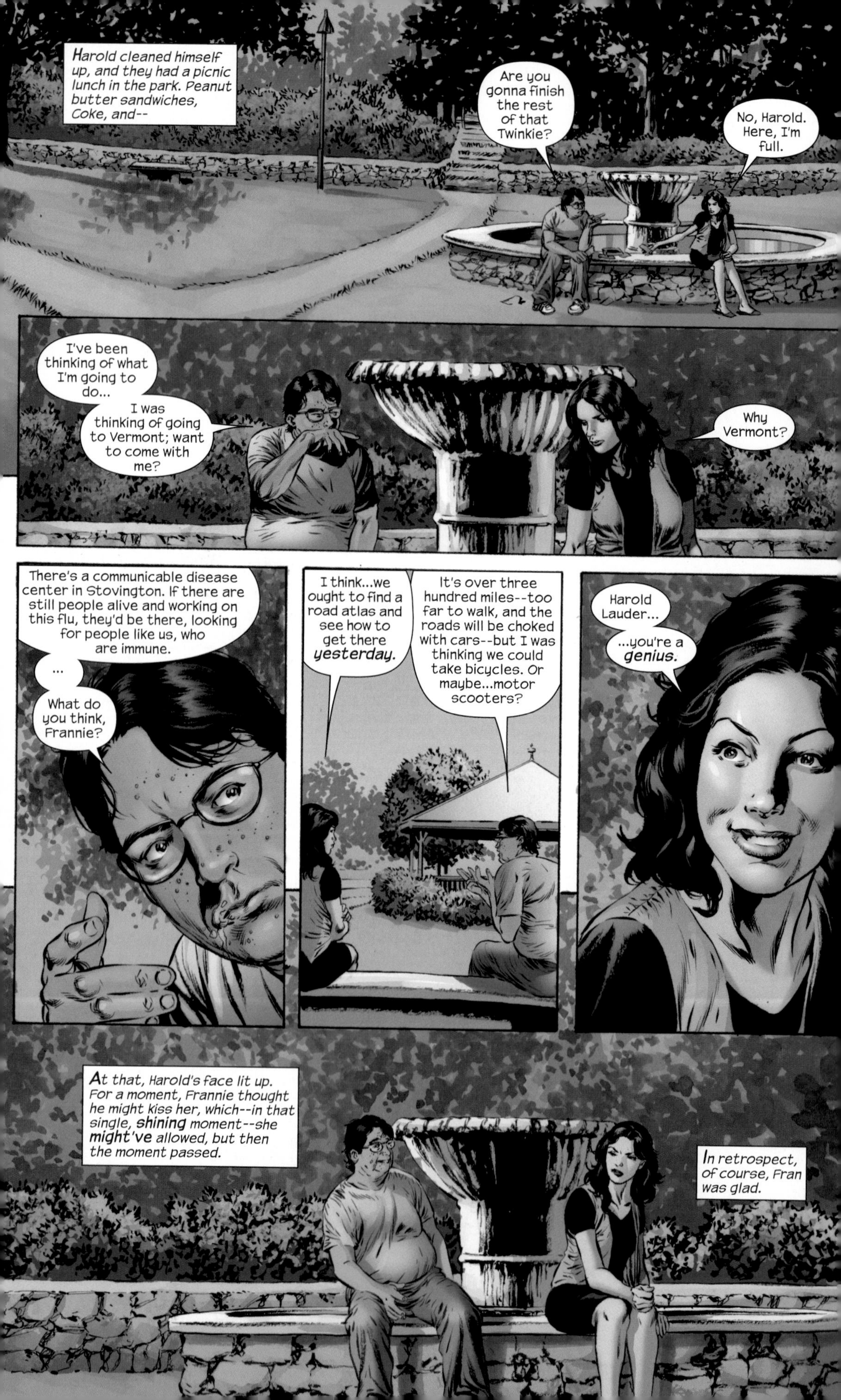

Harold cleaned himself up, and they had a picnic lunch in the park. Peanut butter sandwiches, Coke, and--
Are you gonna finish the rest of that Twinkie?
No, Harold. Here, I'm full.
I've been thinking of what I'm going to do...
I was thinking of going to Vermont; want to come with me?
Why Vermont?
There's a communicable disease center in Stovington. If there are still people alive and working on this flu, they'd be there, looking for people like us, who are immune.
...
What do you think, Frannie?
I think...we ought to find a road atlas and see how to get there yesterday.
It's over three hundred miles--too far to walk, and the roads will be choked with cars--but I was thinking we could take bicycles. Or maybe...motor scooters?
Harold Lauder...
...you're a genius.
At that, Harold's face lit up. For a moment, Frannie thought he might kiss her, which--in that single, shining moment--she might've allowed, but then the moment passed.
In retrospect, of course, Fran was glad.

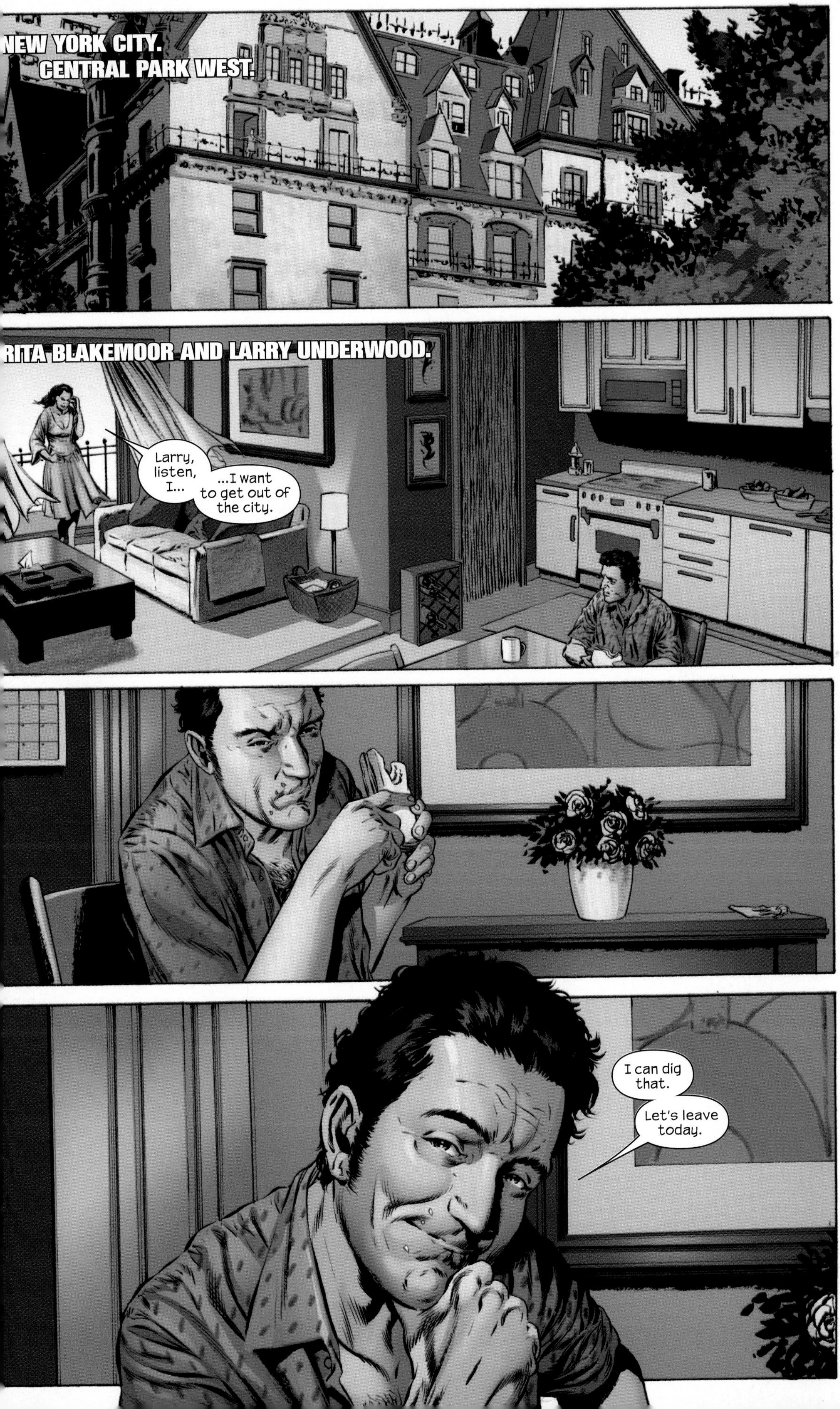

NEW YORK CITY.
CENTRAL PARK WEST.
RITA BLAKEMOOR AND LARRY UNDERWOOD.
Larry, listen, I...
...I want to get out of the city.
I can dig that.
Let's leave today.

chapter THREE

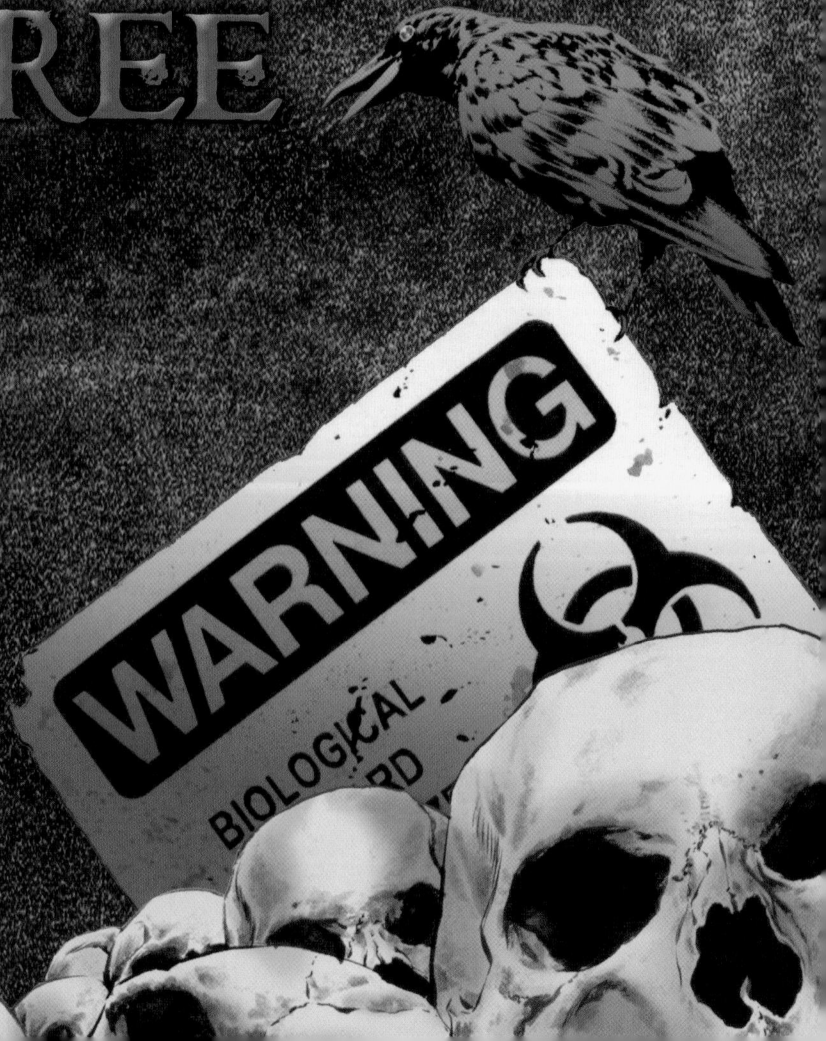
WARNING
BIOLOGICAL

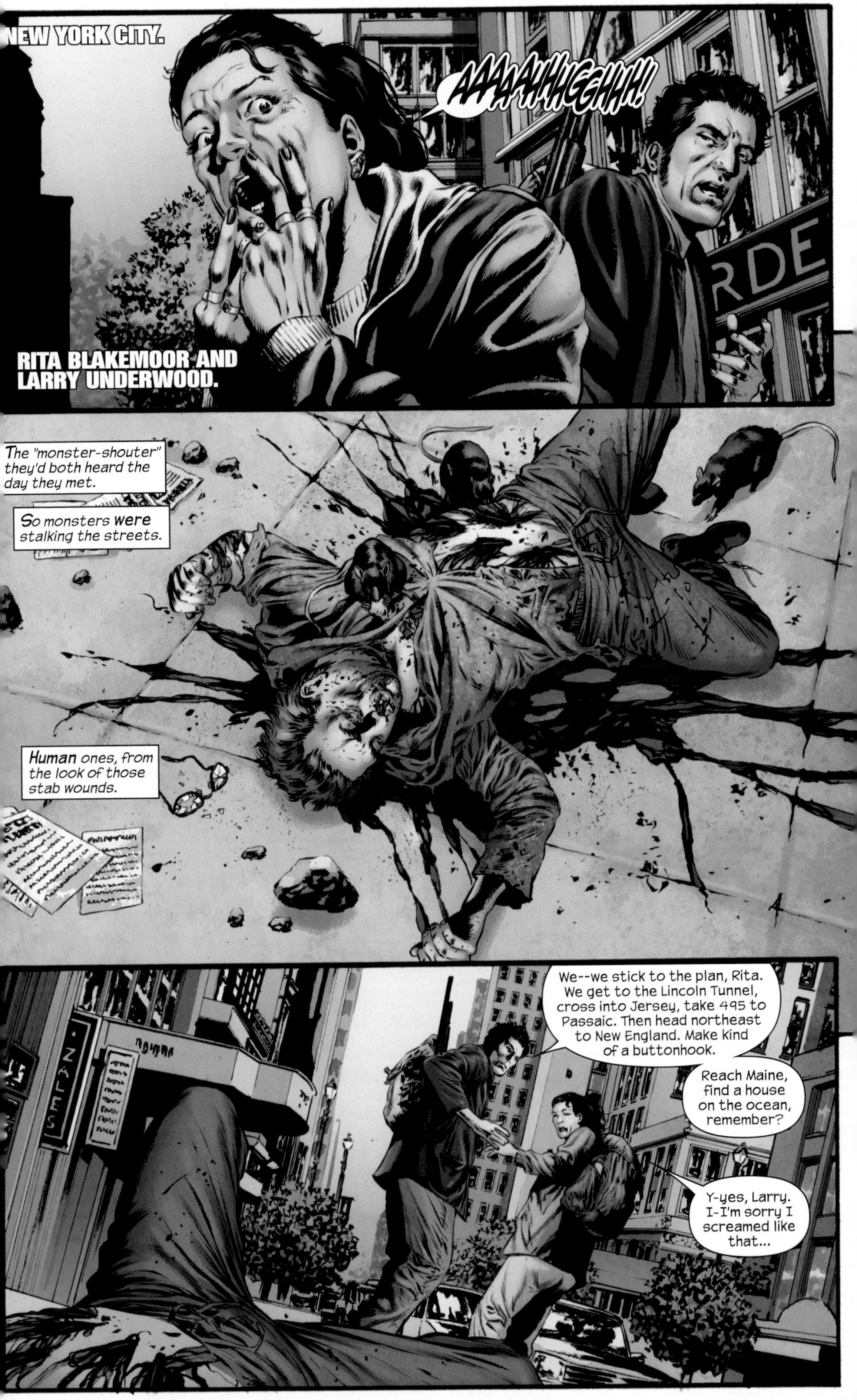

NEW YORK CITY.
AAAAAHHGGHHH!
RITA BLAKEMOOR AND LARRY UNDERWOOD.
The "monster-shouter" they'd both heard the day they met.
So monsters were stalking the streets.
Human ones, from the look of those stab wounds.
ZALES
We--we stick to the plan, Rita. We get to the Lincoln Tunnel, cross into Jersey, take 495 to Passaic. Then head northeast to New England. Make kind of a buttonhook.
Reach Maine, find a house on the ocean, remember?
Y-yes, Larry. I-I'm sorry I screamed like that...

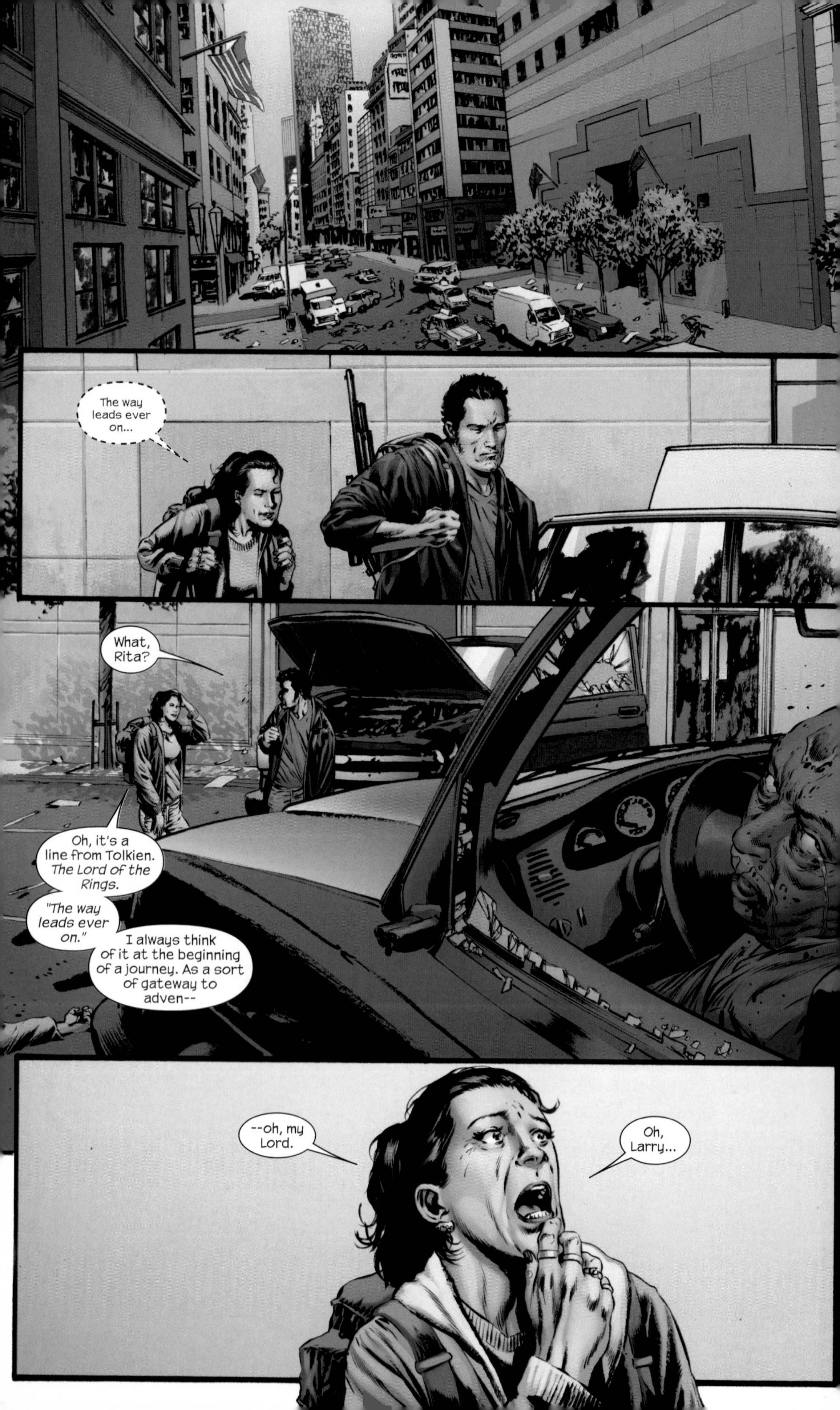

The way leads ever on...
What, Rita?
Oh, it's a line from Tolkien. *The Lord of the Rings.*
"The way leads ever on."
I always think of it at the beginning of a journey. As a sort of gateway to adven--
--oh, my Lord.
Oh, Larry...

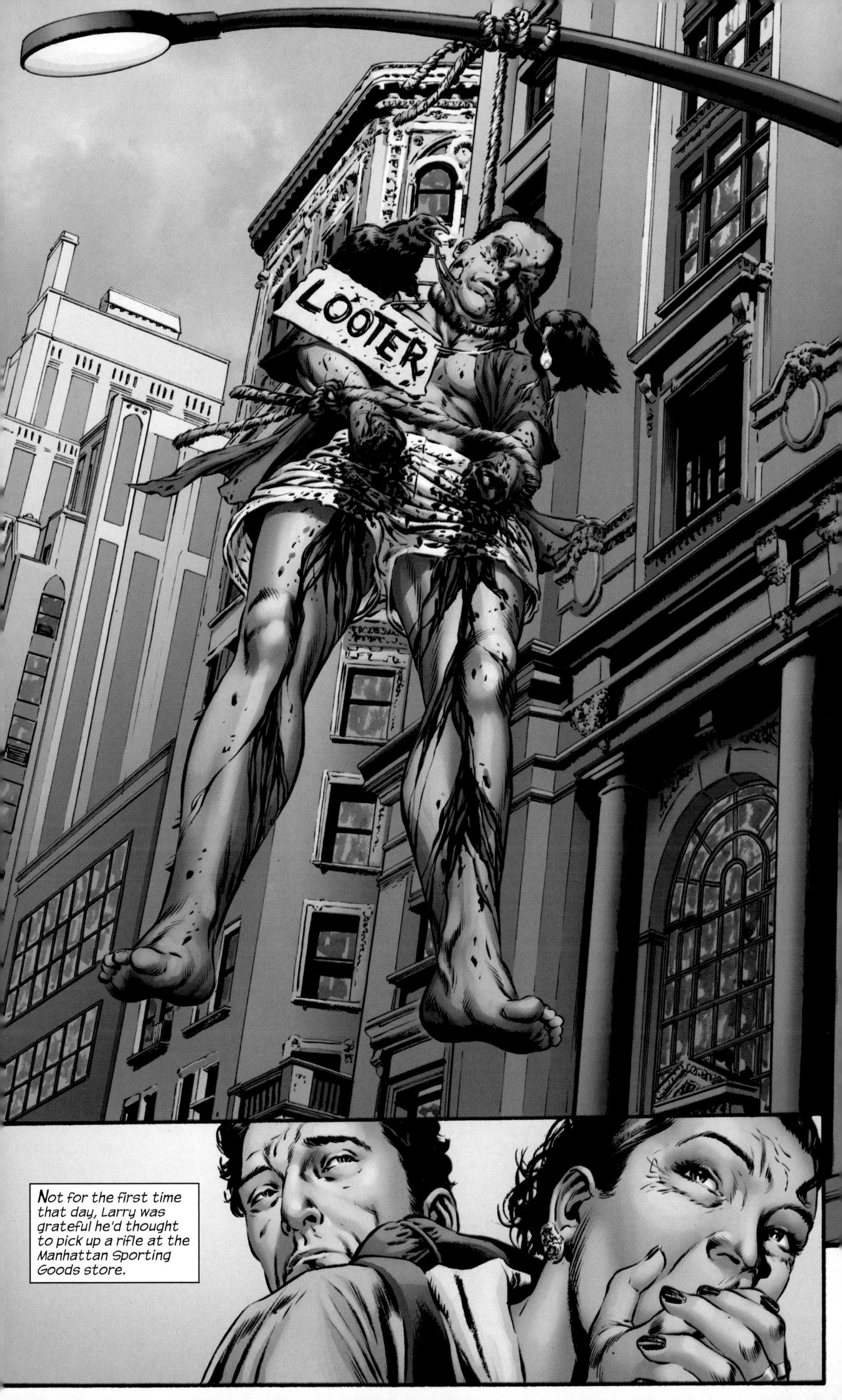
LOOTER
Not for the first time that day, Larry was grateful he'd thought to pick up a rifle at the Manhattan Sporting Goods store.

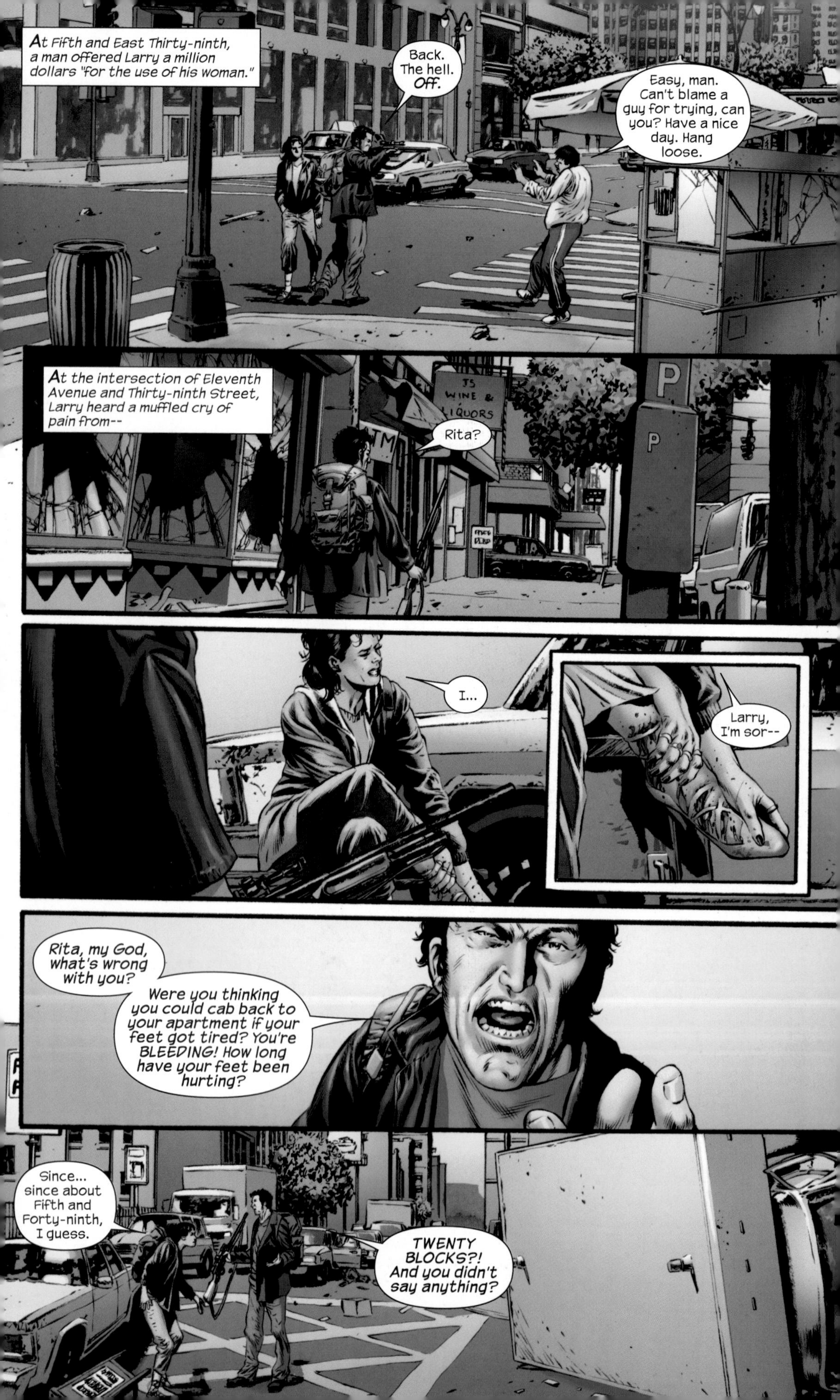

At Fifth and East Thirty-ninth, a man offered Larry a million dollars "for the use of his woman."
Back. The hell. OFF.
Easy, man. Can't blame a guy for trying, can you? Have a nice day. Hang loose.
At the intersection of Eleventh Avenue and Thirty-ninth Street, Larry heard a muffled cry of pain from--
Rita?
I...
Larry, I'm sor--
Rita, my God, what's wrong with you?
Were you thinking you could cab back to your apartment if your feet got tired? You're BLEEDING! How long have your feet been hurting?
Since... since about Fifth and Forty-ninth, I guess.
TWENTY BLOCKS?! And you didn't say anything?

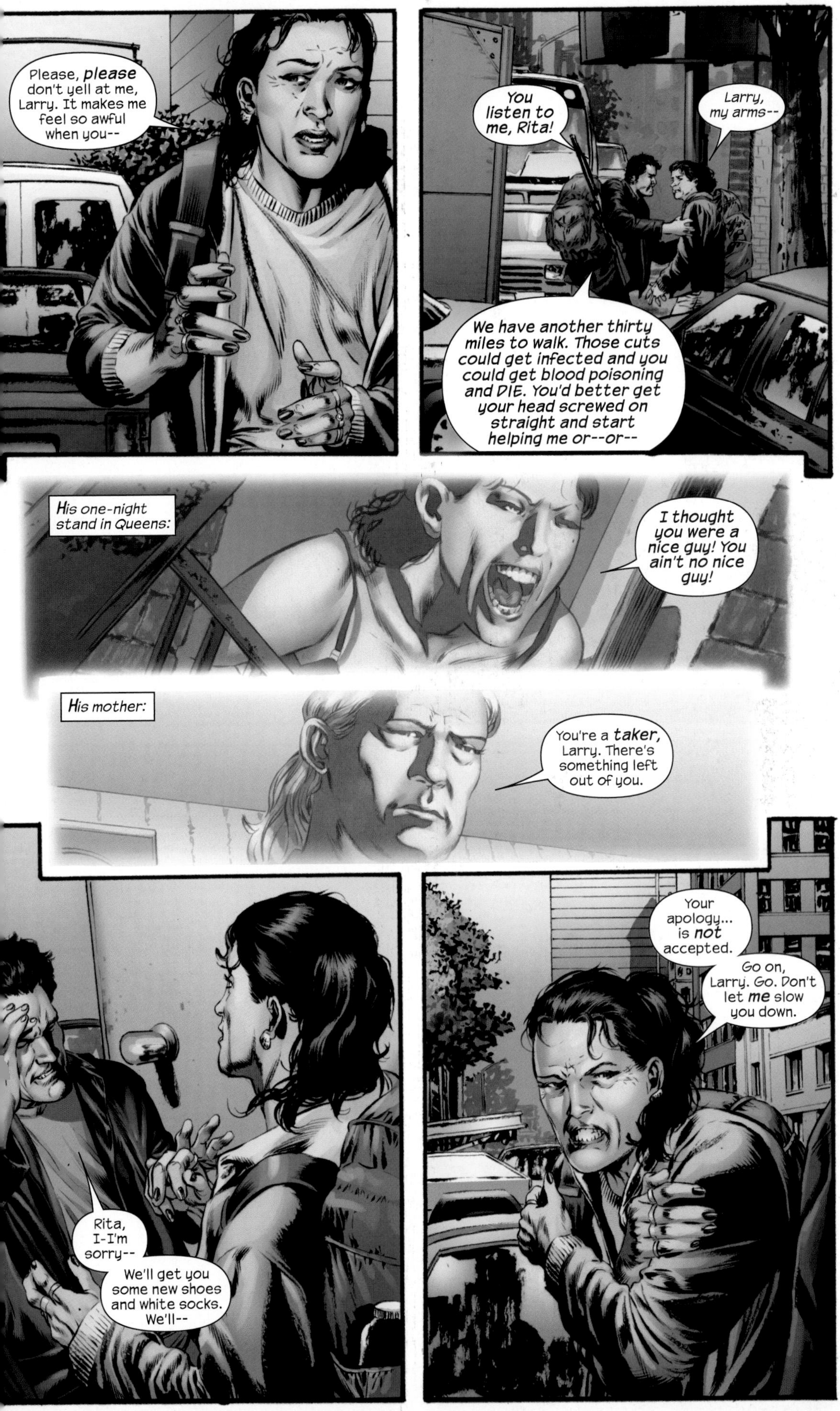
Please, *please* don't yell at me, Larry. It makes me feel so awful when you--
You listen to me, Rita!
Larry, my arms--
We have another thirty miles to walk. Those cuts could get infected and you could get blood poisoning and DIE. You'd better get your head screwed on straight and start helping me or--or--
His one-night stand in Queens:
I thought you were a nice guy! You ain't no nice guy!
His mother:
You're a *taker,* Larry. There's something left out of you.
Rita, I-I'm sorry--
We'll get you some new shoes and white socks. We'll--
Your apology... is *not* accepted.
Go on, Larry. Go. Don't let *me* slow you down.

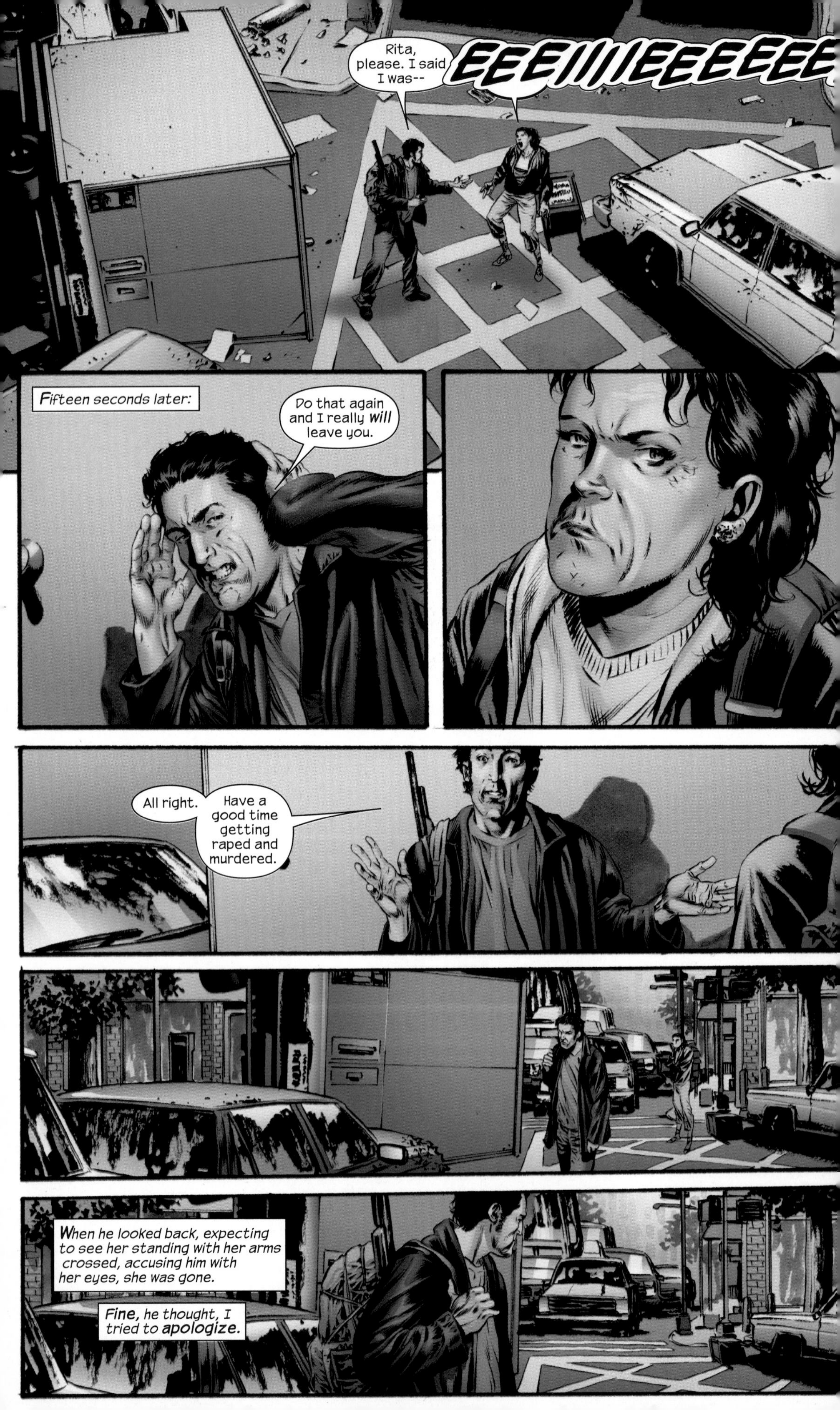
Rita, please. I said I was--
EEEIIIIEEEEEEE
Fifteen seconds later:
Do that again and I really will leave you.
All right.
Have a good time getting raped and murdered.
When he looked back, expecting to see her standing with her arms crossed, accusing him with her eyes, she was gone.
Fine, he thought, I tried to apologize.

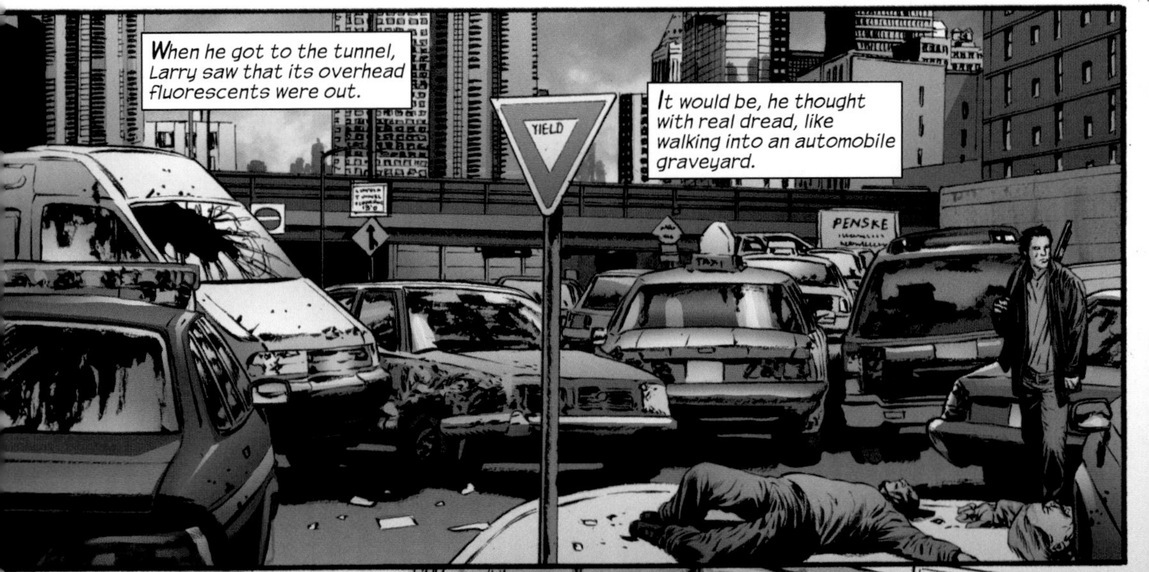
When he got to the tunnel, Larry saw that its overhead fluorescents were out.
It would be, he thought with real dread, like walking into an automobile graveyard.
YIELD
PENSKE

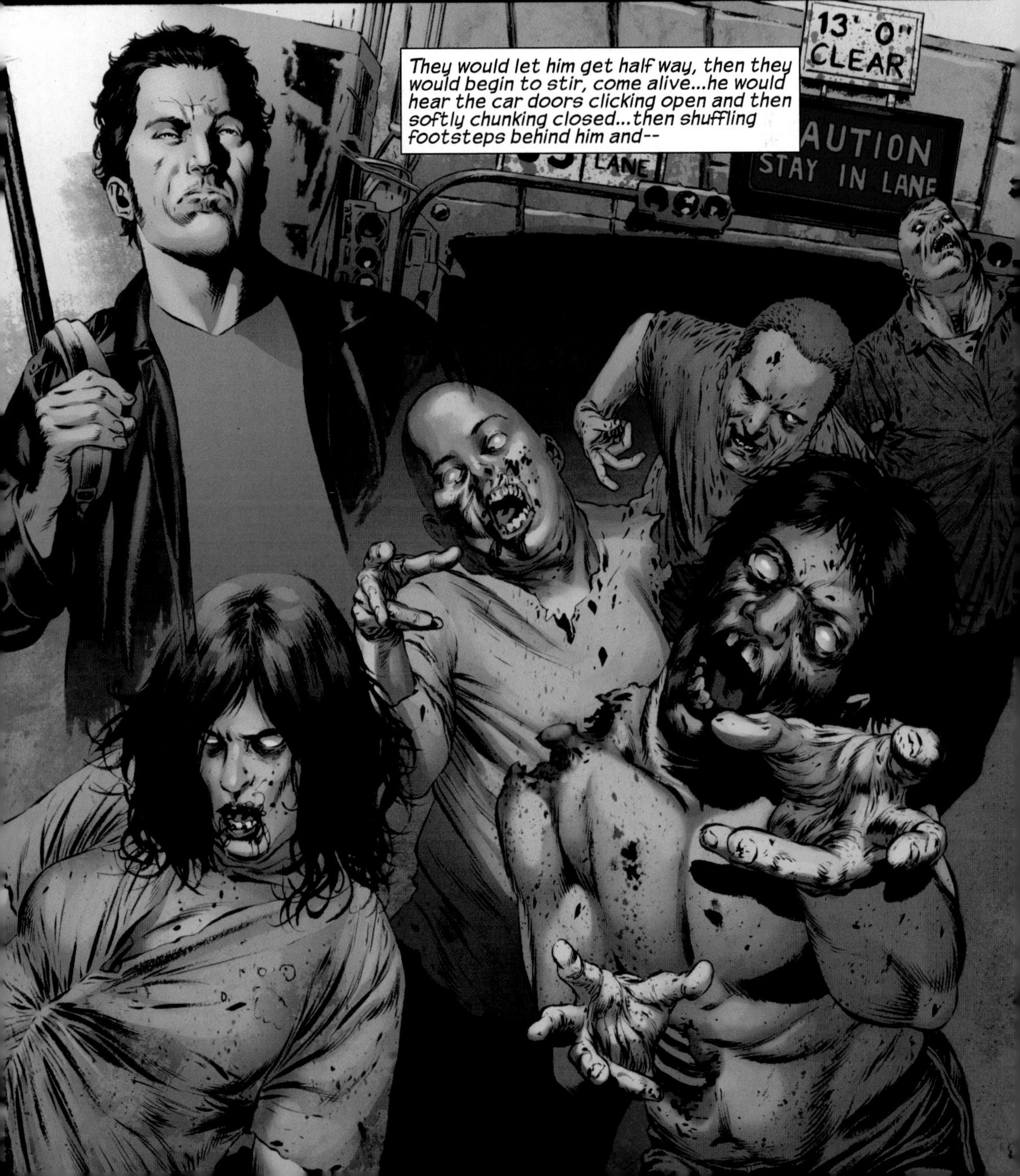
They would let him get half way, then they would begin to stir, come alive...he would hear the car doors clicking open and then softly chunking closed...then shuffling footsteps behind him and--
13'-0" CLEAR
AUTION STAY IN LANE
LANE

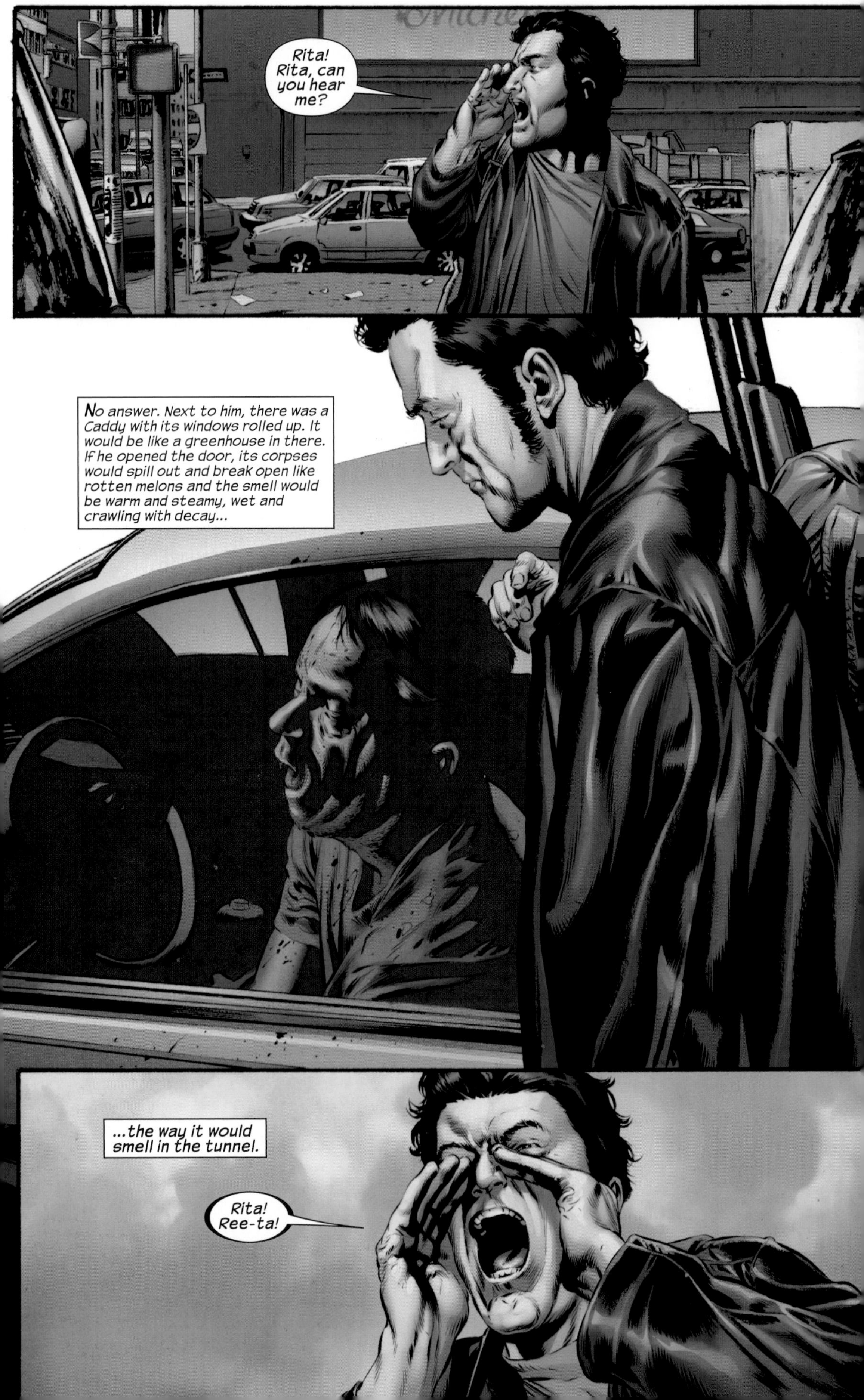
Rita! Rita, can you hear me?
No answer. Next to him, there was a Caddy with its windows rolled up. It would be like a greenhouse in there. If he opened the door, its corpses would spill out and break open like rotten melons and the smell would be warm and steamy, wet and crawling with decay...
...the way it would smell in the tunnel.
Rita! Ree-ta!

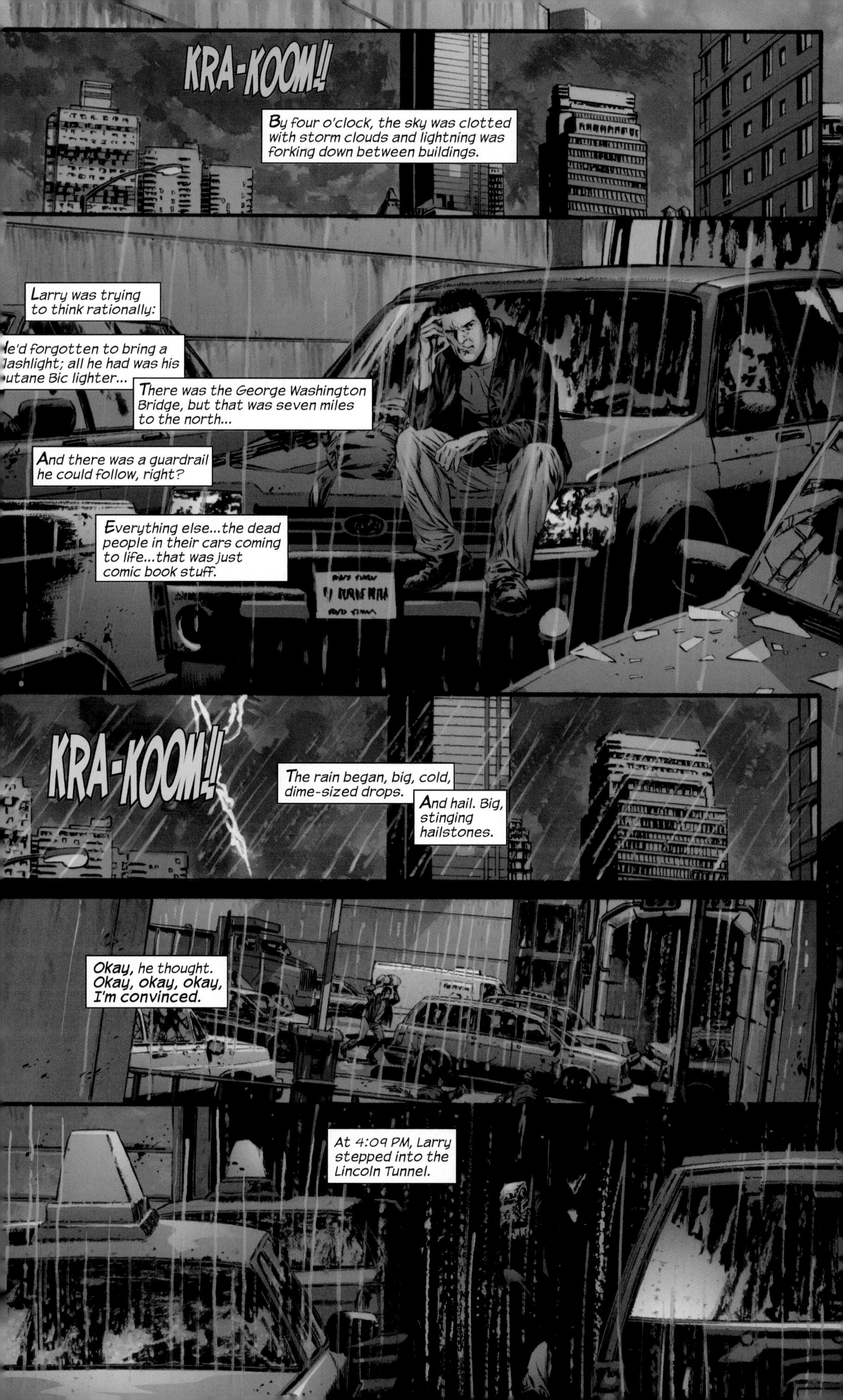
KRA-KOOM!!
By four o'clock, the sky was clotted with storm clouds and lightning was forking down between buildings.
Larry was trying to think rationally:
He'd forgotten to bring a flashlight; all he had was his butane Bic lighter...
There was the George Washington Bridge, but that was seven miles to the north...
And there was a guardrail he could follow, right?
Everything else...the dead people in their cars coming to life...that was just comic book stuff.
KRA-KOOM!!
The rain began, big, cold, dime-sized drops.
And hail. Big, stinging hailstones.
Okay, he thought. Okay, okay, okay, I'm convinced.
At 4:09 PM, Larry stepped into the Lincoln Tunnel.

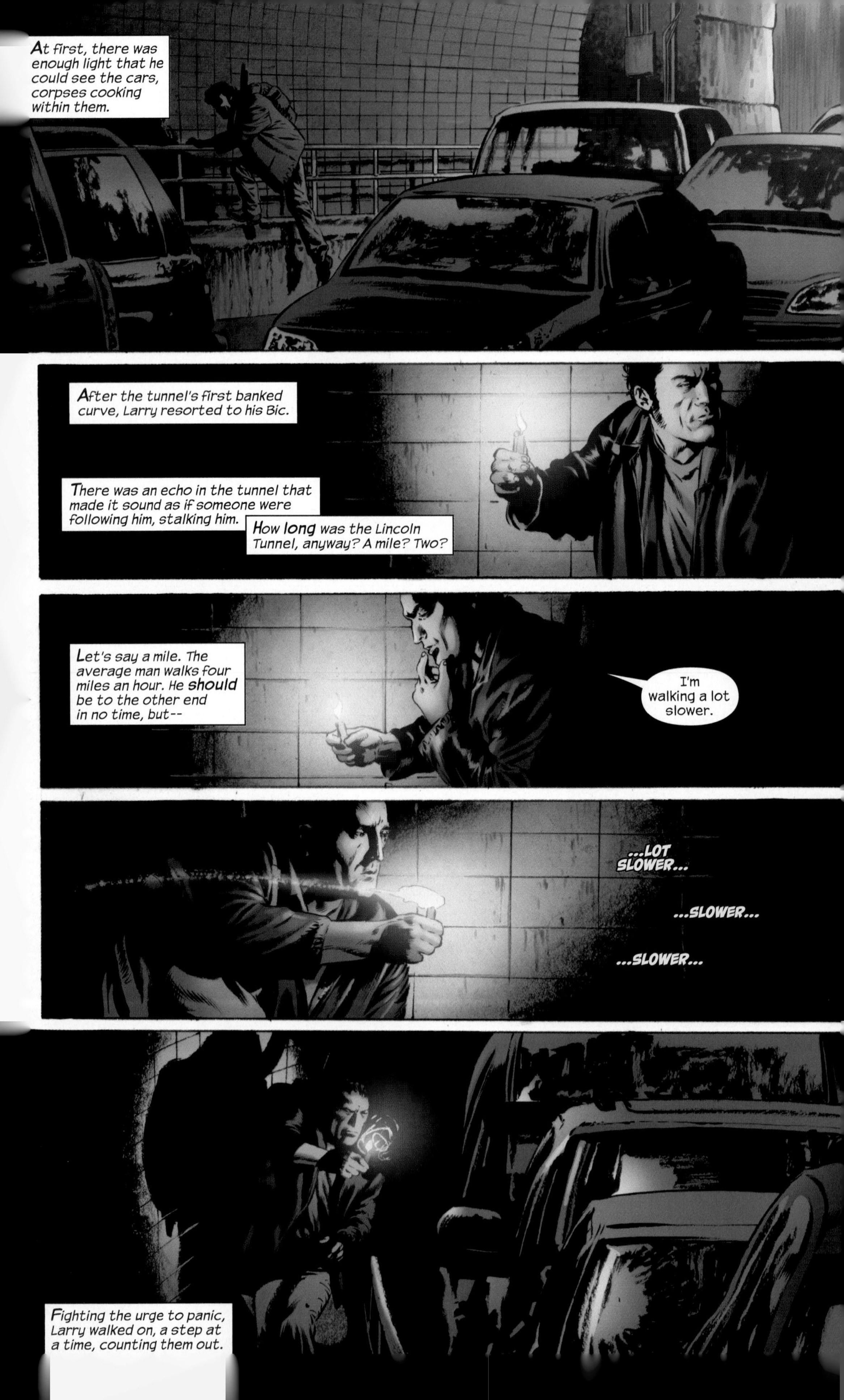
At first, there was enough light that he could see the cars, corpses cooking within them.
After the tunnel's first banked curve, Larry resorted to his Bic.
There was an echo in the tunnel that made it sound as if someone were following him, stalking him.
How long was the Lincoln Tunnel, anyway? A mile? Two?
Let's say a mile. The average man walks four miles an hour. He should be to the other end in no time, but--
I'm walking a lot slower.
...LOT SLOWER...
...SLOWER...
...SLOWER...
Fighting the urge to panic, Larry walked on, a step at a time, counting them out.

Larry was giving his lighter a break, groping his way through the dark, following the handrail--

‹gasp›

--when his foot stepped on something stiff and unyielding.

A horrible sentinel.

A murdered soldier.

The Bic was growing hot in Larry's hand; whether he wanted to or not, he **had** to let it go out.

In the dark, he stepped over the dead soldier, afraid the corpse would reach up and grab him.

Then Larry **ran**--a shuffling sort of run-- afraid that at any second his foot might come in contact with another body, and soon enough...

...it happened.

Six corpses this time. A Hasidic Jewish family. And they might've been sick, but Captain Trips **hadn't** killed them.

They'd been trying to get to Jersey, Larry surmised. Until they reached a command post, a machine-gun emplacement, **something**.

At which point they'd been gunned down. By soldiers? That might still be around?

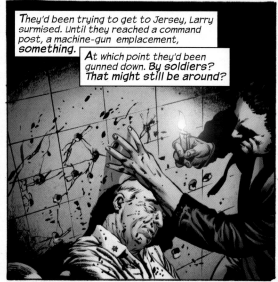

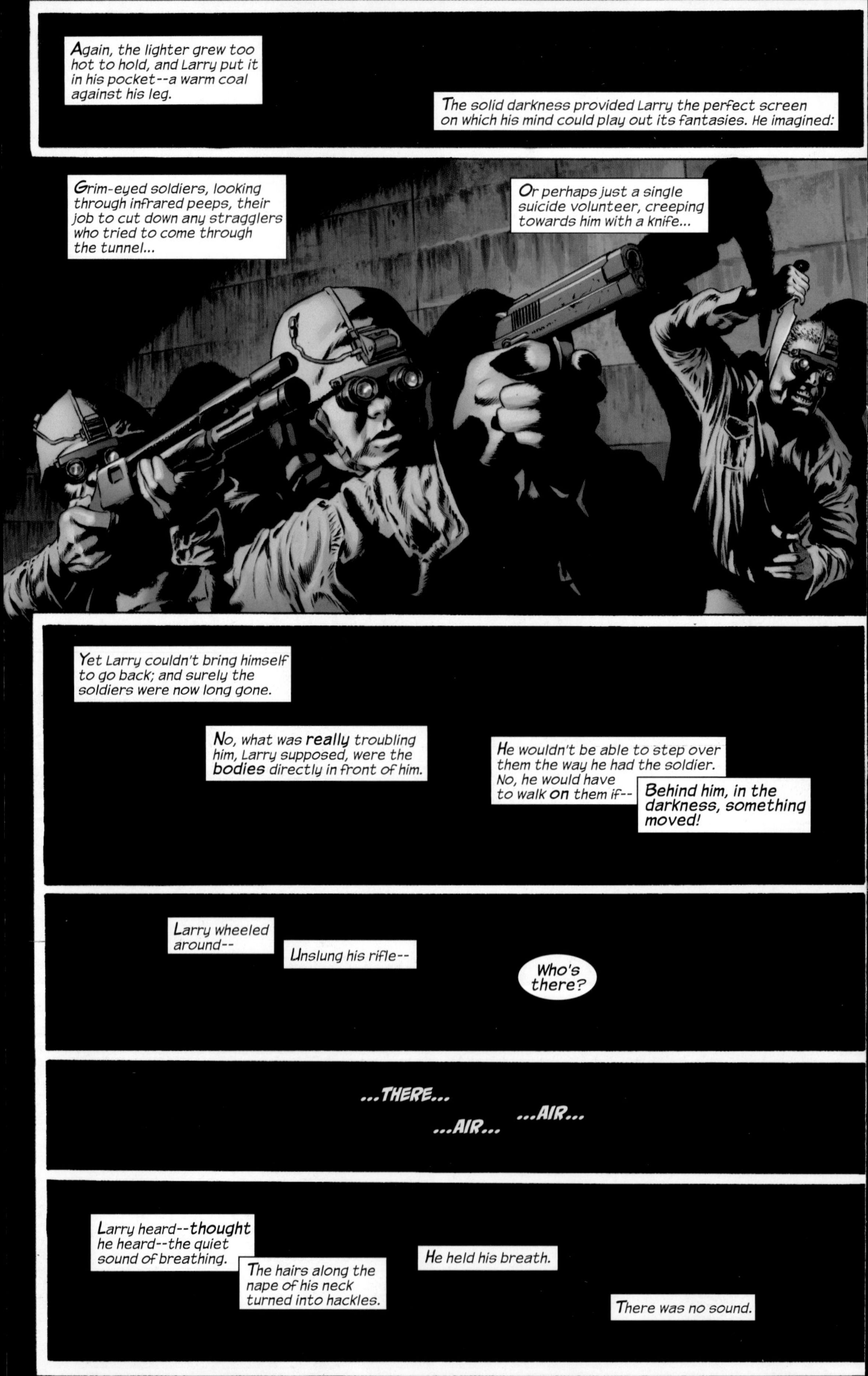
Again, the lighter grew too hot to hold, and Larry put it in his pocket--a warm coal against his leg.
The solid darkness provided Larry the perfect screen on which his mind could play out its fantasies. He imagined:
Grim-eyed soldiers, looking through infrared peeps, their job to cut down any stragglers who tried to come through the tunnel...
Or perhaps just a single suicide volunteer, creeping towards him with a knife...
Yet Larry couldn't bring himself to go back; and surely the soldiers were now long gone.
No, what was **really** troubling him, Larry supposed, were the **bodies** directly in front of him.
He wouldn't be able to step over them the way he had the soldier. No, he would have to walk **on** them if--
Behind him, in the darkness, something moved!
Larry wheeled around--
Unslung his rifle--
Who's there?
...THERE...
...AIR...
...AIR...
Larry heard--**thought** he heard--the quiet sound of breathing.
The hairs along the nape of his neck turned into hackles.
He held his breath.
There was no sound.

He was beginning to dismiss the sound as his imagination when he heard it again: A single, sliding, quiet *footstep*.

Larry fumbled madly for the lighter, pulled it out, and--

CLINK!

CLINK!

CLATTER!

--the Bic had slipped from his hand, tumbling down to the hood of a car below.

Oh, God.

His terror-locked mind gave him a picture of someone or something coming to kill him:

Then the sound of *another* step--

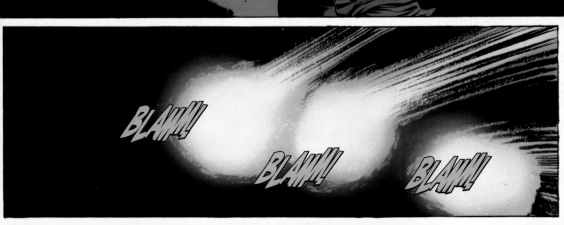

BLAMM!!

BLAMM!!

BLAMM!!

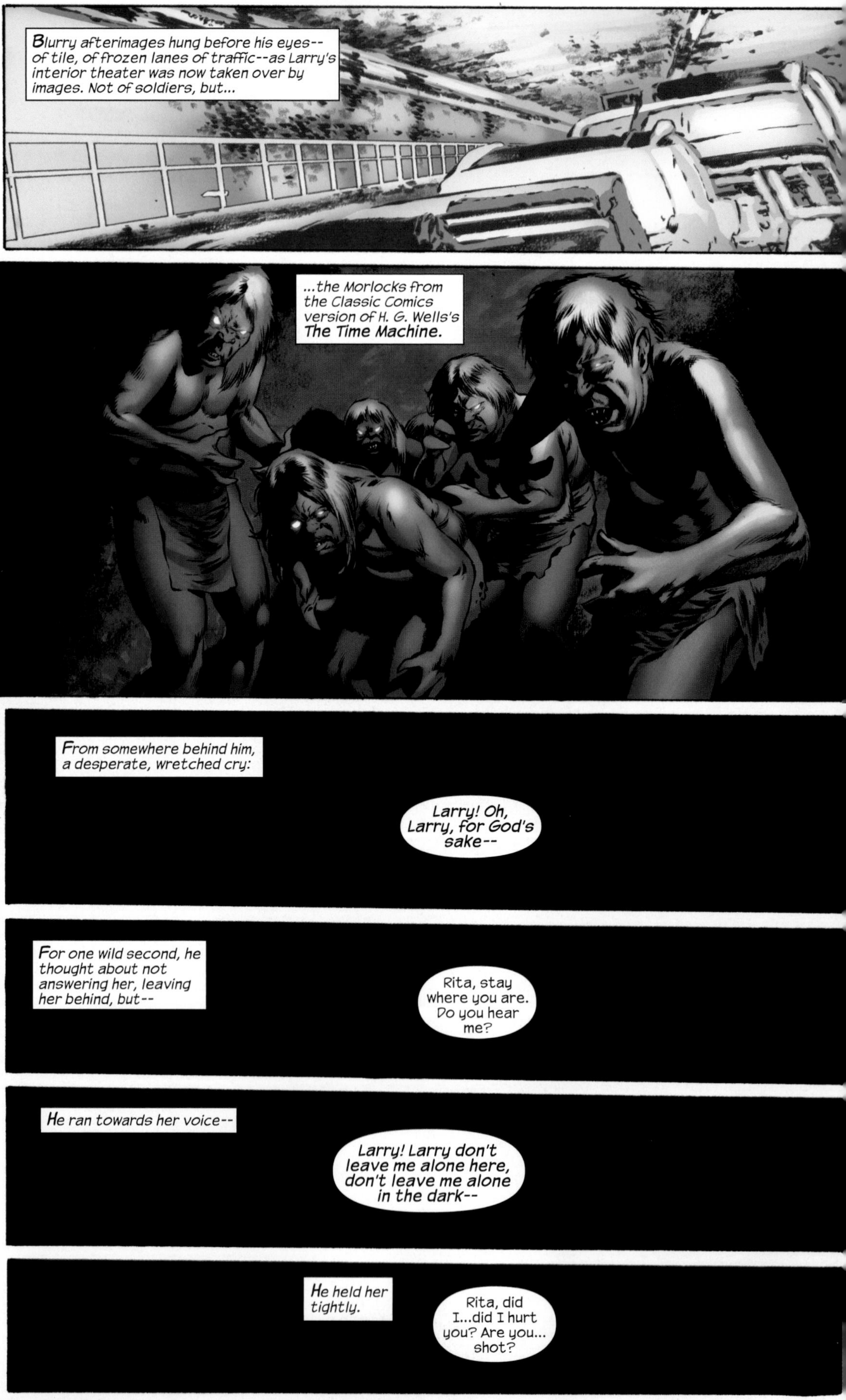

Blurry afterimages hung before his eyes--of tile, of frozen lanes of traffic--as Larry's interior theater was now taken over by images. Not of soldiers, but...
...the Morlocks from the Classic Comics version of H. G. Wells's The Time Machine.
From somewhere behind him, a desperate, wretched cry:
Larry! Oh, Larry, for God's sake--
For one wild second, he thought about not answering her, leaving her behind, but--
Rita, stay where you are. Do you hear me?
He ran towards her voice--
Larry! Larry don't leave me alone here, don't leave me alone in the dark--
He held her tightly.
Rita, did I...did I hurt you? Are you... shot?

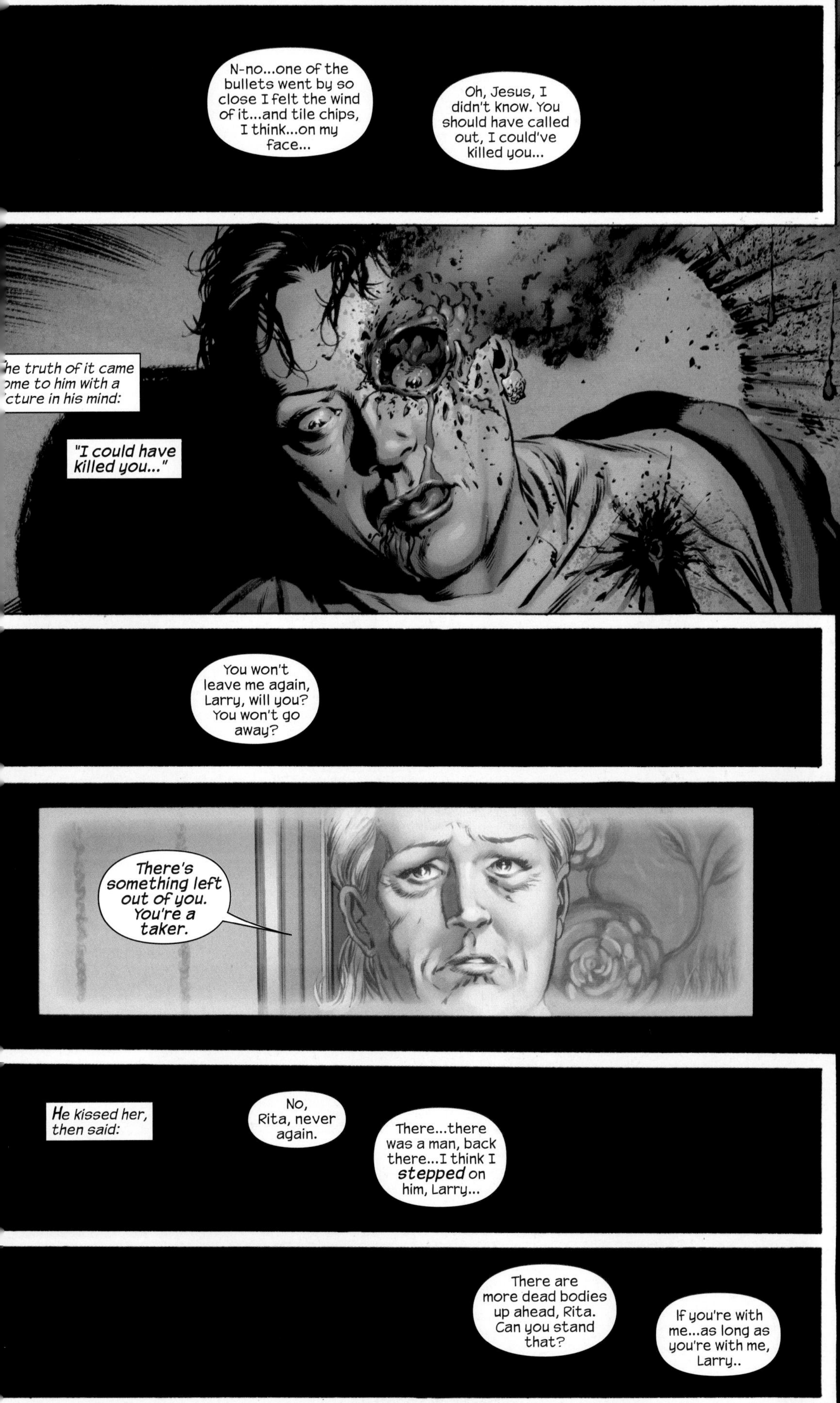
N-no...one of the bullets went by so close I felt the wind of it...and tile chips, I think...on my face...
Oh, Jesus, I didn't know. You should have called out, I could've killed you...
he truth of it came ome to him with a cture in his mind:
"I could have killed you..."
You won't leave me again, Larry, will you? You won't go away?
There's something left out of you. You're a taker.
He kissed her, then said:
No, Rita, never again.
There...there was a man, back there...I think I stepped on him, Larry...
There are more dead bodies up ahead, Rita. Can you stand that?
If you're with me...as long as you're with me, Larry..

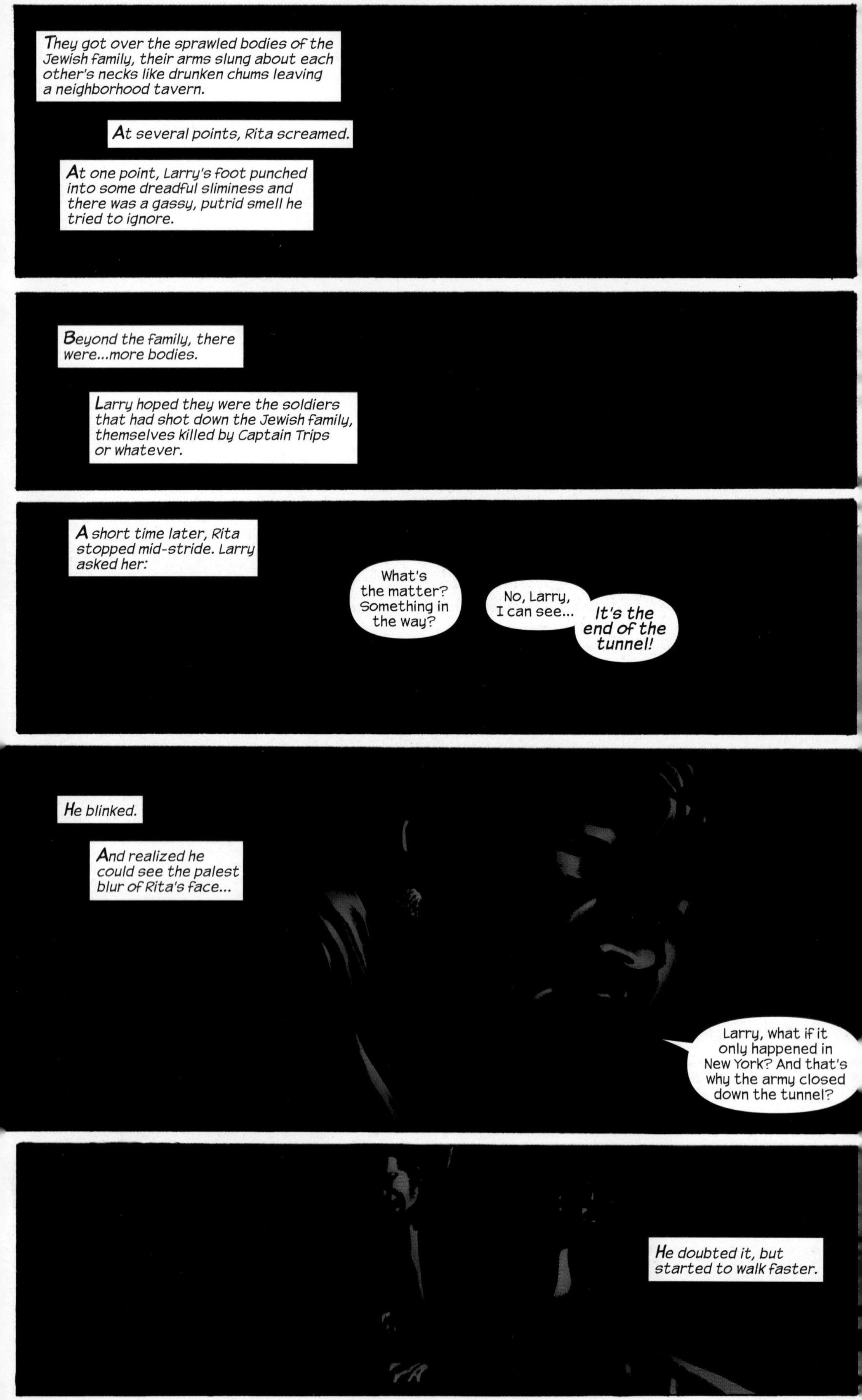

They got over the sprawled bodies of the Jewish family, their arms slung about each other's necks like drunken chums leaving a neighborhood tavern.
At several points, Rita screamed.
At one point, Larry's foot punched into some dreadful sliminess and there was a gassy, putrid smell he tried to ignore.
Beyond the family, there were...more bodies.
Larry hoped they were the soldiers that had shot down the Jewish family, themselves killed by Captain Trips or whatever.
A short time later, Rita stopped mid-stride. Larry asked her:
What's the matter? Something in the way?
No, Larry, I can see...
It's the end of the tunnel!
He blinked.
And realized he could see the palest blur of Rita's face...
Larry, what if it only happened in New York? And that's why the army closed down the tunnel?
He doubted it, but started to walk faster.

The closer they got to the entrance, the more they could see.

Soldiers.

One last sprawling mass of bodies.

Give me your hand--

And don't look inside the cab--

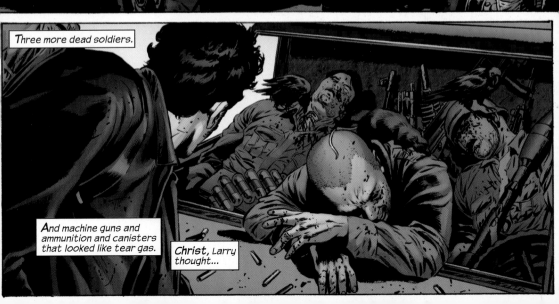

Three more dead soldiers.

And machine guns and ammunition and canisters that looked like tear gas.

Christ, Larry thought...

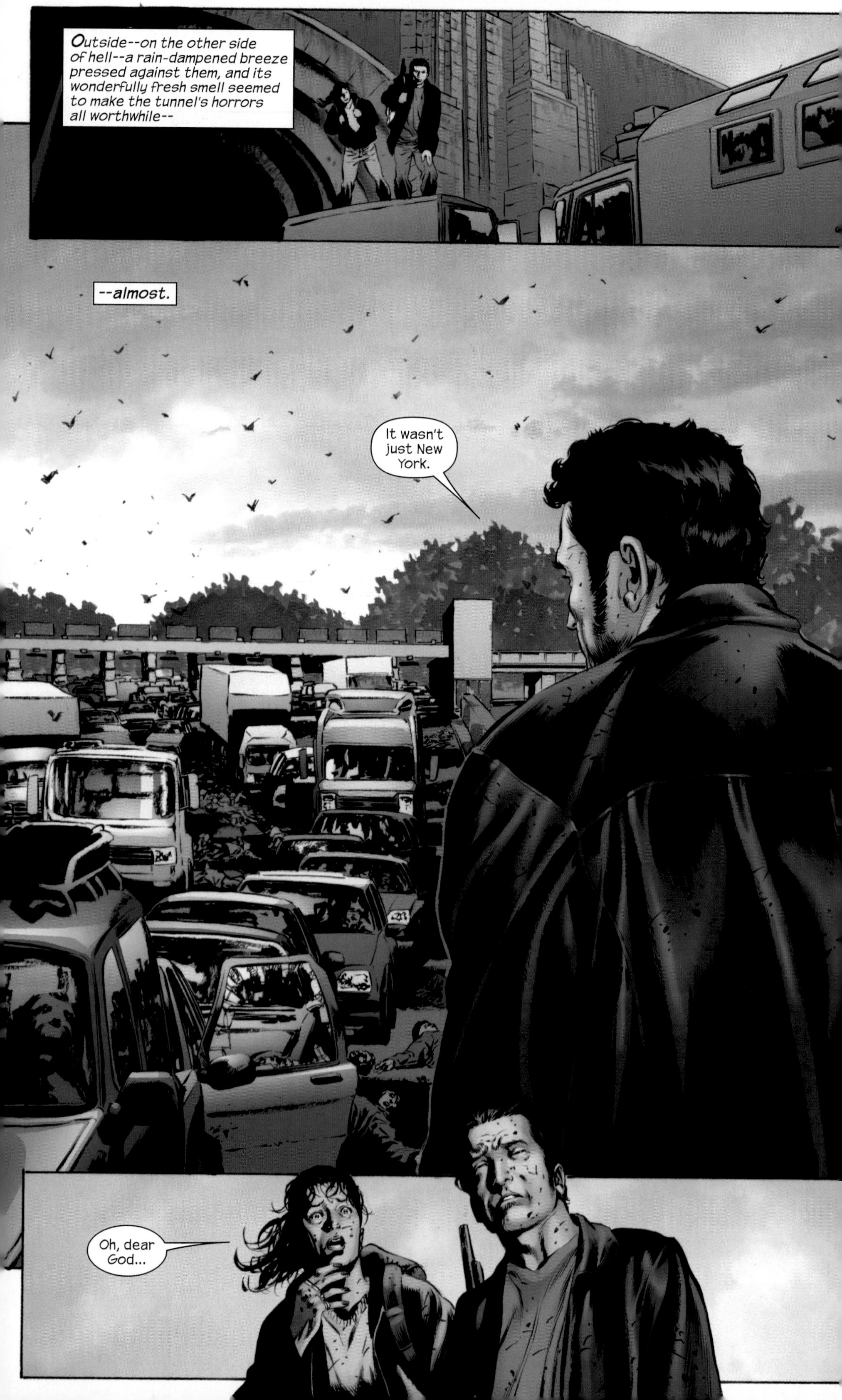
Outside--on the other side of hell--a rain-dampened breeze pressed against them, and its wonderfully fresh smell seemed to make the tunnel's horrors all worthwhile--
--almost.
It wasn't just New York.
Oh, dear God...

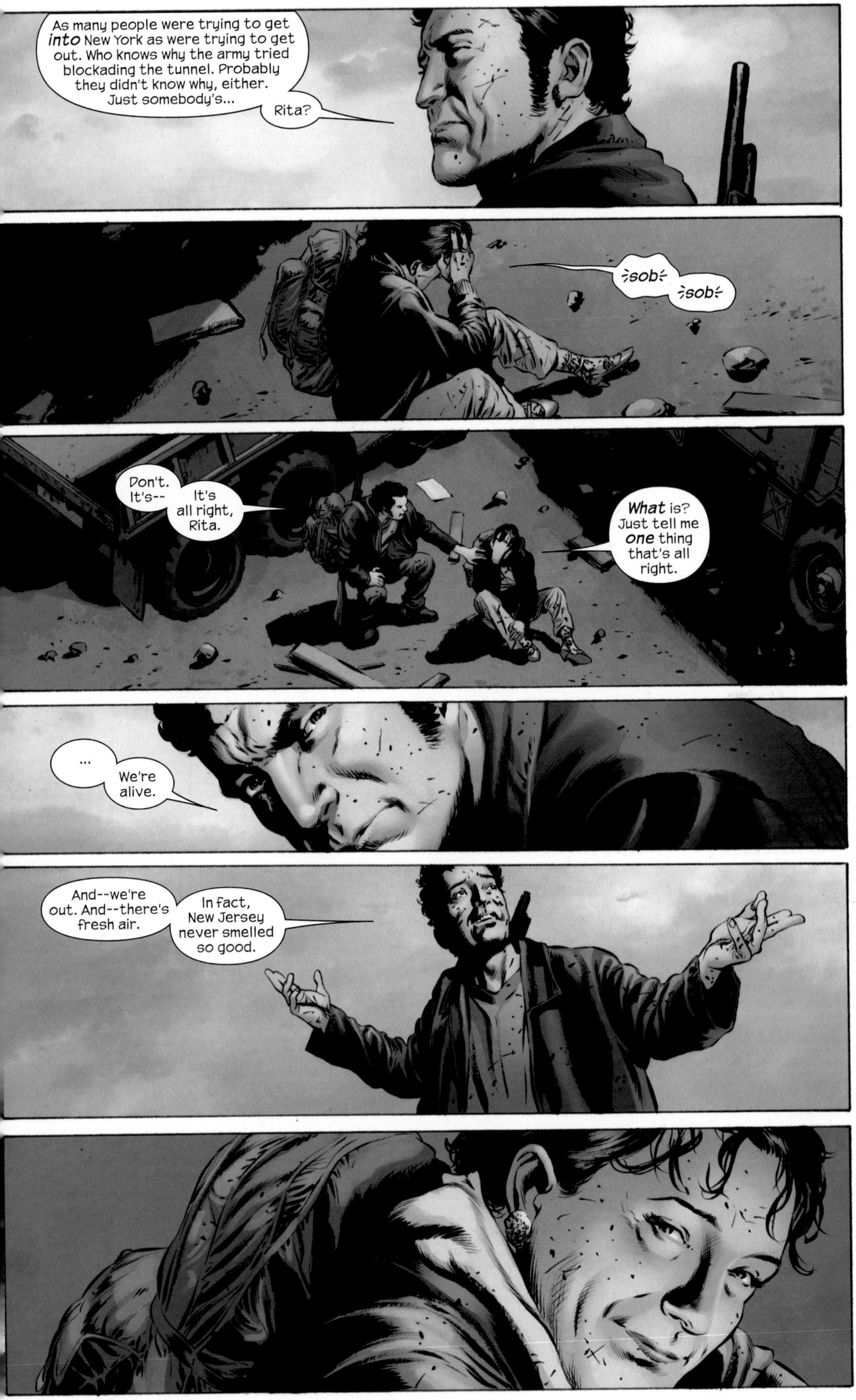

As many people were trying to get *into* New York as were trying to get out. Who knows why the army tried blockading the tunnel. Probably they didn't know why, either. Just somebody's...
Rita?
sob
sob
Don't. It's--
It's all right, Rita.
What is? Just tell me *one* thing that's all right.
...
We're alive.
And--we're out. And--there's fresh air.
In fact, New Jersey never smelled so good.

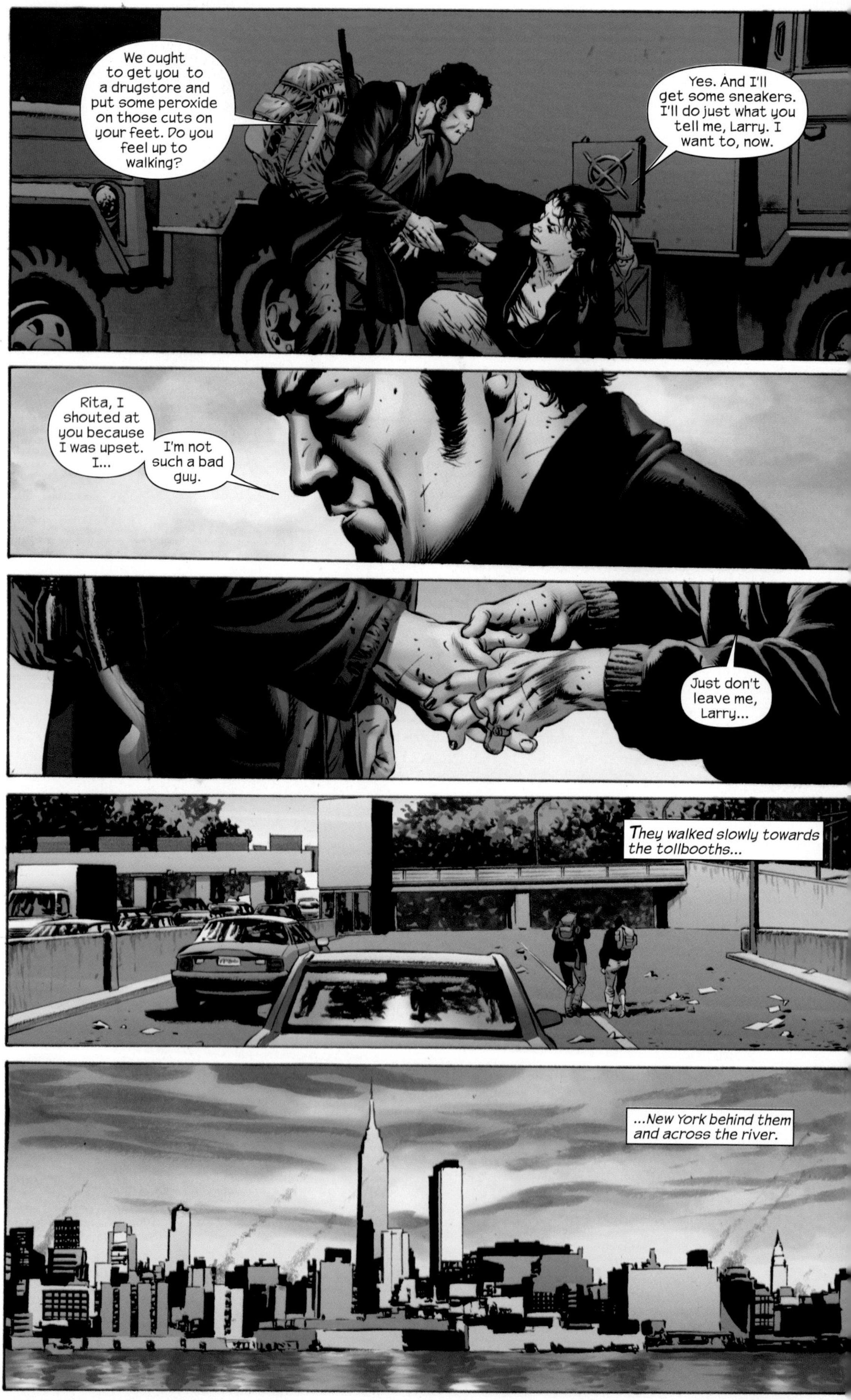

We ought to get you to a drugstore and put some peroxide on those cuts on your feet. Do you feel up to walking?
Yes. And I'll get some sneakers. I'll do just what you tell me, Larry. I want to, now.
Rita, I shouted at you because I was upset. I...
I'm not such a bad guy.
Just don't leave me, Larry...
They walked slowly towards the tollbooths...
...New York behind them and across the river.

OUTSIDE SOUTH RYEGATE, NEW HAMPSHIRE.

ROUTE 302.

Stuart Redman looked at his walk towards the ocean as a kind of...healing process.

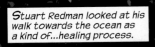

His first two nights on the road, he'd dreamed about Elder, the man who'd been sent to kill him. But last night...the dream hadn't come.

He supposed, in a way, that he might be walking the poison out of his system, little by little. At least, he hoped--

WOOF!
WOOF!

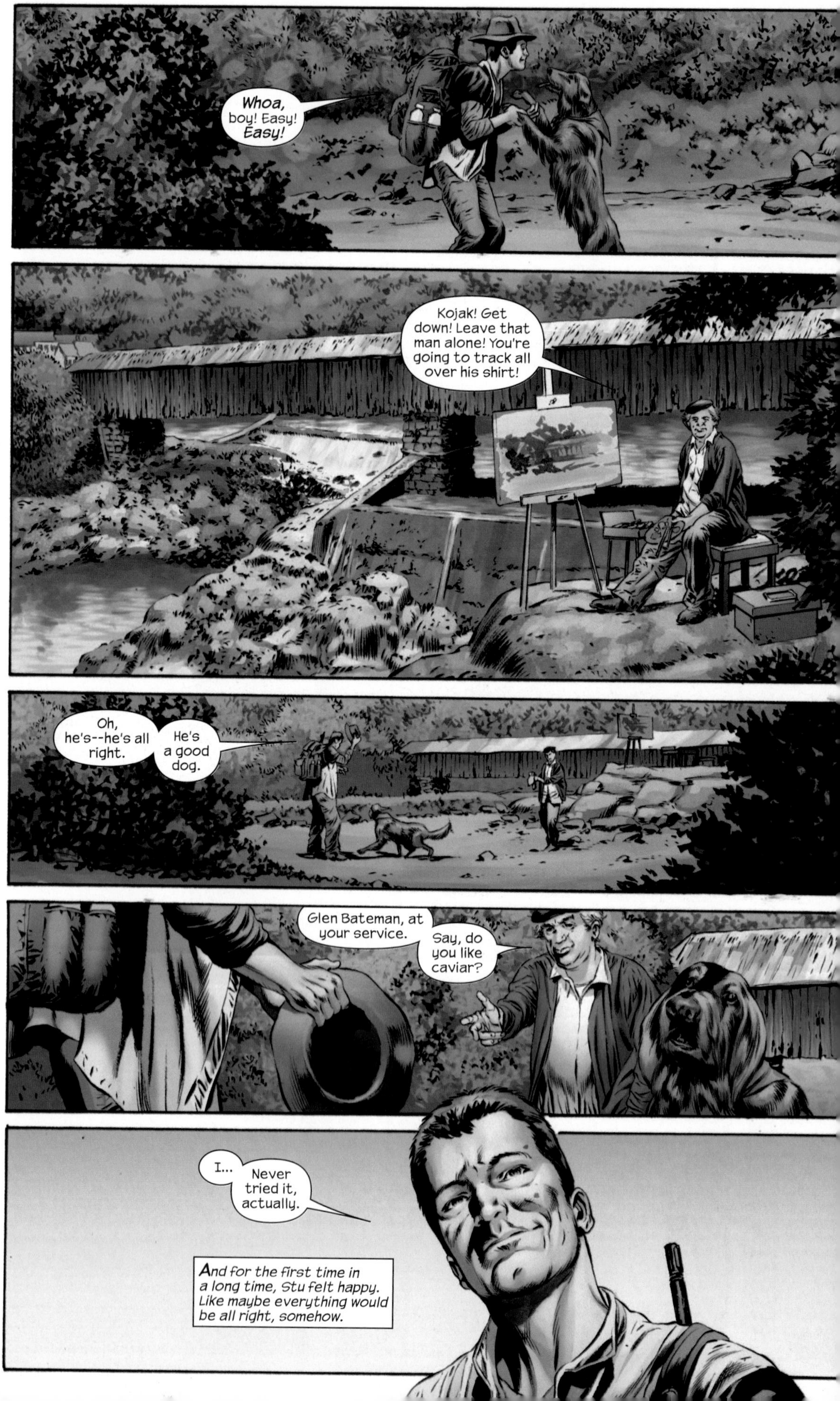

Whoa, boy! Easy! Easy!
Kojak! Get down! Leave that man alone! You're going to track all over his shirt!
Oh, he's--he's all right.
He's a good dog.
Glen Bateman, at your service.
Say, do you like caviar?
I...
Never tried it, actually.
And for the first time in a long time, Stu felt happy. Like maybe everything would be all right, somehow.

chapter FOUR

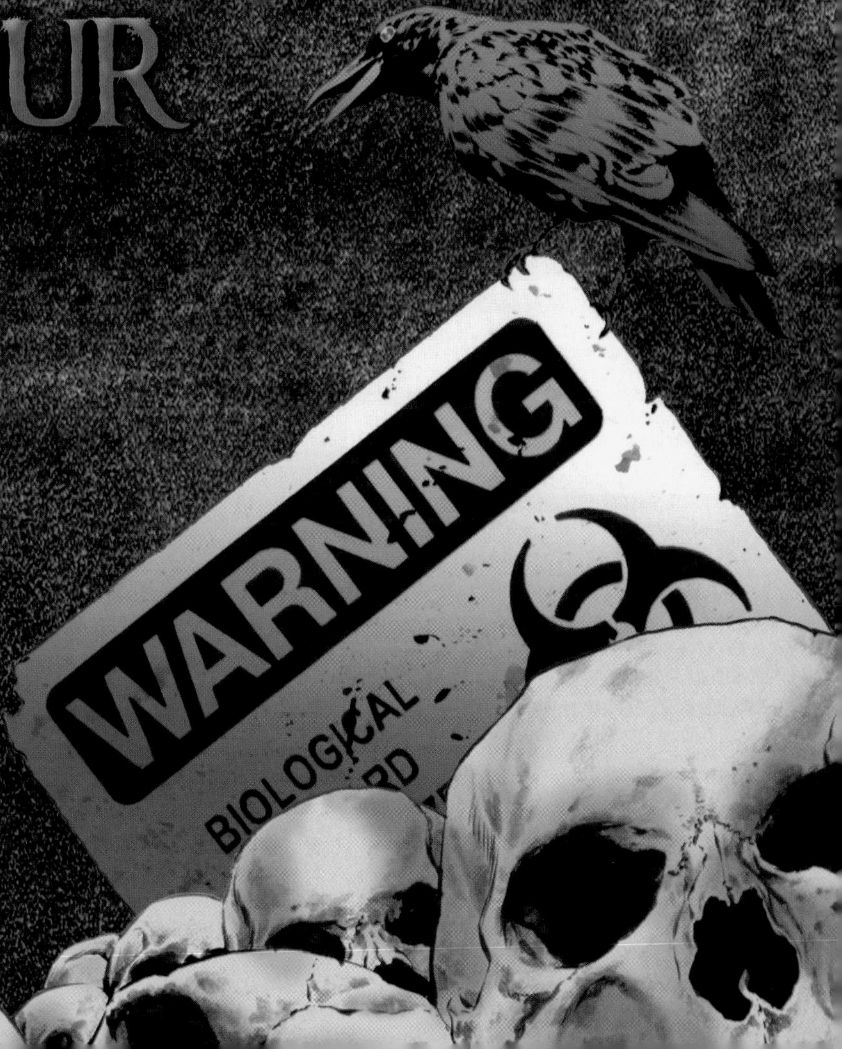
WARNING
BIOLOGICAL

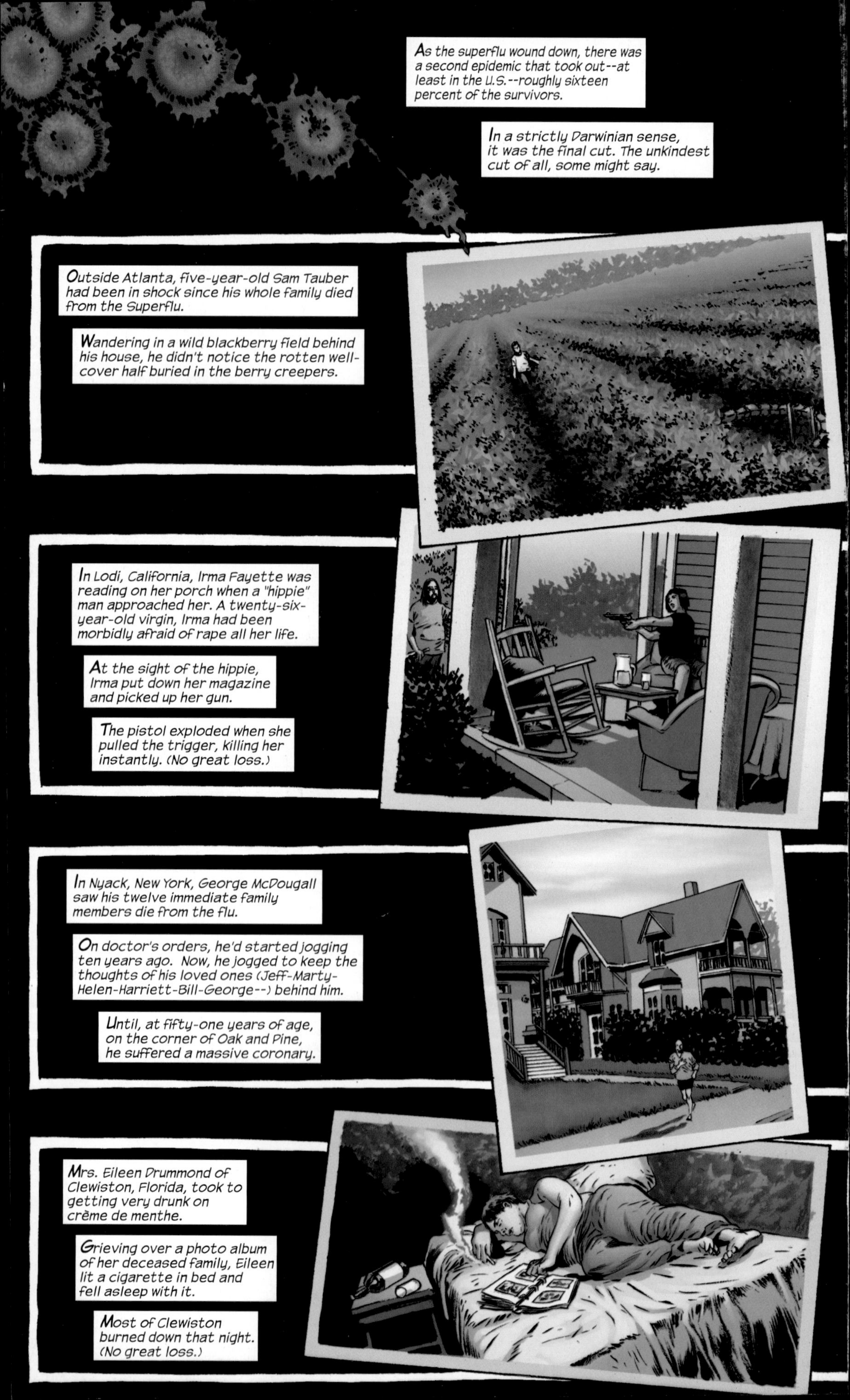

As the superflu wound down, there was a second epidemic that took out--at least in the U.S.--roughly sixteen percent of the survivors.
In a strictly Darwinian sense, it was the final cut. The unkindest cut of all, some might say.
Outside Atlanta, five-year-old Sam Tauber had been in shock since his whole family died from the Superflu.
Wandering in a wild blackberry field behind his house, he didn't notice the rotten well-cover half buried in the berry creepers.
In Lodi, California, Irma Fayette was reading on her porch when a "hippie" man approached her. A twenty-six-year-old virgin, Irma had been morbidly afraid of rape all her life.
At the sight of the hippie, Irma put down her magazine and picked up her gun.
The pistol exploded when she pulled the trigger, killing her instantly. (No great loss.)
In Nyack, New York, George McDougall saw his twelve immediate family members die from the flu.
On doctor's orders, he'd started jogging ten years ago. Now, he jogged to keep the thoughts of his loved ones (Jeff-Marty-Helen-Harriett-Bill-George--) behind him.
Until, at fifty-one years of age, on the corner of Oak and Pine, he suffered a massive coronary.
Mrs. Eileen Drummond of Clewiston, Florida, took to getting very drunk on crème de menthe.
Grieving over a photo album of her deceased family, Eileen lit a cigarette in bed and fell asleep with it.
Most of Clewiston burned down that night. (No great loss.)

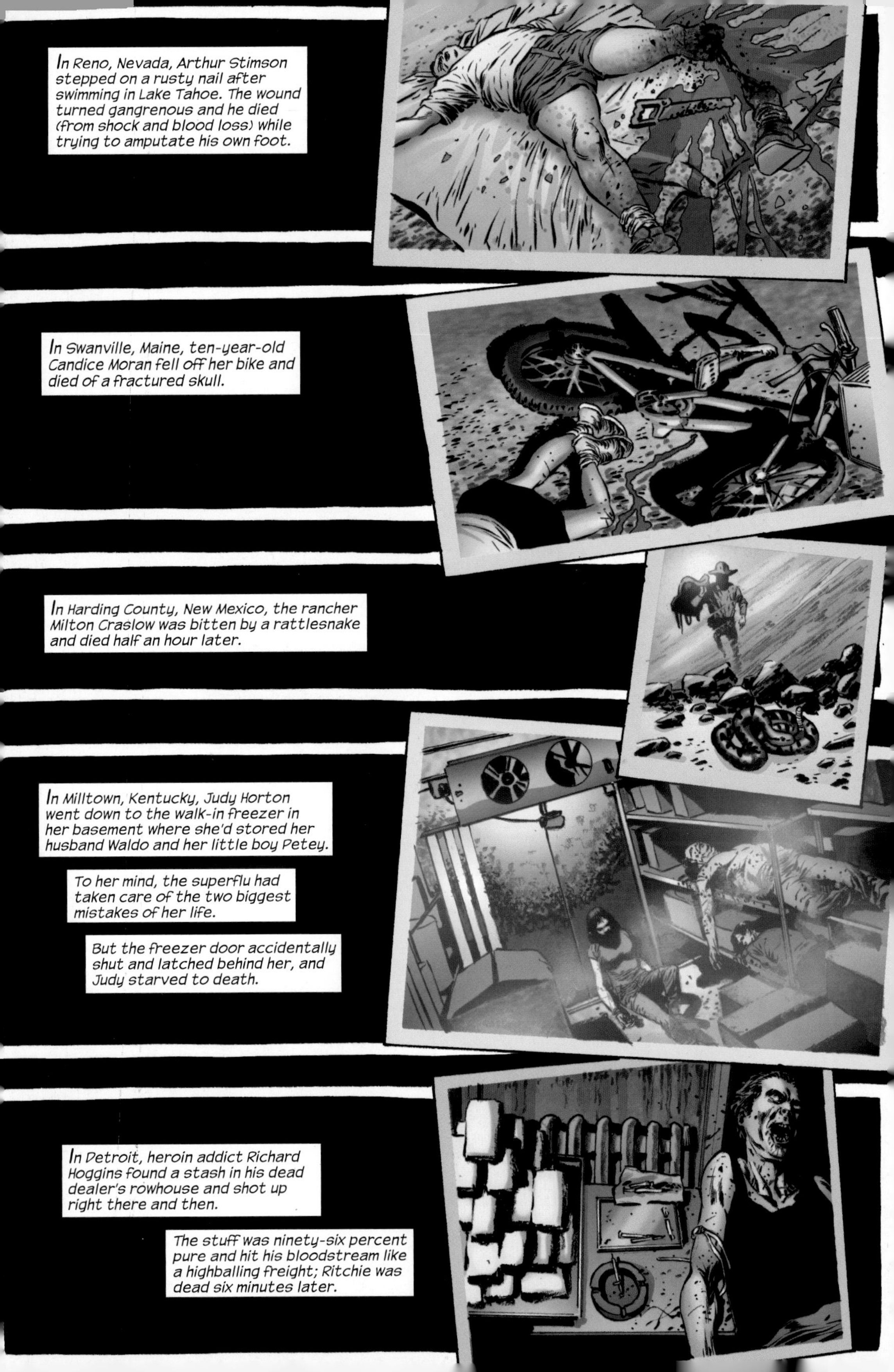
In Reno, Nevada, Arthur Stimson stepped on a rusty nail after swimming in Lake Tahoe. The wound turned gangrenous and he died (from shock and blood loss) while trying to amputate his own foot.
In Swanville, Maine, ten-year-old Candice Moran fell off her bike and died of a fractured skull.
In Harding County, New Mexico, the rancher Milton Craslow was bitten by a rattlesnake and died half an hour later.
In Milltown, Kentucky, Judy Horton went down to the walk-in freezer in her basement where she'd stored her husband Waldo and her little boy Petey.
To her mind, the superflu had taken care of the two biggest mistakes of her life.
But the freezer door accidentally shut and latched behind her, and Judy starved to death.
In Detroit, heroin addict Richard Hoggins found a stash in his dead dealer's rowhouse and shot up right there and then.
The stuff was ninety-six percent pure and hit his bloodstream like a highballing freight; Ritchie was dead six minutes later.

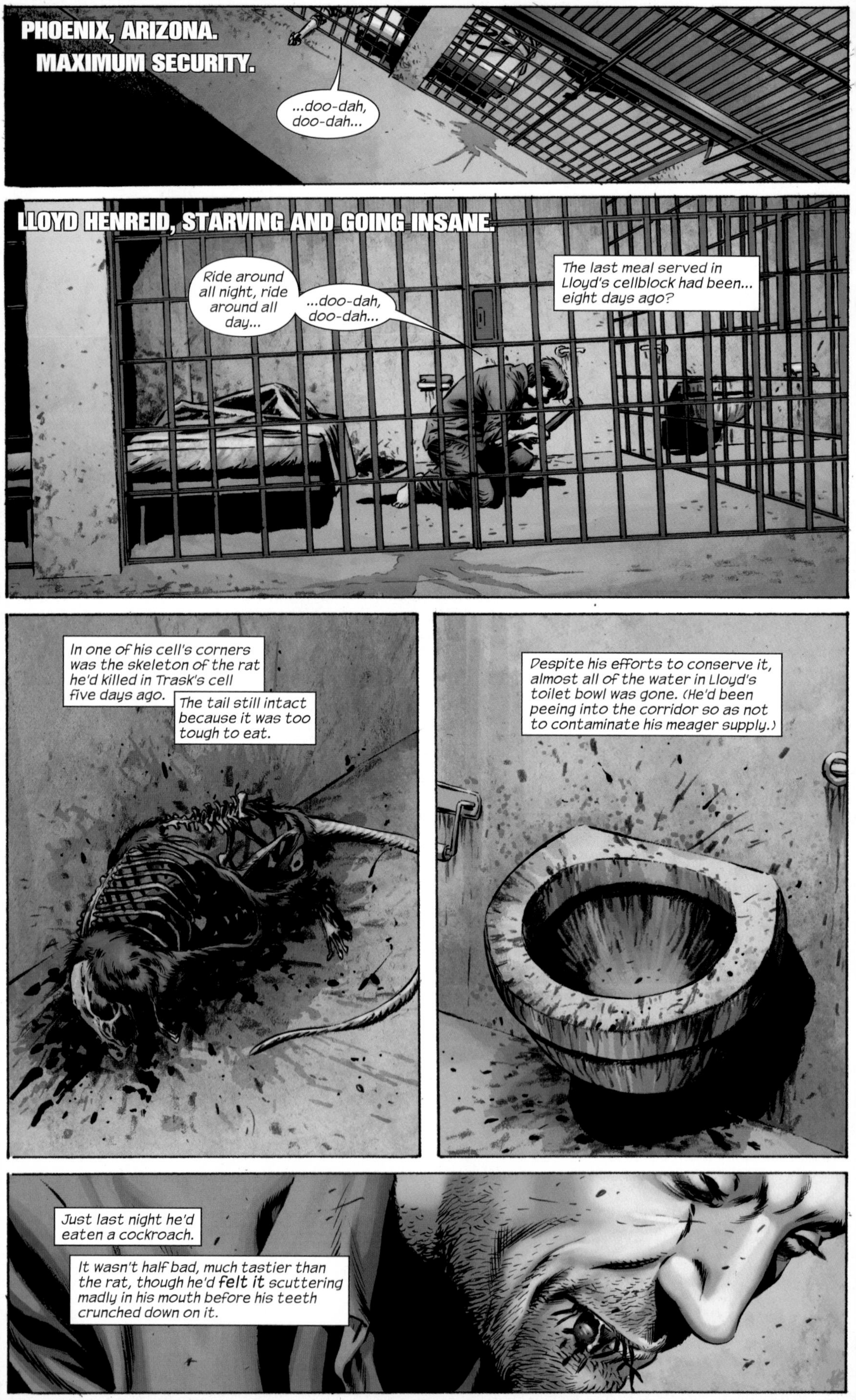
PHOENIX, ARIZONA.
MAXIMUM SECURITY.
...doo-dah, doo-dah...
LLOYD HENREID, STARVING AND GOING INSANE.
Ride around all night, ride around all day...
...doo-dah, doo-dah...
The last meal served in Lloyd's cellblock had been... eight days ago?
In one of his cell's corners was the skeleton of the rat he'd killed in Trask's cell five days ago.
The tail still intact because it was too tough to eat.
Despite his efforts to conserve it, almost all of the water in Lloyd's toilet bowl was gone. (He'd been peeing into the corridor so as not to contaminate his meager supply.)
Just last night he'd eaten a cockroach.
It wasn't half bad, much tastier than the rat, though he'd felt it scuttering madly in his mouth before his teeth crunched down on it.

Lloyd didn't **want** to eat Trask. He didn't **want** to become a cannibal. It was like the rat. He wanted to have Trask within reach **just in case.**

...doo-dah, doo-dah...

...doo-dah...

The main reason Lloyd was still alive?

He was too full of **hate** to die.

And all his hate had coalesced into one simple, imagistic concept: THE KEY.

THE KEY was your reward for following the rules.

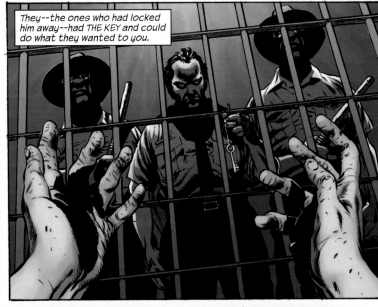

They--the ones who had locked him away--had THE KEY and could do what they wanted to you.

But not this. Not leave him to die a slow, horrible death.

Please...

If only **he** had THE KEY...

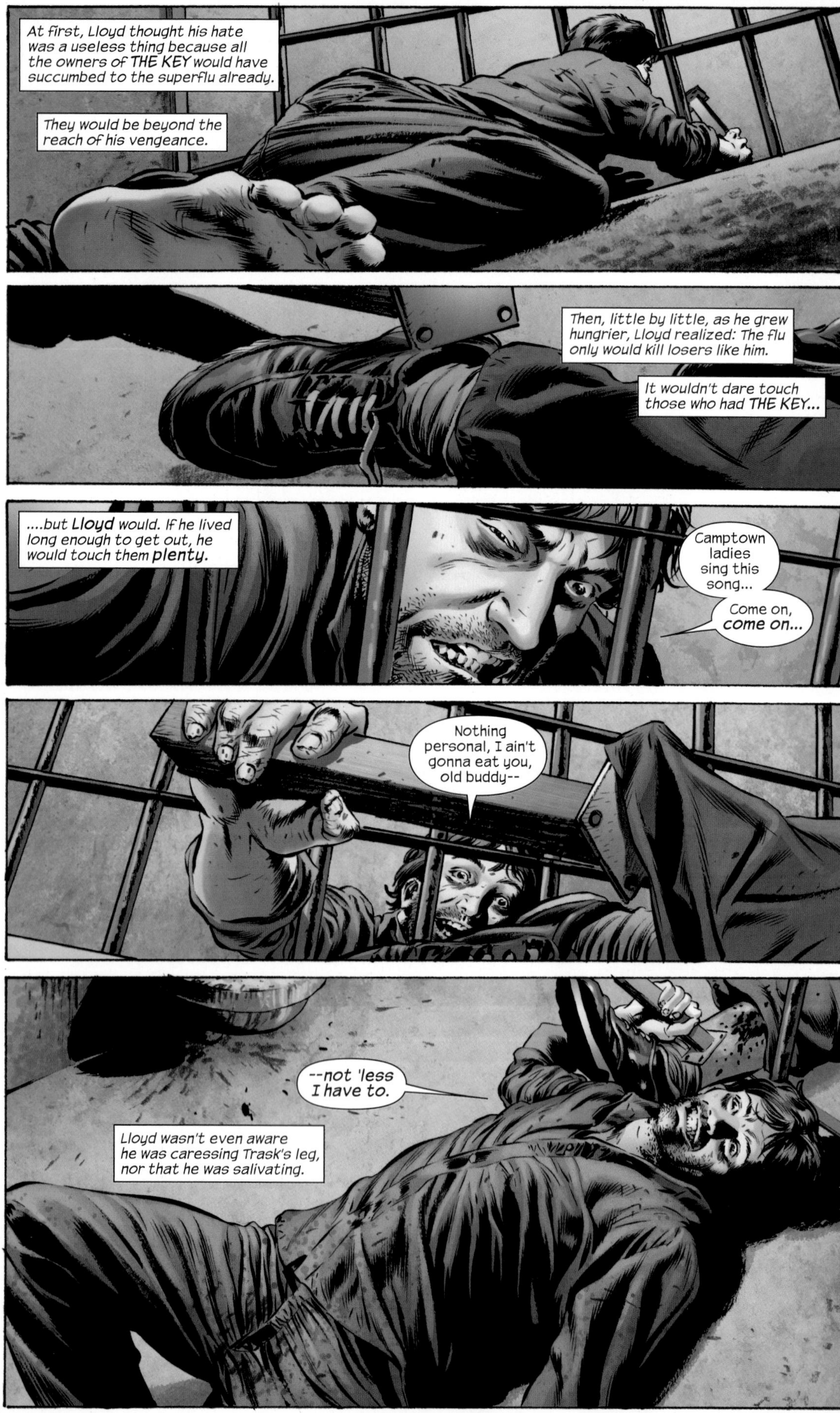

At first, Lloyd thought his hate was a useless thing because all the owners of THE KEY would have succumbed to the superflu already.
They would be beyond the reach of his vengeance.
Then, little by little, as he grew hungrier, Lloyd realized: The flu only would kill losers like him.
It wouldn't dare touch those who had THE KEY...
....but Lloyd would. If he lived long enough to get out, he would touch them plenty.
Camptown ladies sing this song...
Come on, come on...
Nothing personal, I ain't gonna eat you, old buddy--
--not 'less I have to.
Lloyd wasn't even aware he was caressing Trask's leg, nor that he was salivating.

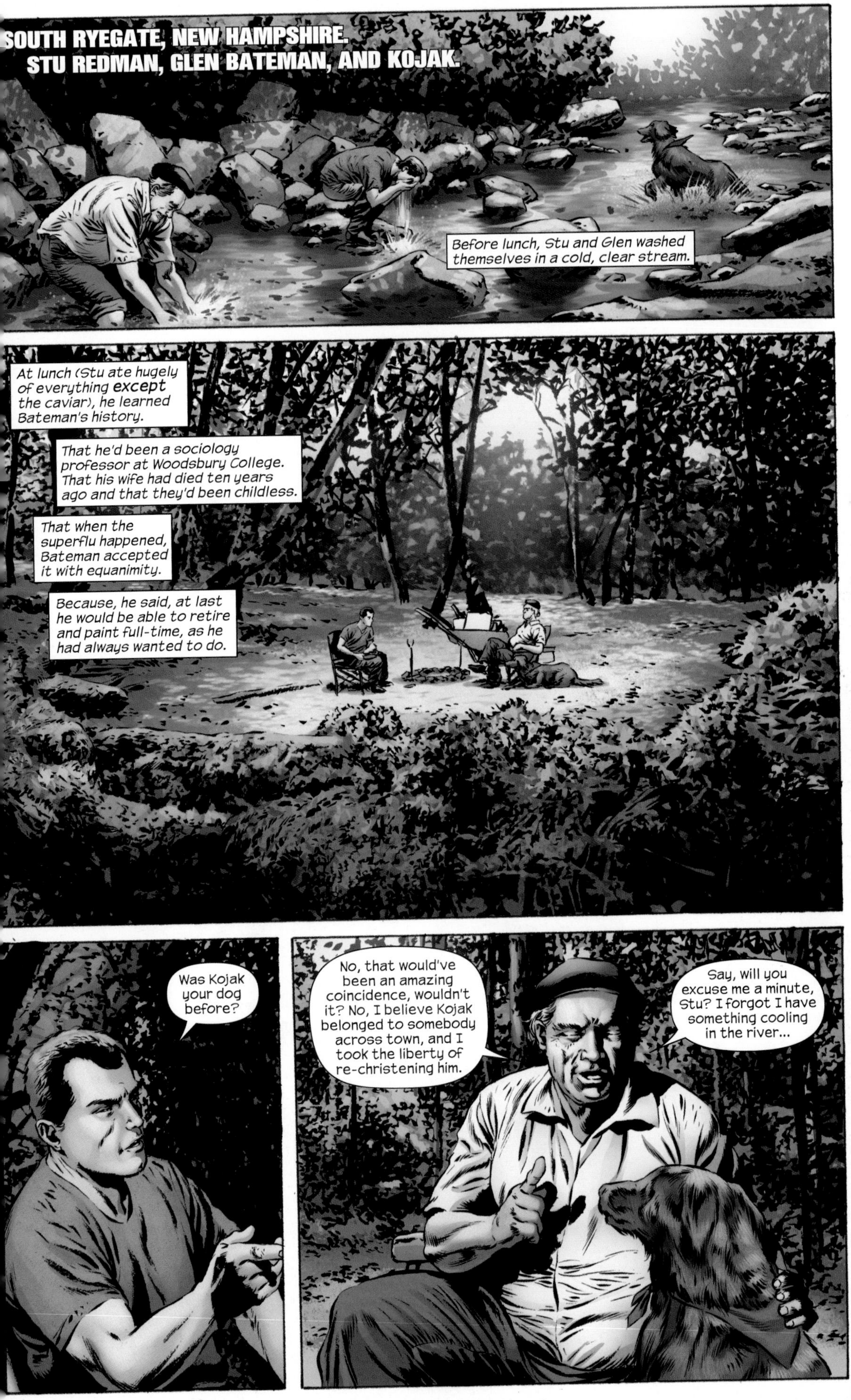

SOUTH RYEGATE, NEW HAMPSHIRE.
STU REDMAN, GLEN BATEMAN, AND KOJAK.
Before lunch, Stu and Glen washed themselves in a cold, clear stream.
At lunch (Stu ate hugely of everything **except** the caviar), he learned Bateman's history.
That he'd been a sociology professor at Woodsbury College. That his wife had died ten years ago and that they'd been childless.
That when the superflu happened, Bateman accepted it with equanimity.
Because, he said, at last he would be able to retire and paint full-time, as he had always wanted to do.
Was Kojak your dog before?
No, that would've been an amazing coincidence, wouldn't it? No, I believe Kojak belonged to somebody across town, and I took the liberty of re-christening him.
Say, will you excuse me a minute, Stu? I forgot I have something cooling in the river...

CLICK!

SSSSHHHHHH!!

These were supposed to go with the meal. Stupid of me.

They taste just as good afterwards.

...

Bubonic plague-- the Black Death-- decimated Europe near the end of the fourteenth century. The dancing sickness took place during the latter part of the fifteenth.

Whooping cough near the end of the seventeenth. The first outbreaks of influenza happened near the end of the nineteenth.

Hell, we're so used to the idea of the flu now, but what everyone forgets is that *a hundred years ago it didn't exist...*

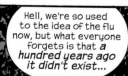

What are you getting at, Glen?

Let's walk for a bit.

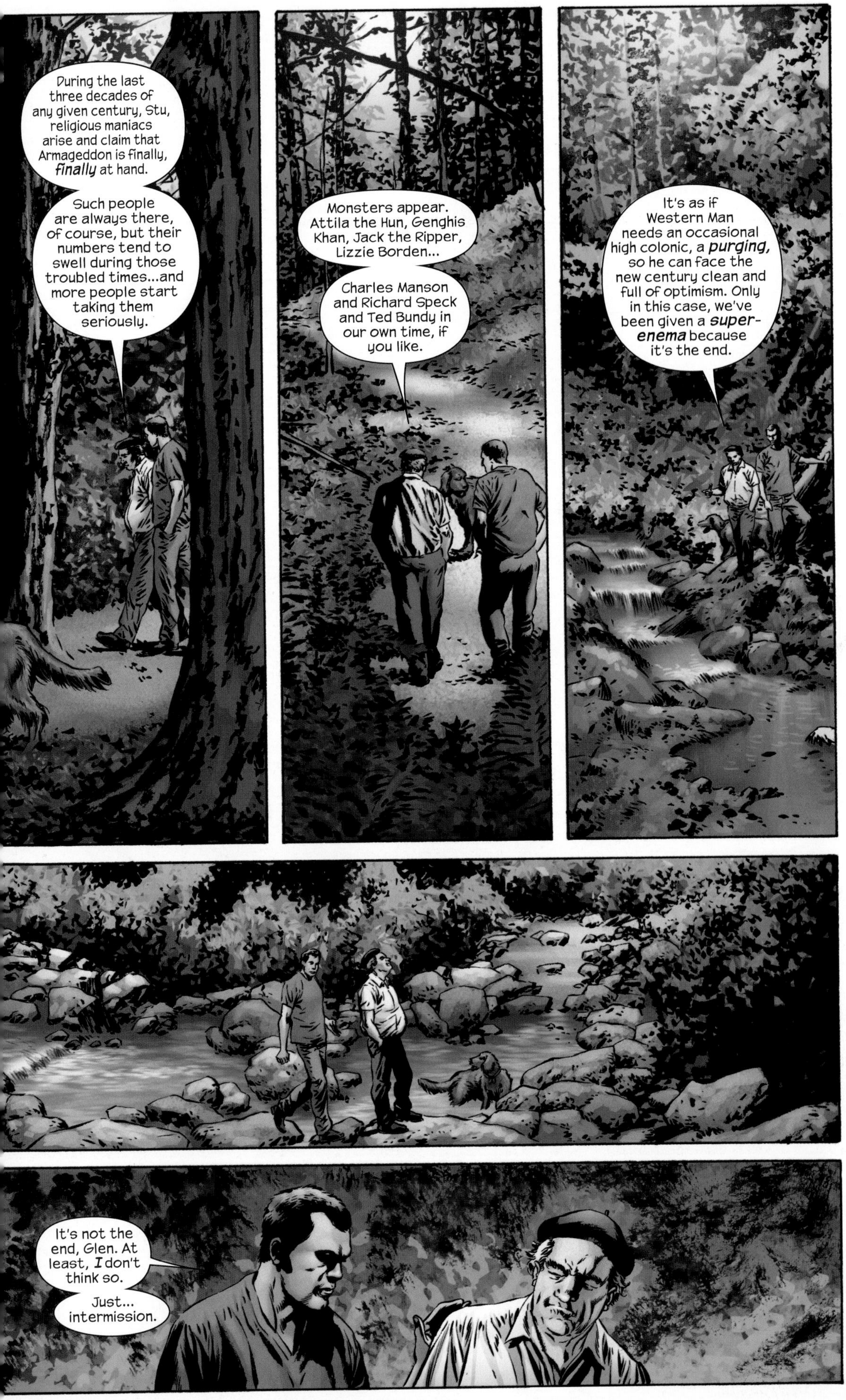
During the last three decades of any given century, Stu, religious maniacs arise and claim that Armageddon is finally, *finally* at hand.
Such people are always there, of course, but their numbers tend to swell during those troubled times...and more people start taking them seriously.
Monsters appear. Attila the Hun, Genghis Khan, Jack the Ripper, Lizzie Borden...
Charles Manson and Richard Speck and Ted Bundy in our own time, if you like.
It's as if Western Man needs an occasional high colonic, a *purging,* so he can face the new century clean and full of optimism. Only in this case, we've been given a *super-enema* because it's the end.
It's not the end, Glen. At least, *I* don't think so.
Just... intermission.

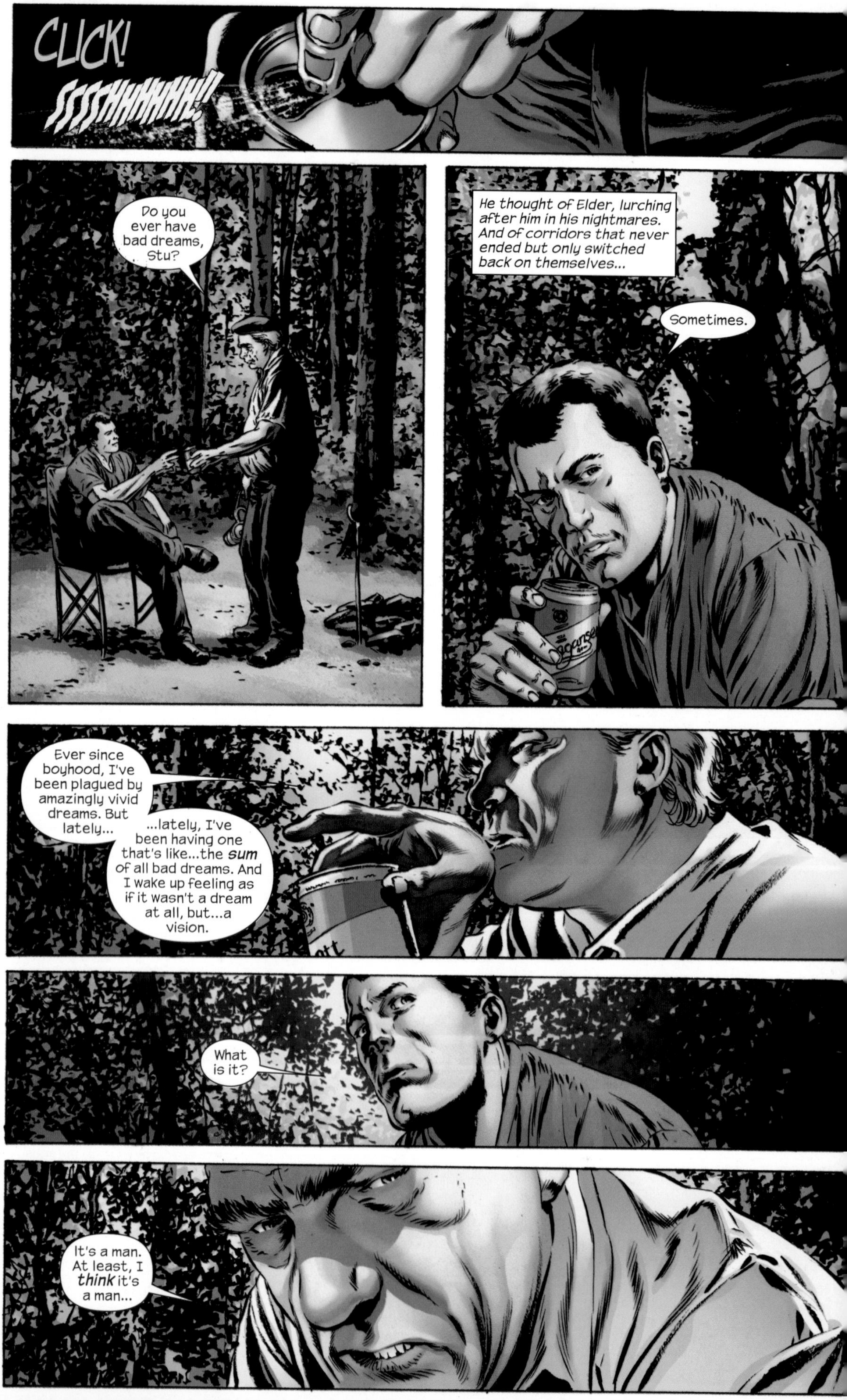
CLICK!
SSSSHHHHHH!!
Do you ever have bad dreams, Stu?
He thought of Elder, lurching after him in his nightmares. And of corridors that never ended but only switched back on themselves...
Sometimes.
Ever since boyhood, I've been plagued by amazingly vivid dreams. But lately...
...lately, I've been having one that's like...the *sum* of all bad dreams. And I wake up feeling as if it wasn't a dream at all, but...a vision.
What is it?
It's a man. At least, I ***think*** it's a man...

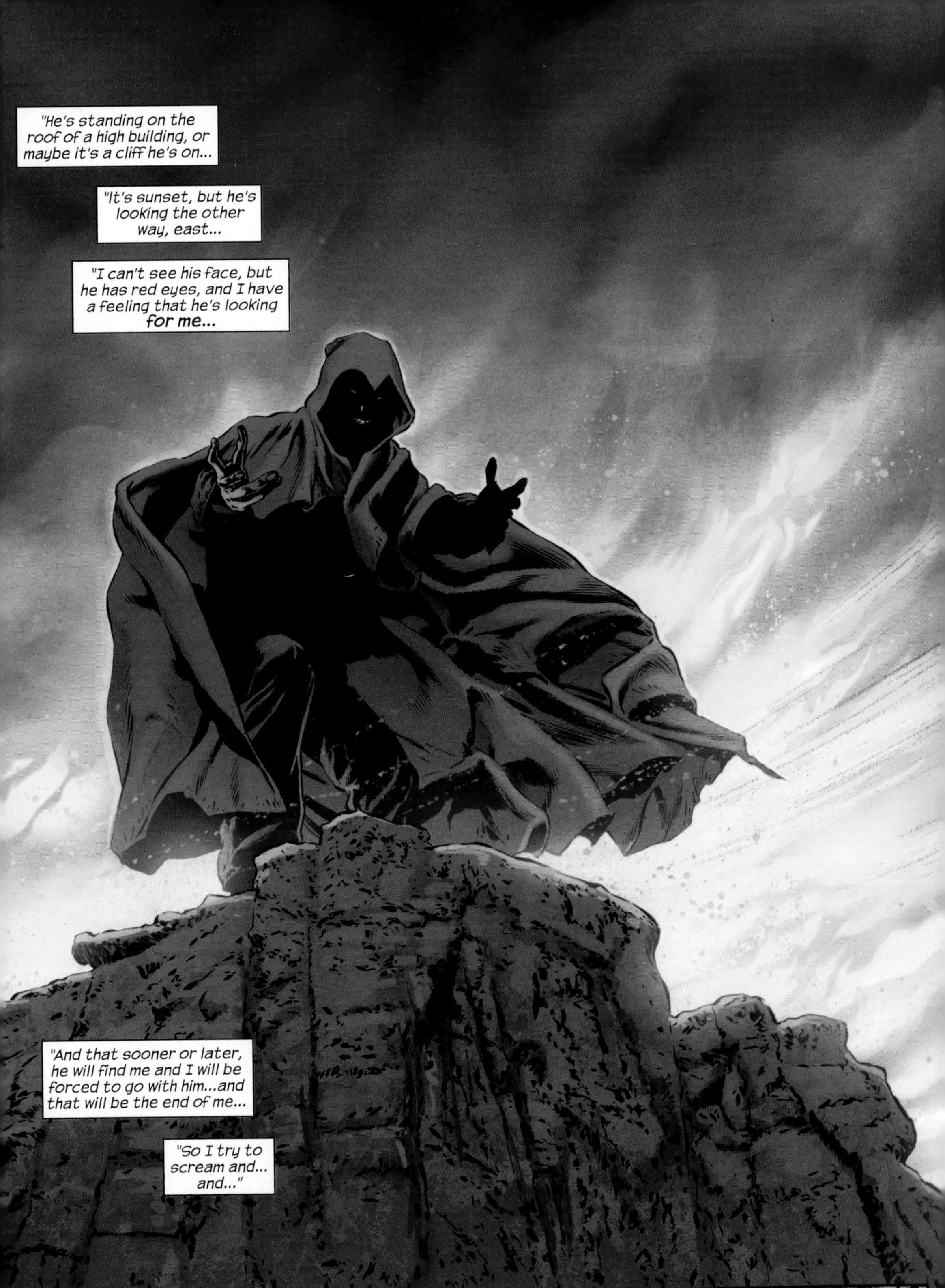
"He's standing on the roof of a high building, or maybe it's a cliff he's on...
"It's sunset, but he's looking the other way, east...
"I can't see his face, but he has red eyes, and I have a feeling that he's looking for me...
"And that sooner or later, he will find me and I will be forced to go with him...and that will be the end of me...
"So I try to scream and... and..."

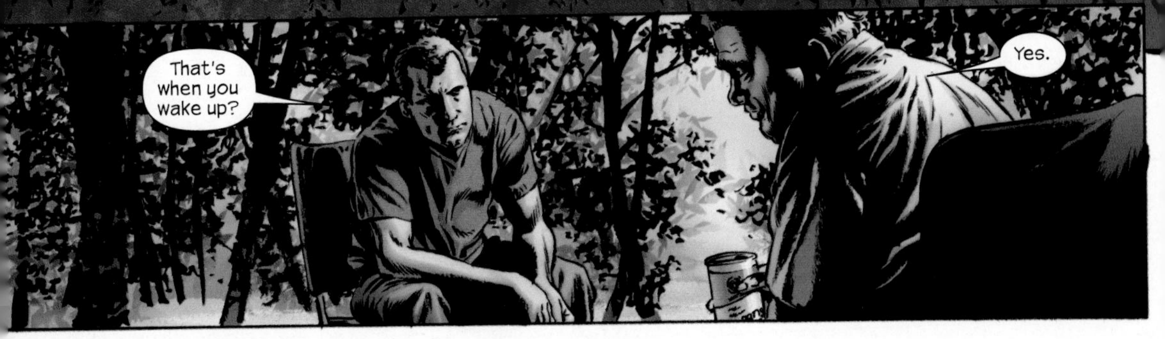
That's when you wake up?
Yes.

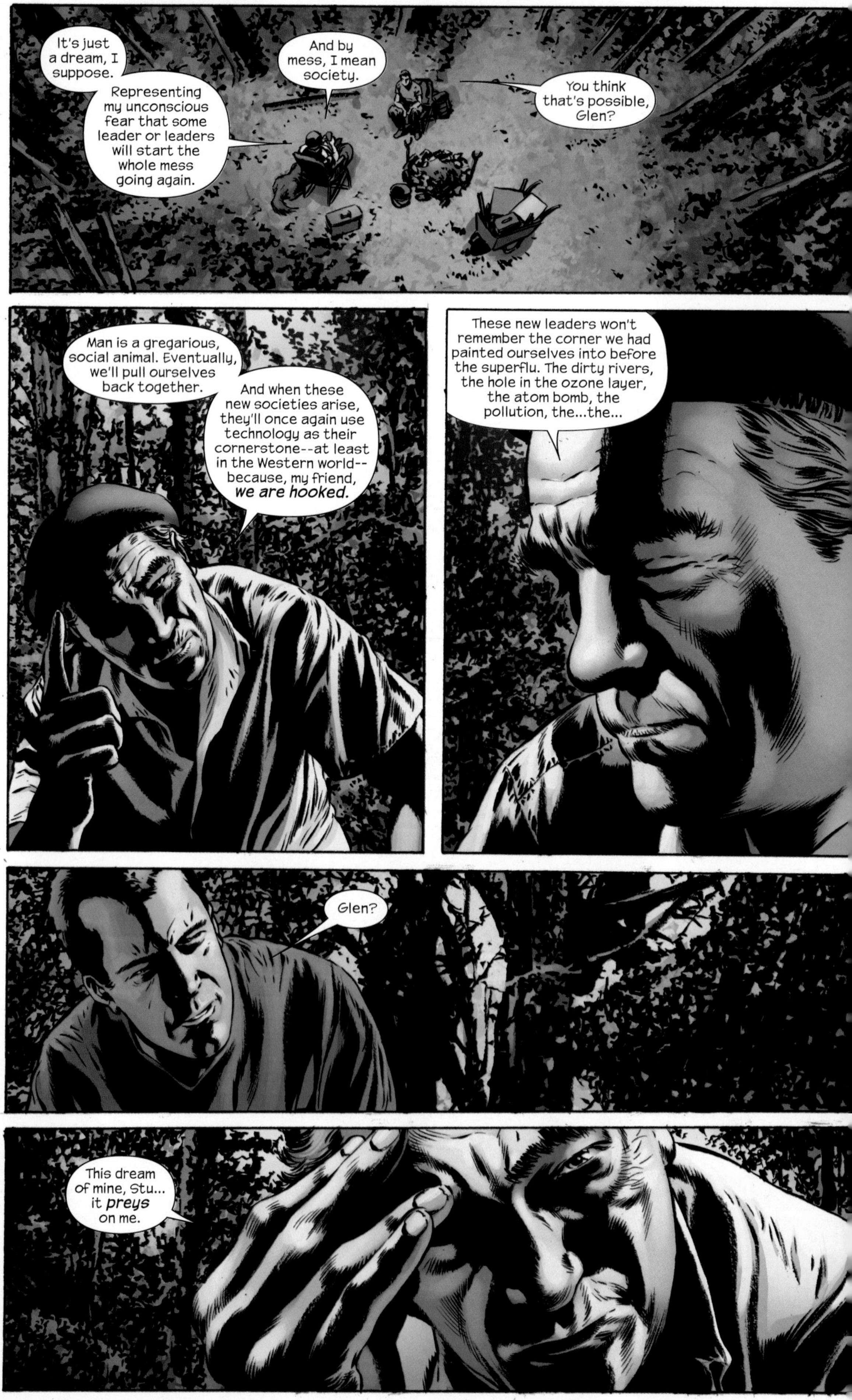
It's just a dream, I suppose.
Representing my unconscious fear that some leader or leaders will start the whole mess going again.
And by mess, I mean society.
You think that's possible, Glen?
Man is a gregarious, social animal. Eventually, we'll pull ourselves back together.
And when these new societies arise, they'll once again use technology as their cornerstone--at least in the Western world--because, my friend, *we are hooked.*
These new leaders won't remember the corner we had painted ourselves into before the superflu. The dirty rivers, the hole in the ozone layer, the atom bomb, the pollution, the...the...
Glen?
This dream of mine, Stu... it *preys* on me.

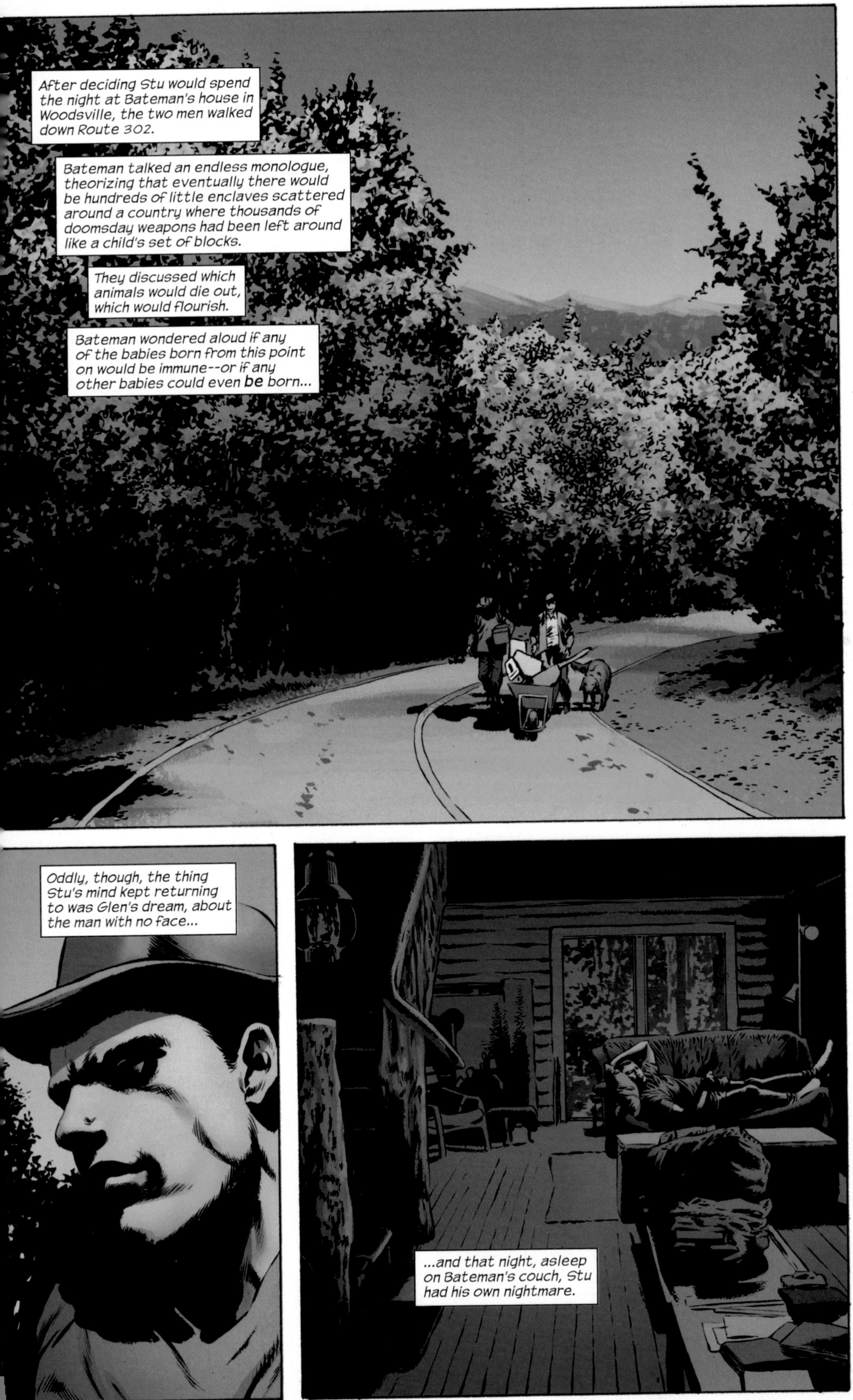
After deciding Stu would spend the night at Bateman's house in Woodsville, the two men walked down Route 302.
Bateman talked an endless monologue, theorizing that eventually there would be hundreds of little enclaves scattered around a country where thousands of doomsday weapons had been left around like a child's set of blocks.
They discussed which animals would die out, which would flourish.
Bateman wondered aloud if any of the babies born from this point on would be immune--or if any other babies could even **be** born...
Oddly, though, the thing Stu's mind kept returning to was Glen's dream, about the man with no face...
...and that night, asleep on Bateman's couch, Stu had his own nightmare.

He was back in Stovington. Elder was dead. Everyone was dead. It was a tomb--

--and he couldn't find his way out.

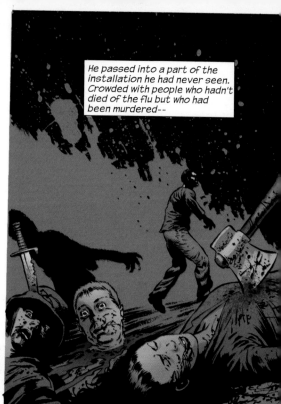

He passed into a part of the installation he had never seen. Crowded with people who hadn't died of the flu but who had been murdered--

He glimpsed a sign on a locked room--

Then, blessedly, he saw a door to the outside world, standing open. Beyond it, the sweet, fragrant night.

In his dream, Stu plunged towards it...

...but as he neared it, a figure stepped into the doorway, blocking his escape.

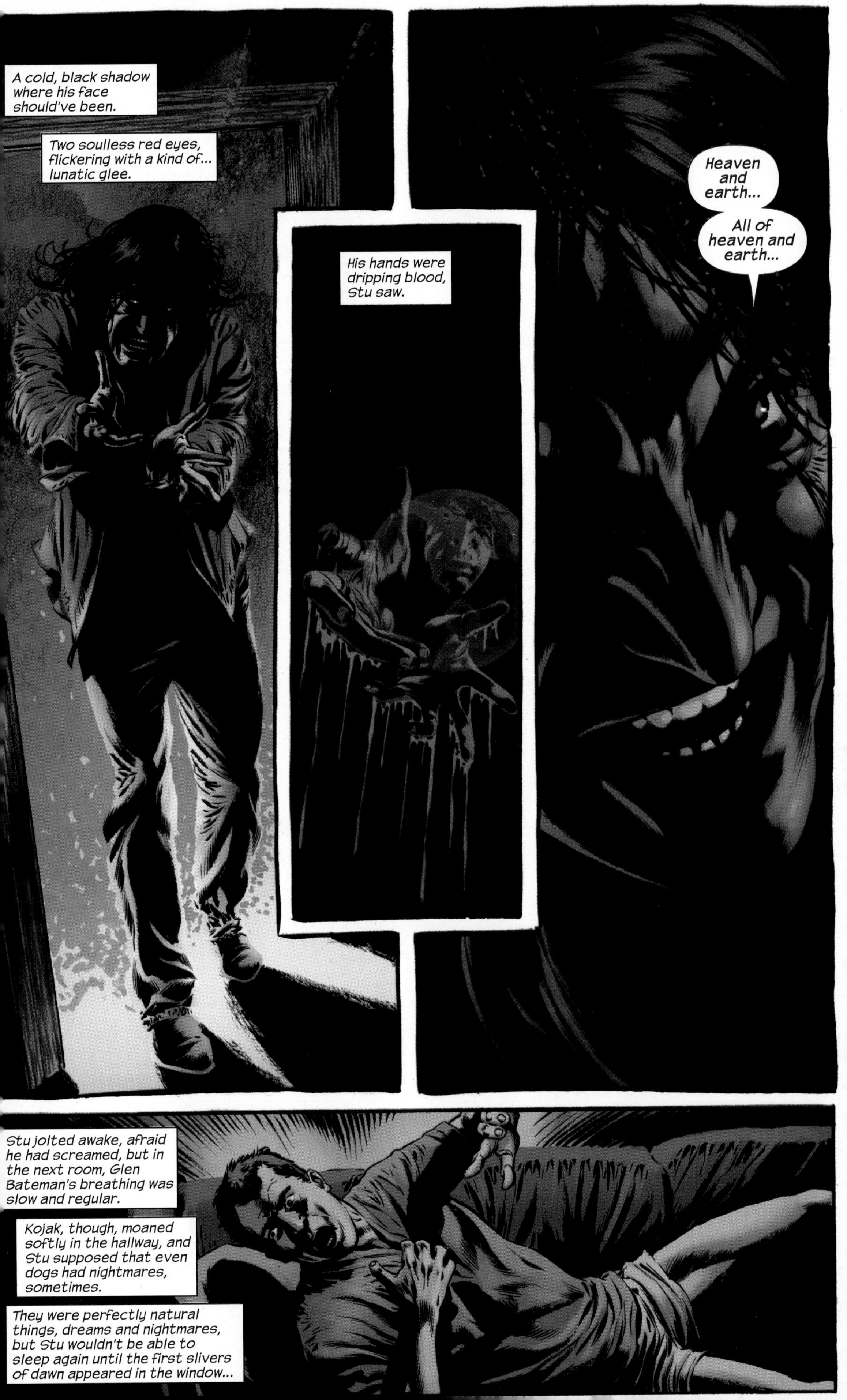
A cold, black shadow where his face should've been.
Two soulless red eyes, flickering with a kind of... lunatic glee.
His hands were dripping blood, Stu saw.
Heaven and earth...
All of heaven and earth...
Stu jolted awake, afraid he had screamed, but in the next room, Glen Bateman's breathing was slow and regular.
Kojak, though, moaned softly in the hallway, and Stu supposed that even dogs had nightmares, sometimes.
They were perfectly natural things, dreams and nightmares, but Stu wouldn't be able to sleep again until the first slivers of dawn appeared in the window...

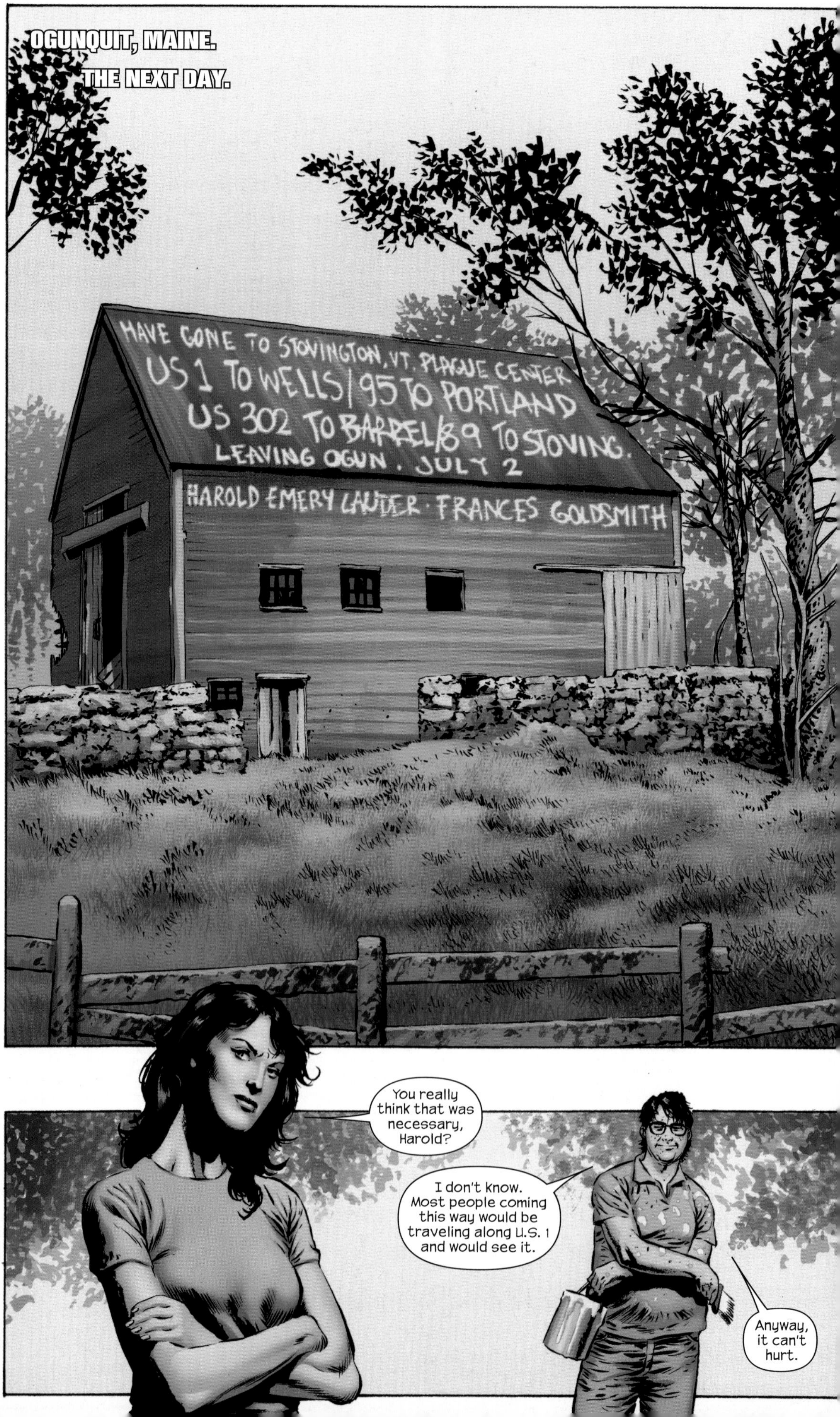
OGUNQUIT, MAINE.
THE NEXT DAY.
HAVE GONE TO STOVINGTON, VT. PLAGUE CENTER
US 1 TO WELLS/95 TO PORTLAND
US 302 TO BARREL/89 TO STOVING.
LEAVING OGUN. JULY 2
HAROLD EMERY LAUDER · FRANCES GOLDSMITH
You really think that was necessary, Harold?
I don't know. Most people coming this way would be traveling along U.S. 1 and would see it.
Anyway, it can't hurt.

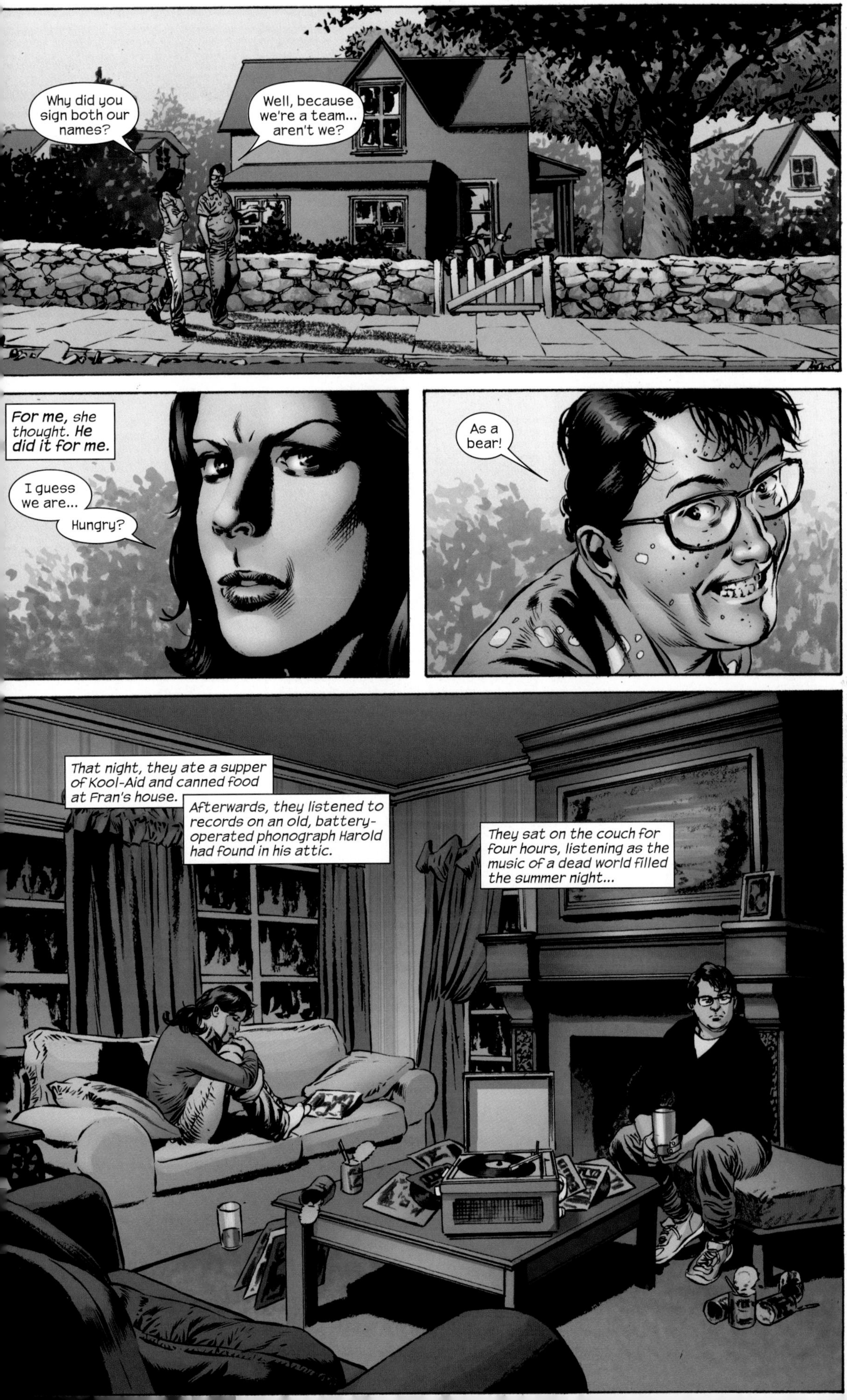
Why did you sign both our names?
Well, because we're a team... aren't we?
For me, she thought. He did it for me.
I guess we are...
Hungry?
As a bear!
That night, they ate a supper of Kool-Aid and canned food at Fran's house.
Afterwards, they listened to records on an old, battery-operated phonograph Harold had found in his attic.
They sat on the couch for four hours, listening as the music of a dead world filled the summer night...

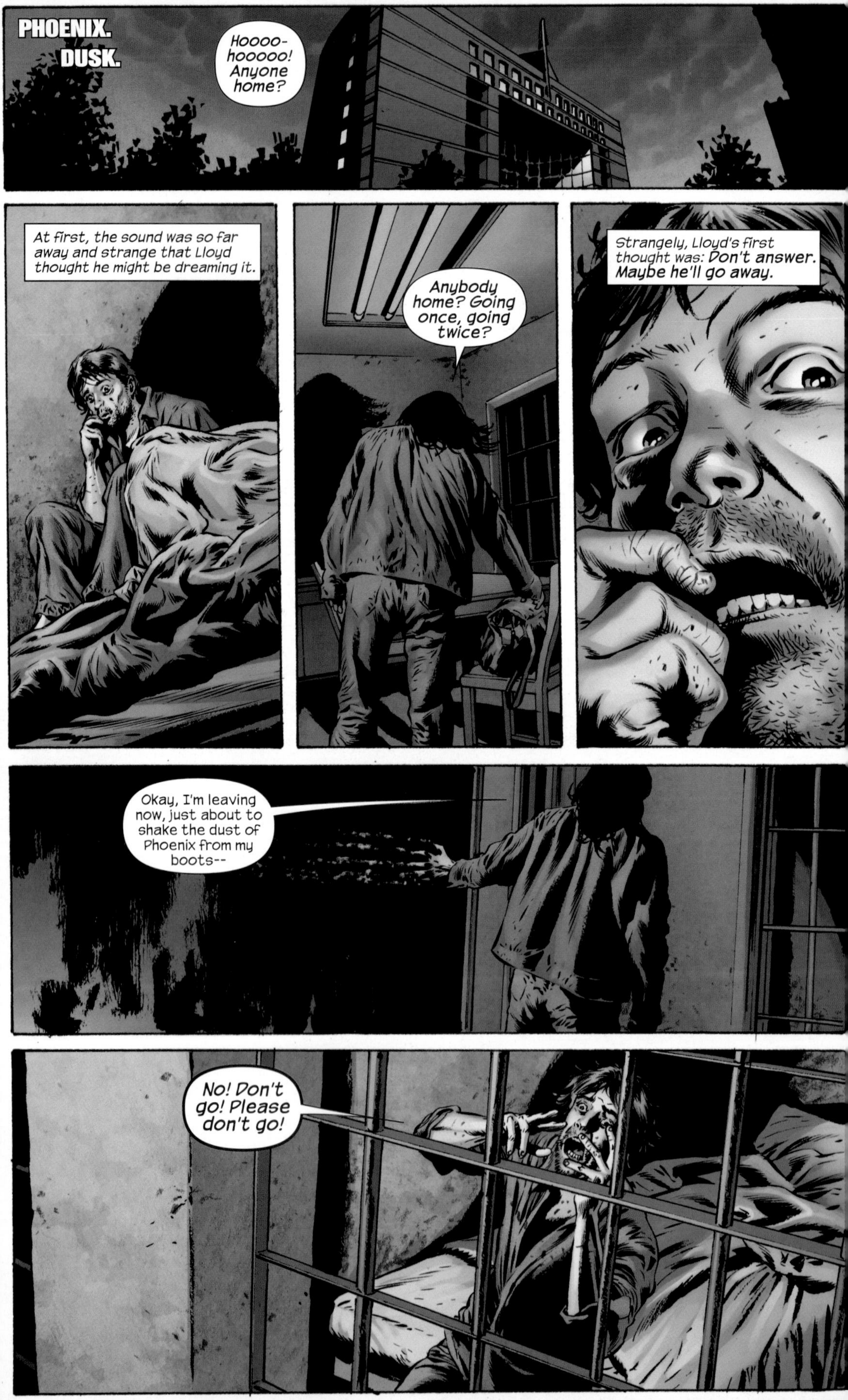
PHOENIX.
DUSK.
Hoooo-hooooo! Anyone home?
At first, the sound was so far away and strange that Lloyd thought he might be dreaming it.
Anybody home? Going once, going twice?
Strangely, Lloyd's first thought was: Don't answer. Maybe he'll go away.
Okay, I'm leaving now, just about to shake the dust of Phoenix from my boots--
No! Don't go! Please don't go!

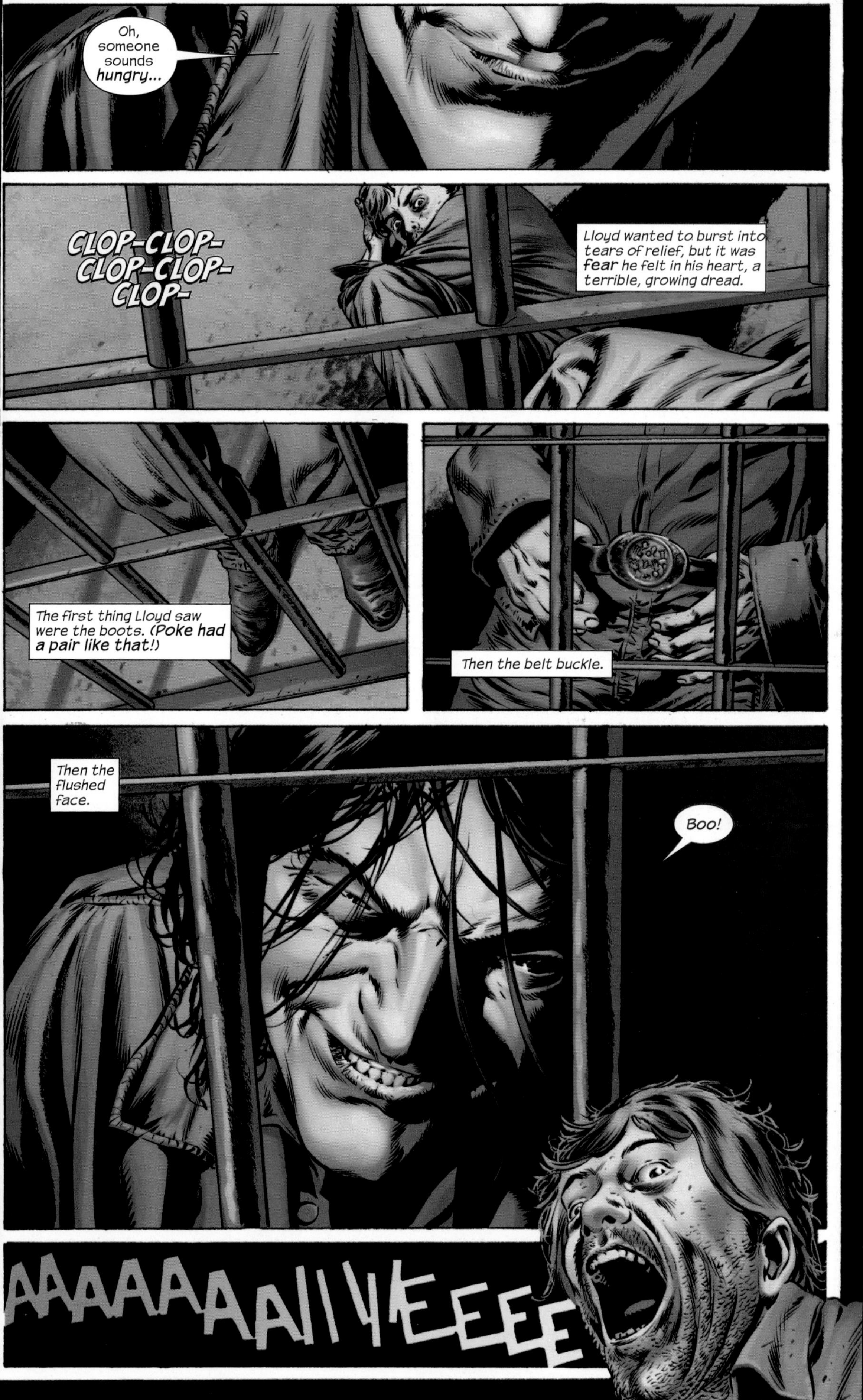

Oh, someone sounds hungry...
CLOP-CLOP-CLOP-CLOP-CLOP-
Lloyd wanted to burst into tears of relief, but it was fear he felt in his heart, a terrible, growing dread.
The first thing Lloyd saw were the boots. (Poke had a pair like that!)
Then the belt buckle.
Then the flushed face.
Boo!
AAAAAAAIIYEEEE

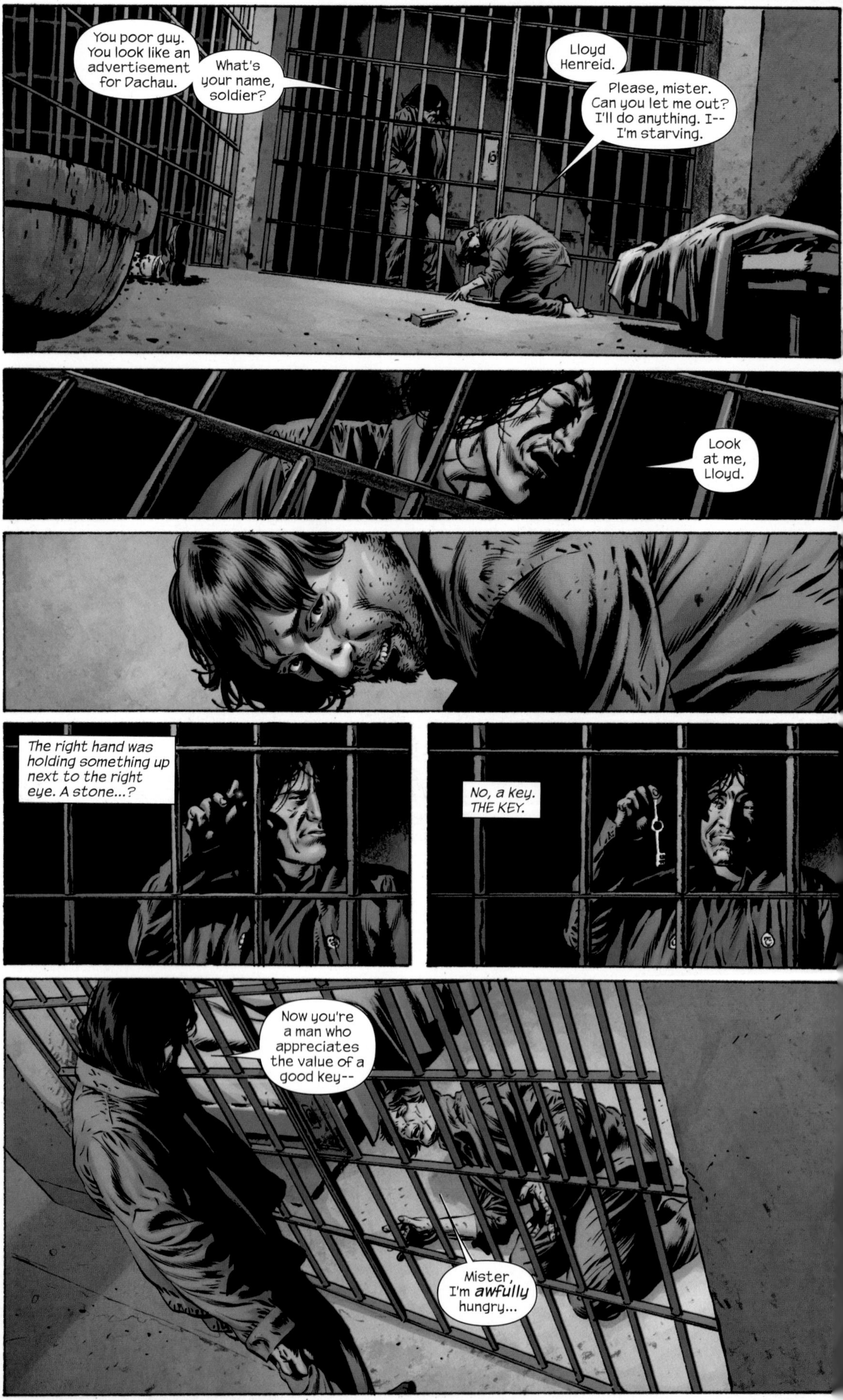

You poor guy. You look like an advertisement for Dachau.
What's your name, soldier?
Lloyd Henreid.
Please, mister. Can you let me out? I'll do anything. I-- I'm starving.
Look at me, Lloyd.
The right hand was holding something up next to the right eye. A stone...?
No, a key. THE KEY.
Now you're a man who appreciates the value of a good key--
Mister, I'm awfully hungry...

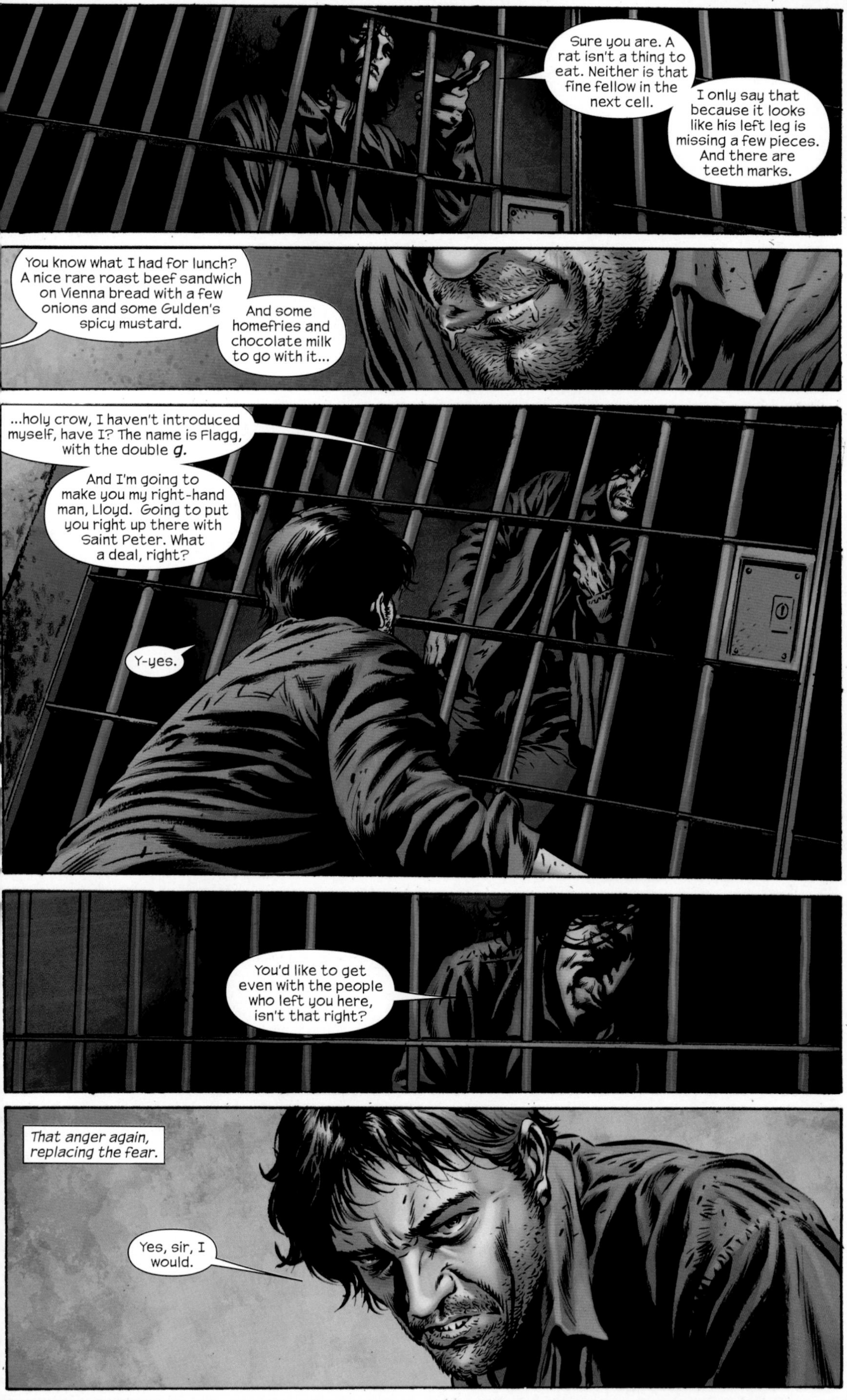
Sure you are. A rat isn't a thing to eat. Neither is that fine fellow in the next cell.
I only say that because it looks like his left leg is missing a few pieces. And there are teeth marks.
You know what I had for lunch? A nice rare roast beef sandwich on Vienna bread with a few onions and some Gulden's spicy mustard.
And some homefries and chocolate milk to go with it...
...holy crow, I haven't introduced myself, have I? The name is Flagg, with the double g.
And I'm going to make you my right-hand man, Lloyd. Going to put you right up there with Saint Peter. What a deal, right?
Y-yes.
You'd like to get even with the people who left you here, isn't that right?
That anger again, replacing the fear.
Yes, sir, I would.

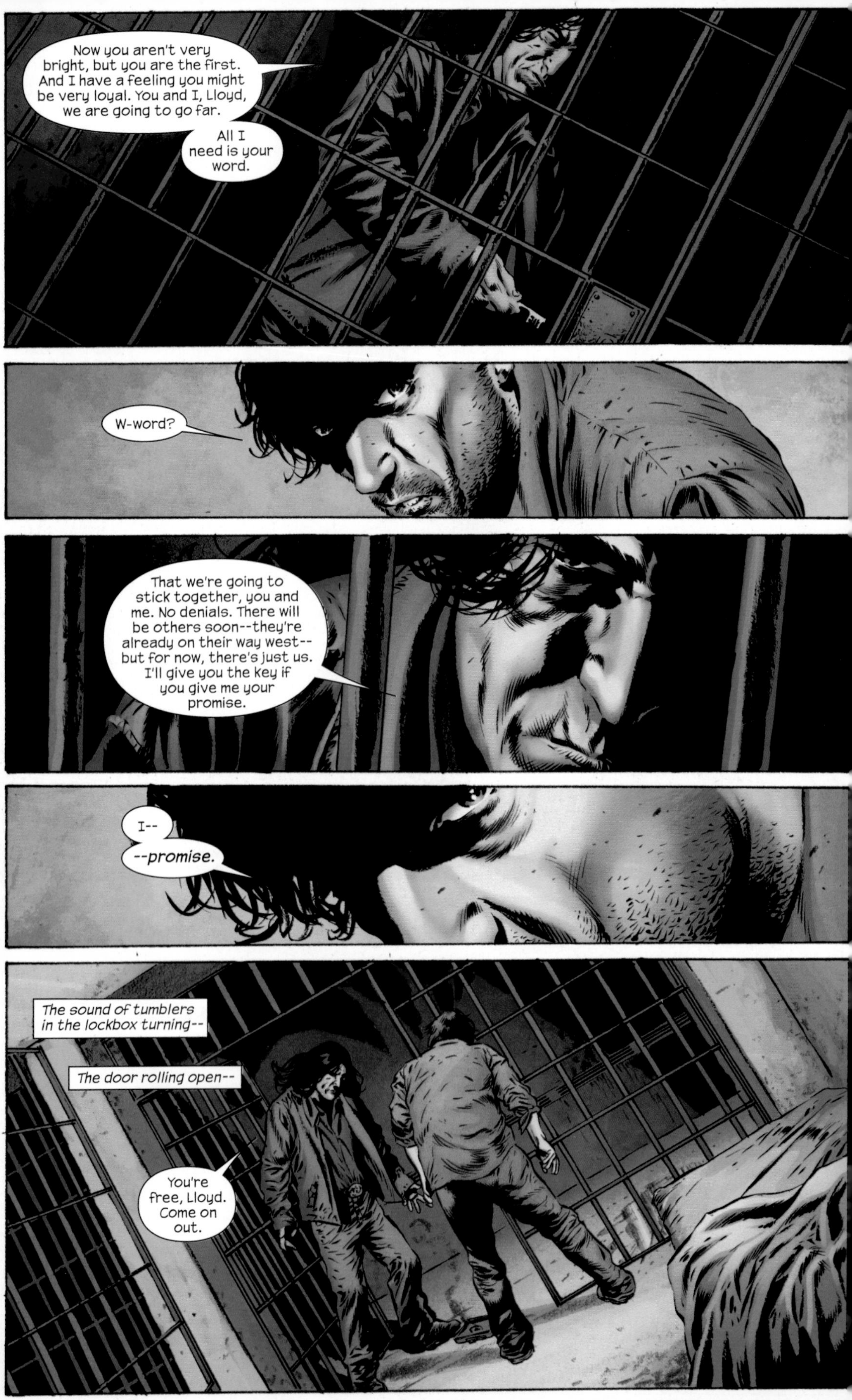
Now you aren't very bright, but you are the first. And I have a feeling you might be very loyal. You and I, Lloyd, we are going to go far.
All I need is your word.
W-word?
That we're going to stick together, you and me. No denials. There will be others soon--they're already on their way west--but for now, there's just us. I'll give you the key if you give me your promise.
I--
--promise.
The sound of tumblers in the lockbox turning--
The door rolling open--
You're free, Lloyd. Come on out.

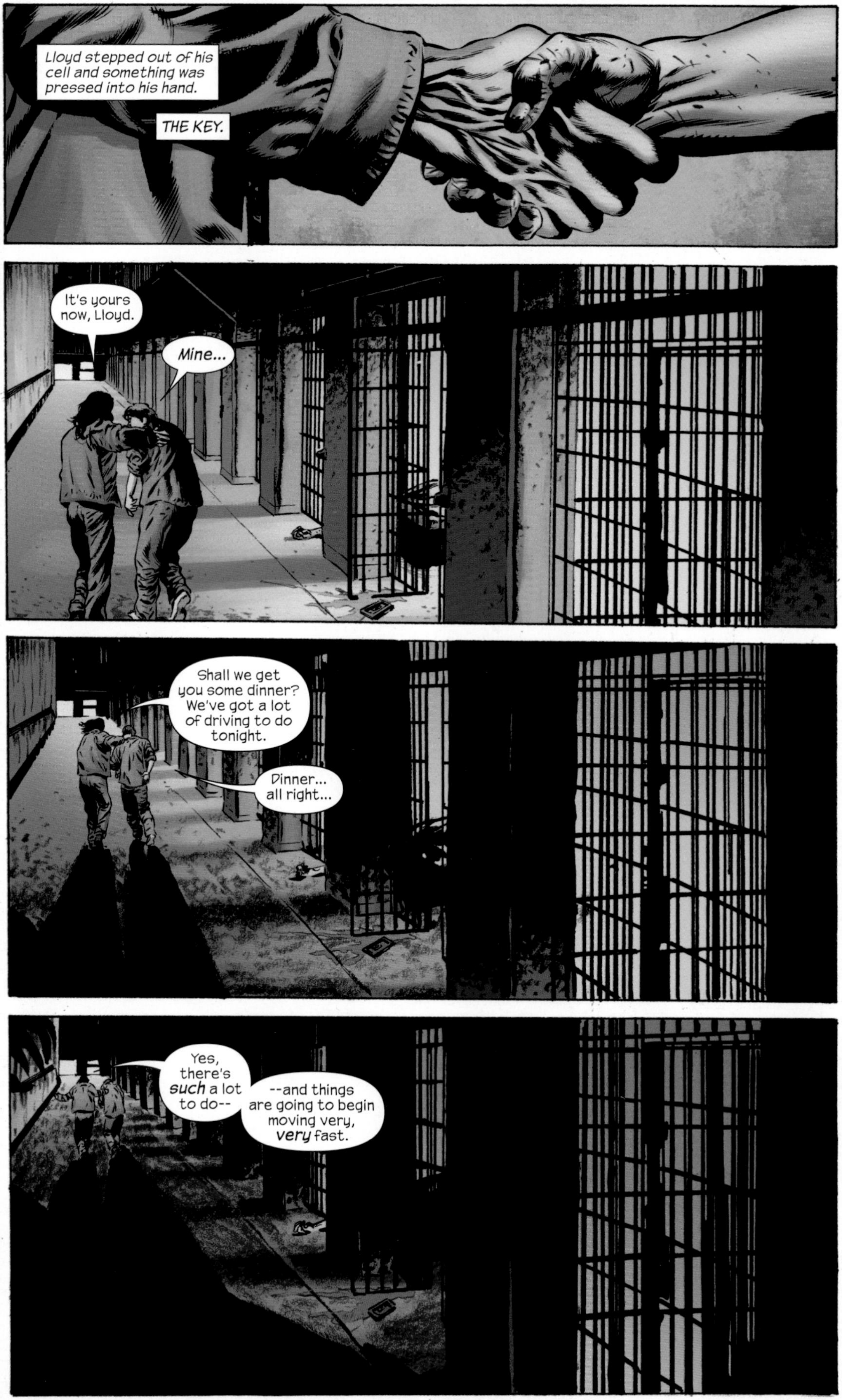
Lloyd stepped out of his cell and something was pressed into his hand.
THE KEY.
It's yours now, Lloyd.
Mine...
Shall we get you some dinner? We've got a lot of driving to do tonight.
Dinner... all right...
Yes, there's *such* a lot to do--
--and things are going to begin moving very, *very* fast.

chapter FIVE

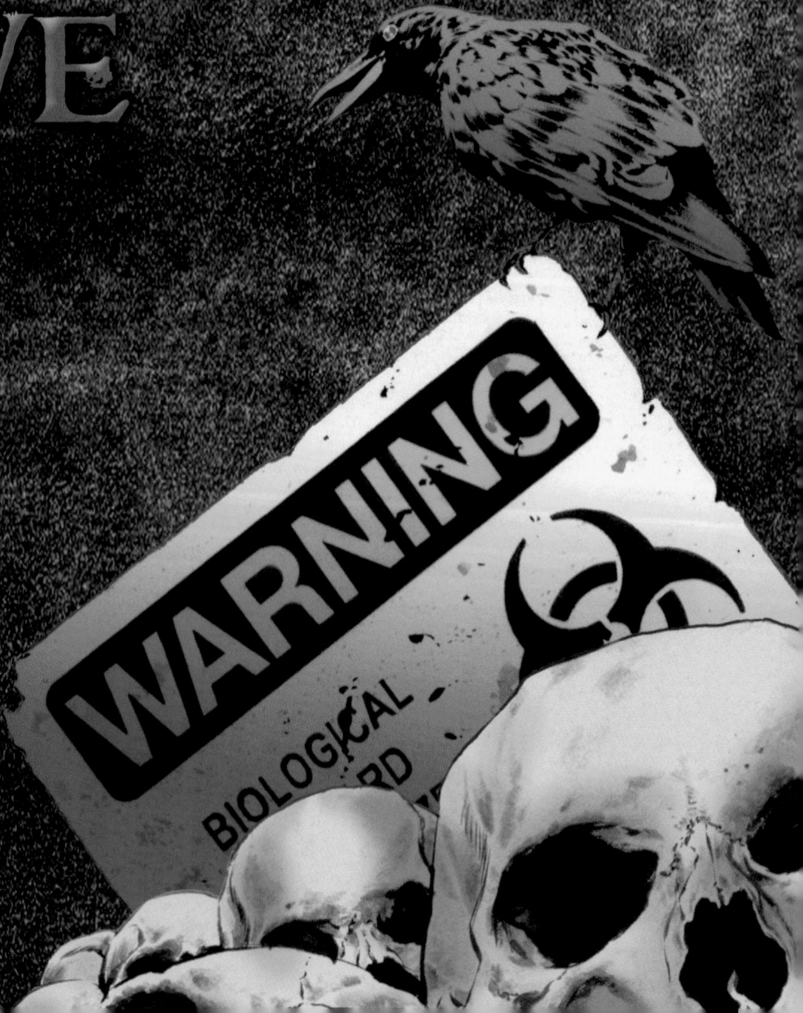
WARNING
BIOLOGICAL

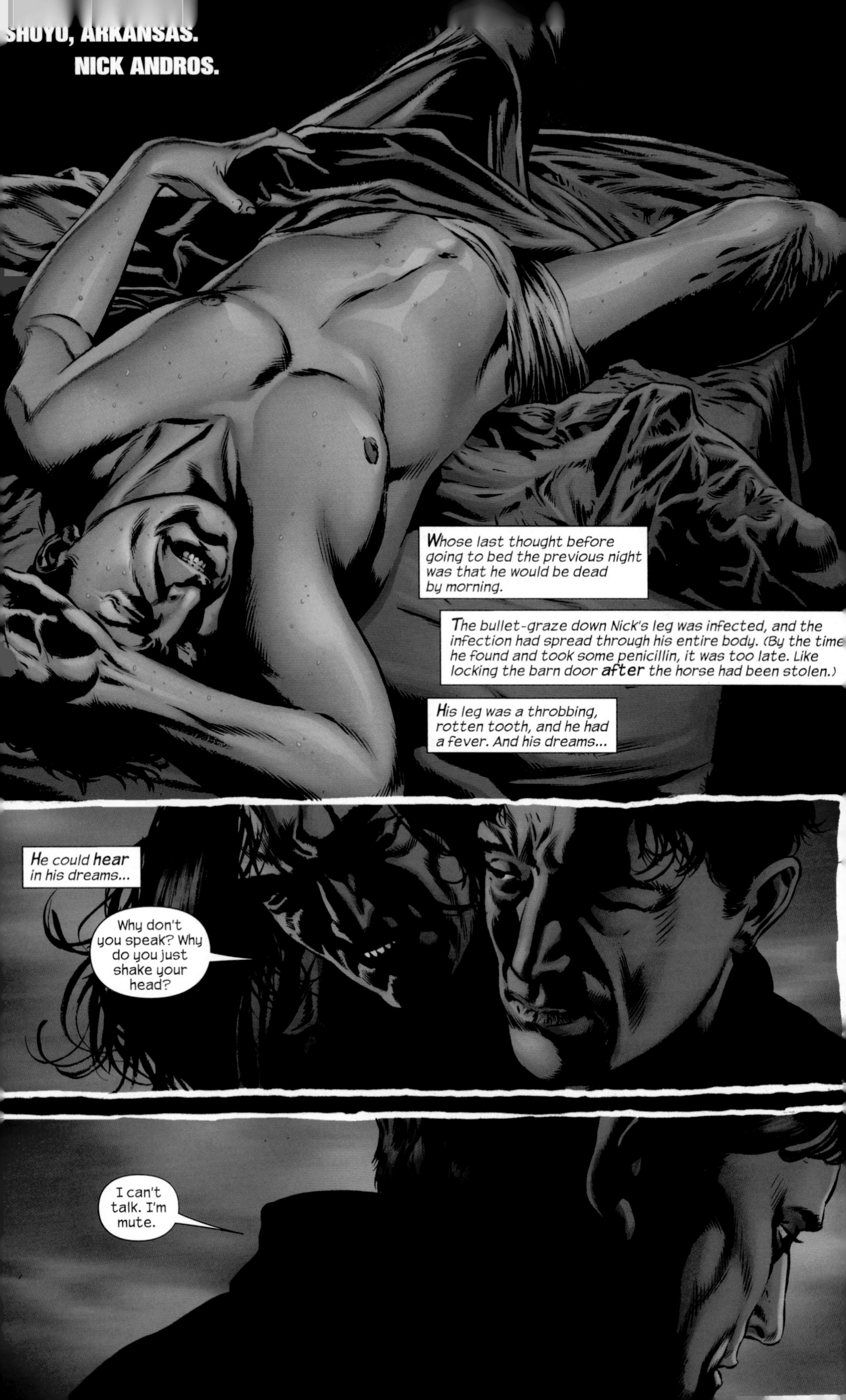
SHOYO, ARKANSAS.
NICK ANDROS.
Whose last thought before going to bed the previous night was that he would be dead by morning.
The bullet-graze down Nick's leg was infected, and the infection had spread through his entire body. (By the time he found and took some penicillin, it was too late. Like locking the barn door after the horse had been stolen.)
His leg was a throbbing, rotten tooth, and he had a fever. And his dreams...
He could hear in his dreams...
Why don't you speak? Why do you just shake your head?
I can't talk. I'm mute.

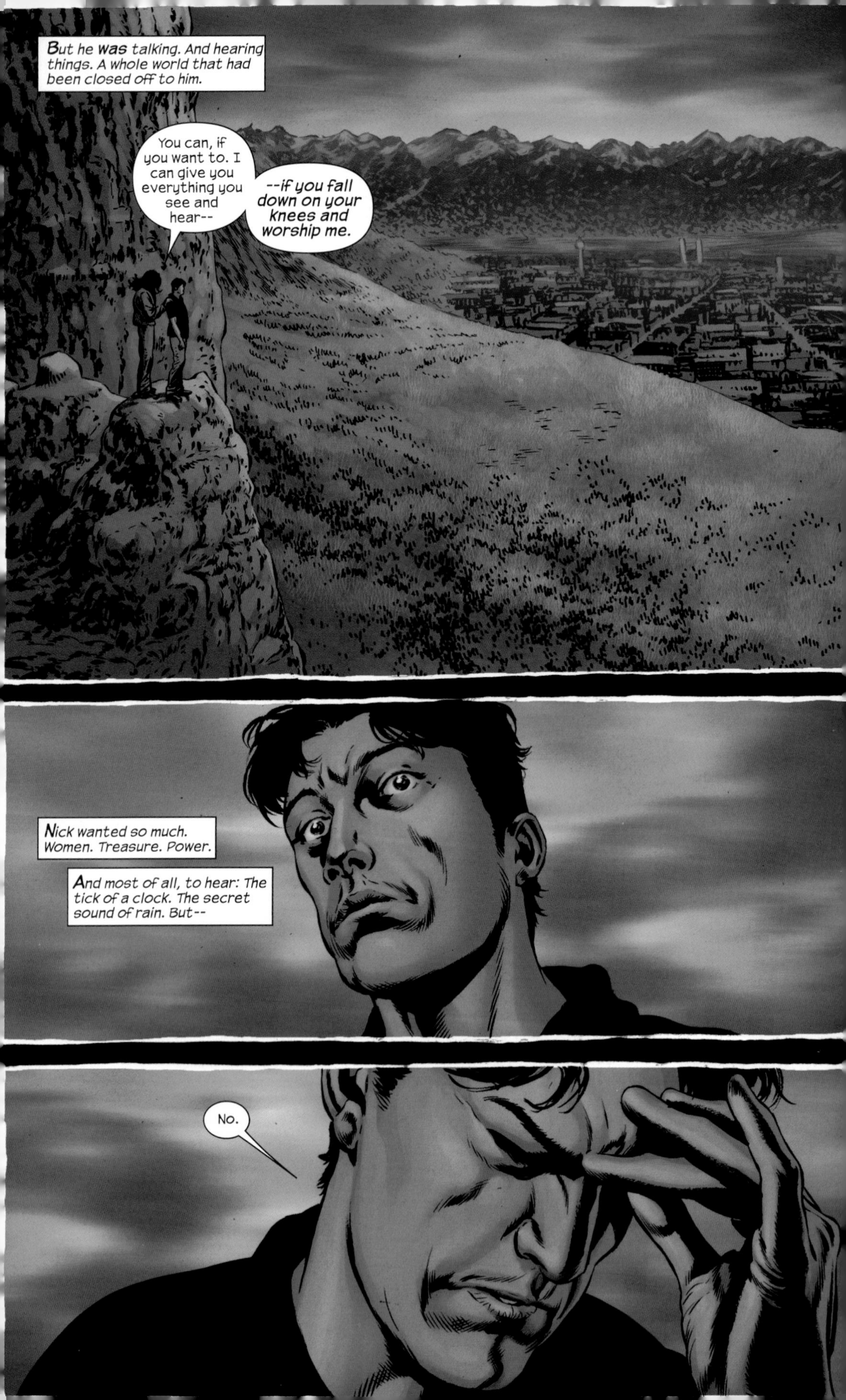
But he was talking. And hearing things. A whole world that had been closed off to him.
You can, if you want to. I can give you everything you see and hear--
--if you fall down on your knees and worship me.
Nick wanted so much. Women. Treasure. Power.
And most of all, to hear: The tick of a clock. The secret sound of rain. But--
No.

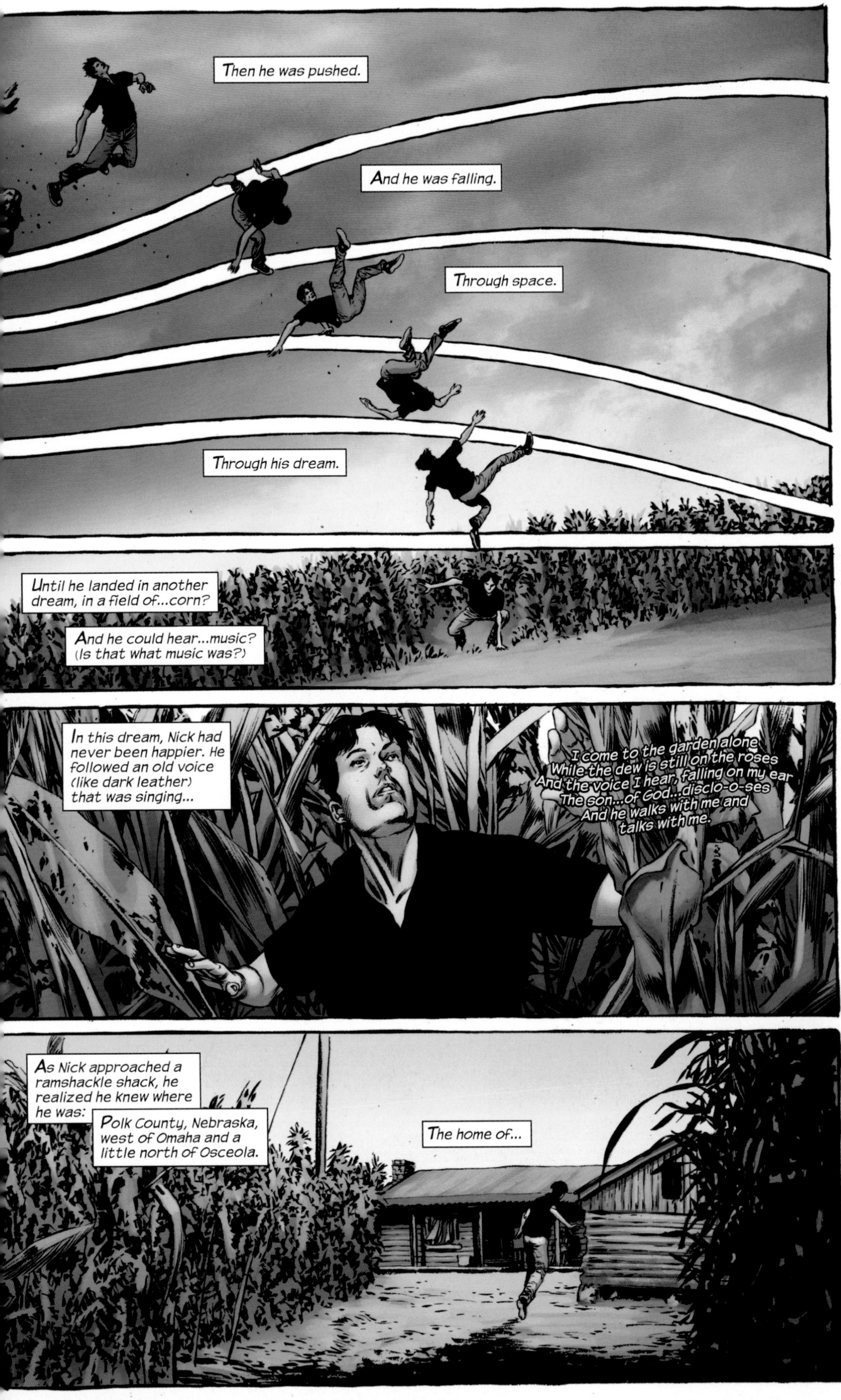

Then he was pushed.
And he was falling.
Through space.
Through his dream.
Until he landed in another dream, in a field of...corn?
And he could hear...music? (Is that what music was?)
In this dream, Nick had never been happier. He followed an old voice (like dark leather) that was singing...
I come to the garden alone While the dew is still on the roses And the voice I hear, falling on my ear The son...of God...disclo-o-ses And he walks with me and talks with me.
As Nick approached a ramshackle shack, he realized he knew where he was:
Polk County, Nebraska, west of Omaha and a little north of Osceola.
The home of...

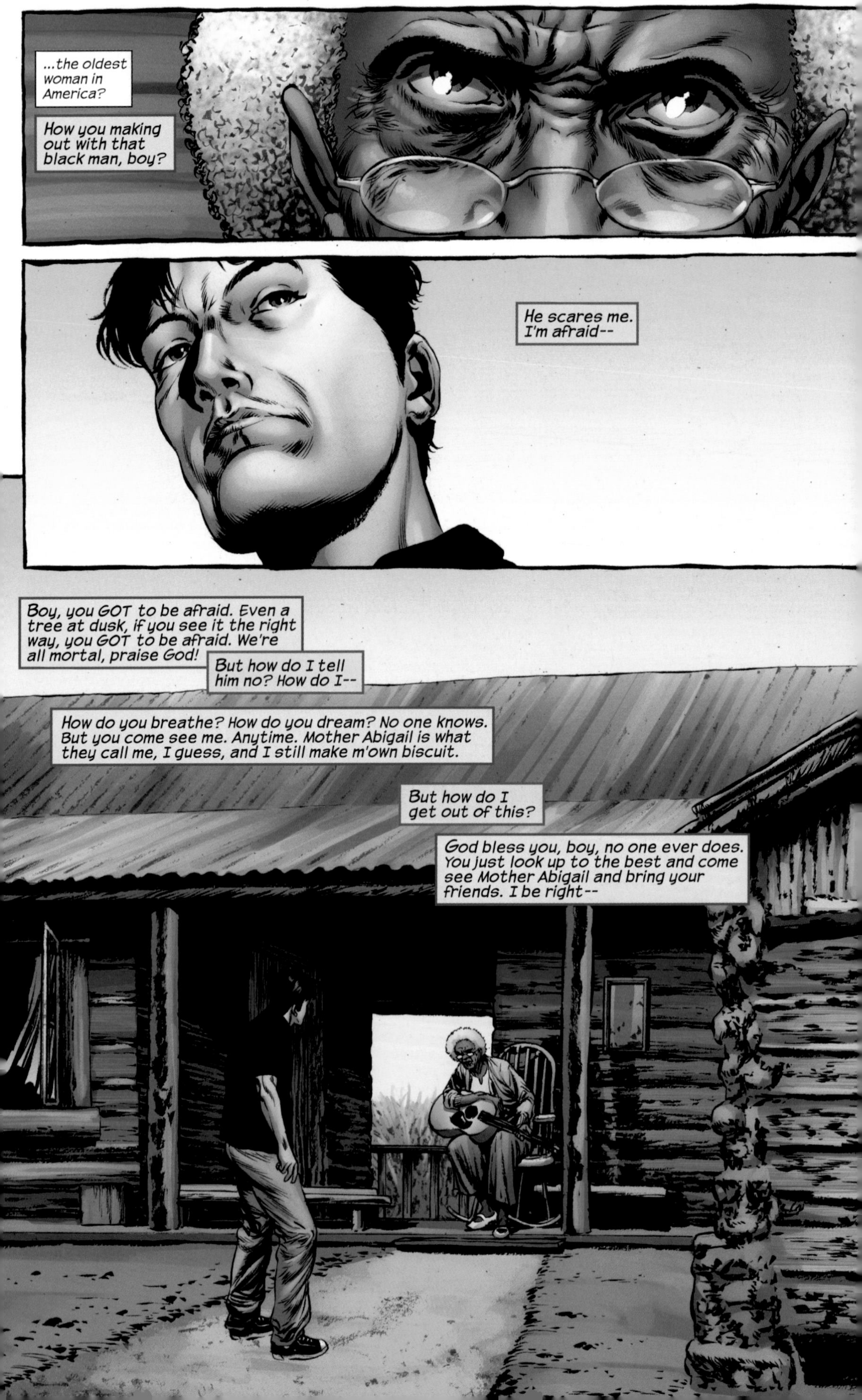
...the oldest woman in America?
How you making out with that black man, boy?
He scares me. I'm afraid--
Boy, you GOT to be afraid. Even a tree at dusk, if you see it the right way, you GOT to be afraid. We're all mortal, praise God!
But how do I tell him no? How do I--
How do you breathe? How do you dream? No one knows. But you come see me. Anytime. Mother Abigail is what they call me, I guess, and I still make m'own biscuit.
But how do I get out of this?
God bless you, boy, no one ever does. You just look up to the best and come see Mother Abigail and bring your friends. I be right--

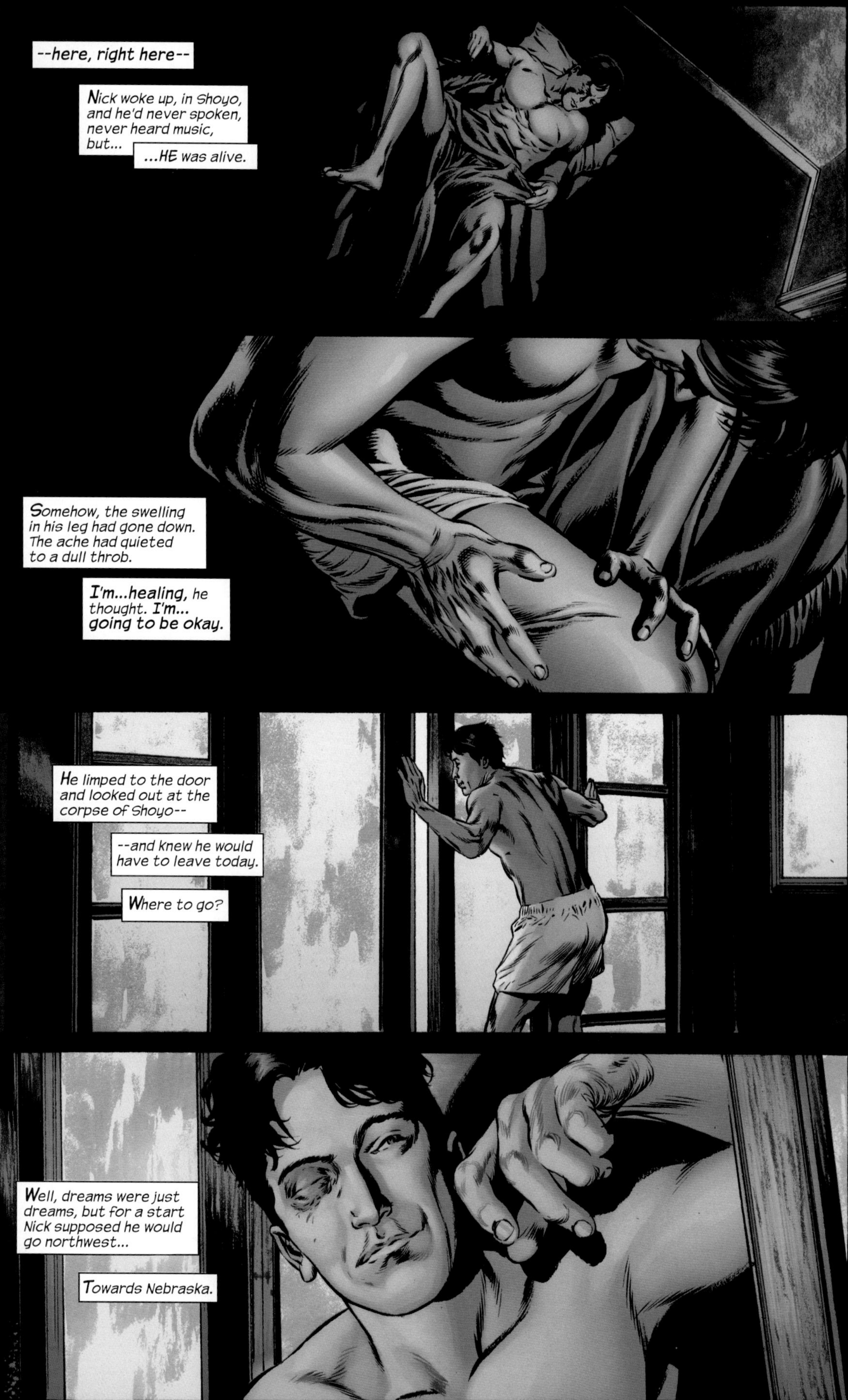
--here, right here--
Nick woke up, in Shoyo, and he'd never spoken, never heard music, but...
...HE was alive.
Somehow, the swelling in his leg had gone down. The ache had quieted to a dull throb.
I'm...healing, he thought. I'm... going to be okay.
He limped to the door and looked out at the corpse of Shoyo--
--and knew he would have to leave today.
Where to go?
Well, dreams were just dreams, but for a start Nick supposed he would go northwest...
Towards Nebraska.

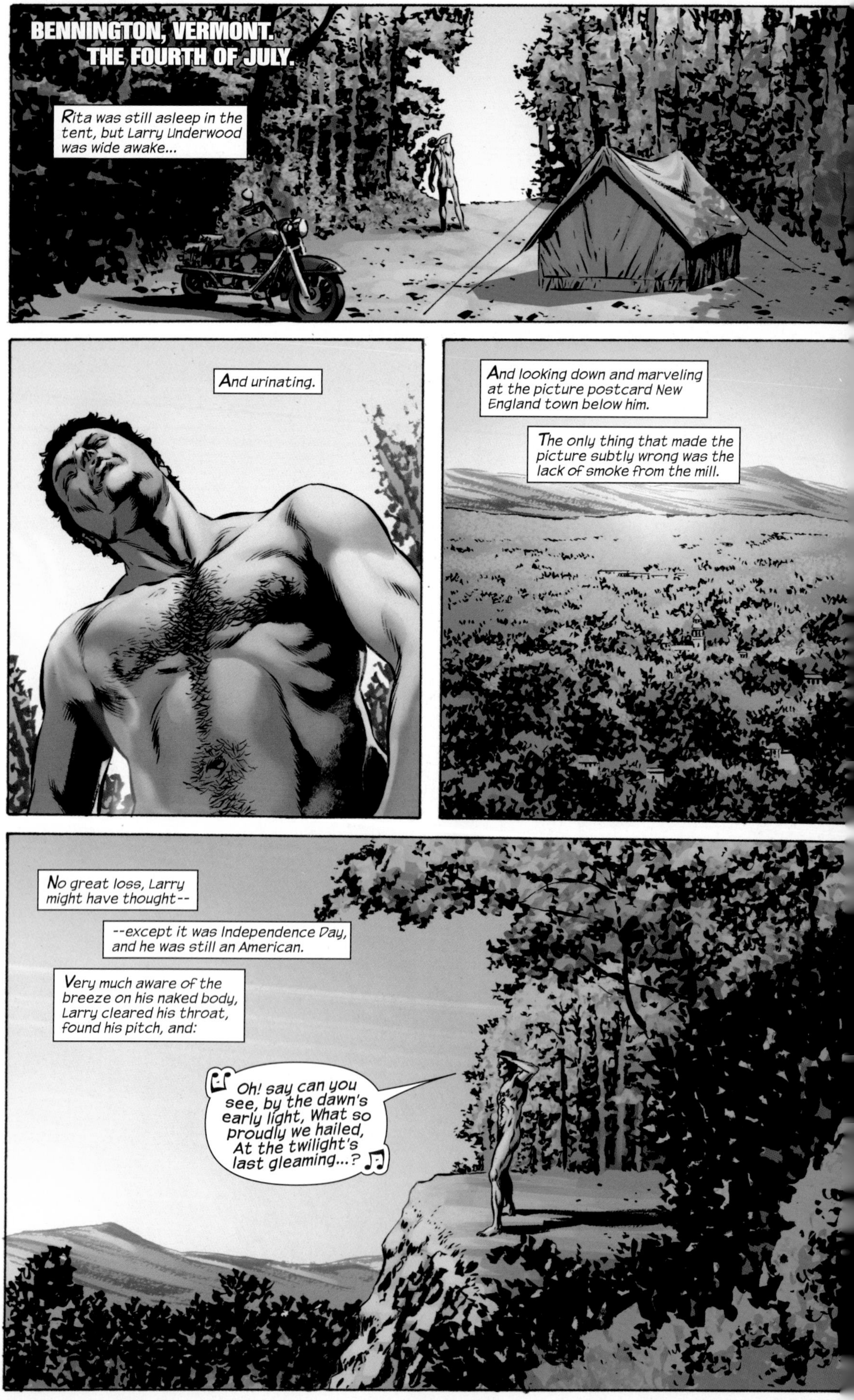
BENNINGTON, VERMONT. THE FOURTH OF JULY.
Rita was still asleep in the tent, but Larry Underwood was wide awake...
And urinating.
And looking down and marveling at the picture postcard New England town below him.
The only thing that made the picture subtly wrong was the lack of smoke from the mill.
No great loss, Larry might have thought--
--except it was Independence Day, and he was still an American.
Very much aware of the breeze on his naked body, Larry cleared his throat, found his pitch, and:
Oh! say can you see, by the dawn's early light, What so proudly we hailed, At the twilight's last gleaming...?

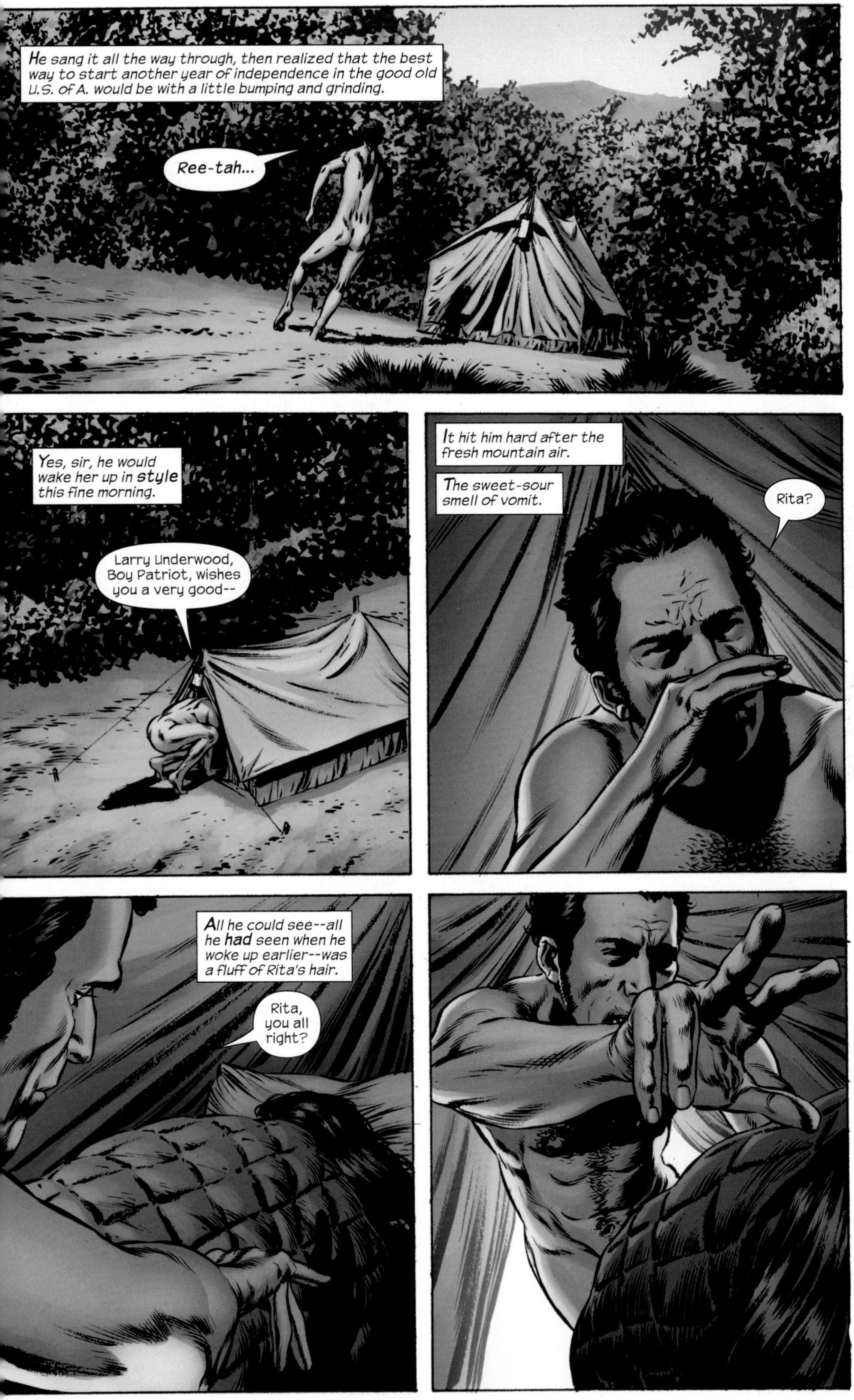
He sang it all the way through, then realized that the best way to start another year of independence in the good old U.S. of A. would be with a little bumping and grinding.
Ree-tah...
Yes, sir, he would wake her up in style this fine morning.
Larry Underwood, Boy Patriot, wishes you a very good--
It hit him hard after the fresh mountain air.
The sweet-sour smell of vomit.
Rita?
All he could see--all he had seen when he woke up earlier--was a fluff of Rita's hair.
Rita, you all right?

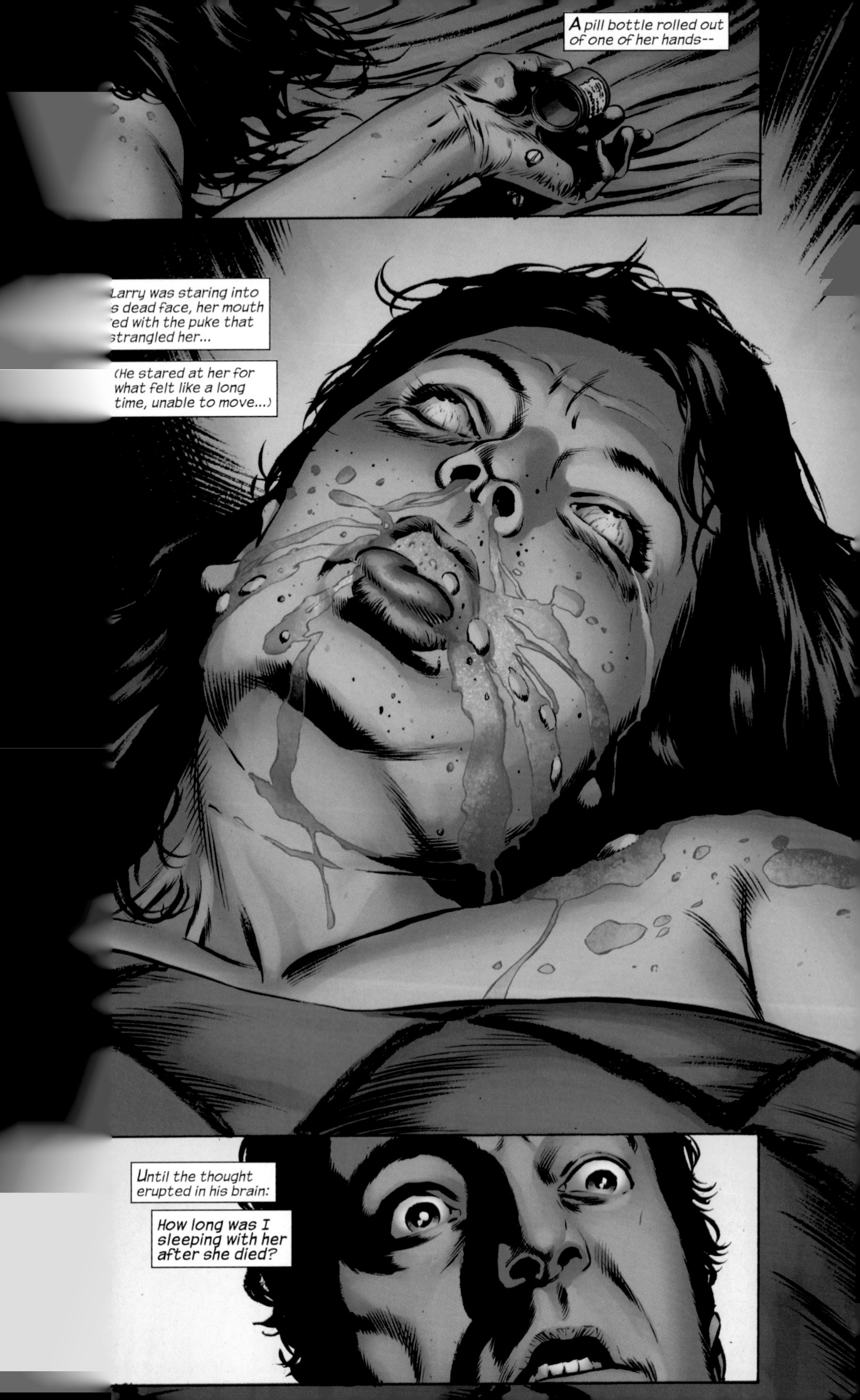

A pill bottle rolled out of one of her hands--
Larry was staring into s dead face, her mouth ed with the puke that strangled her...
(He stared at her for what felt like a long time, unable to move...)
Until the thought erupted in his brain:
How long was I sleeping with her after she died?

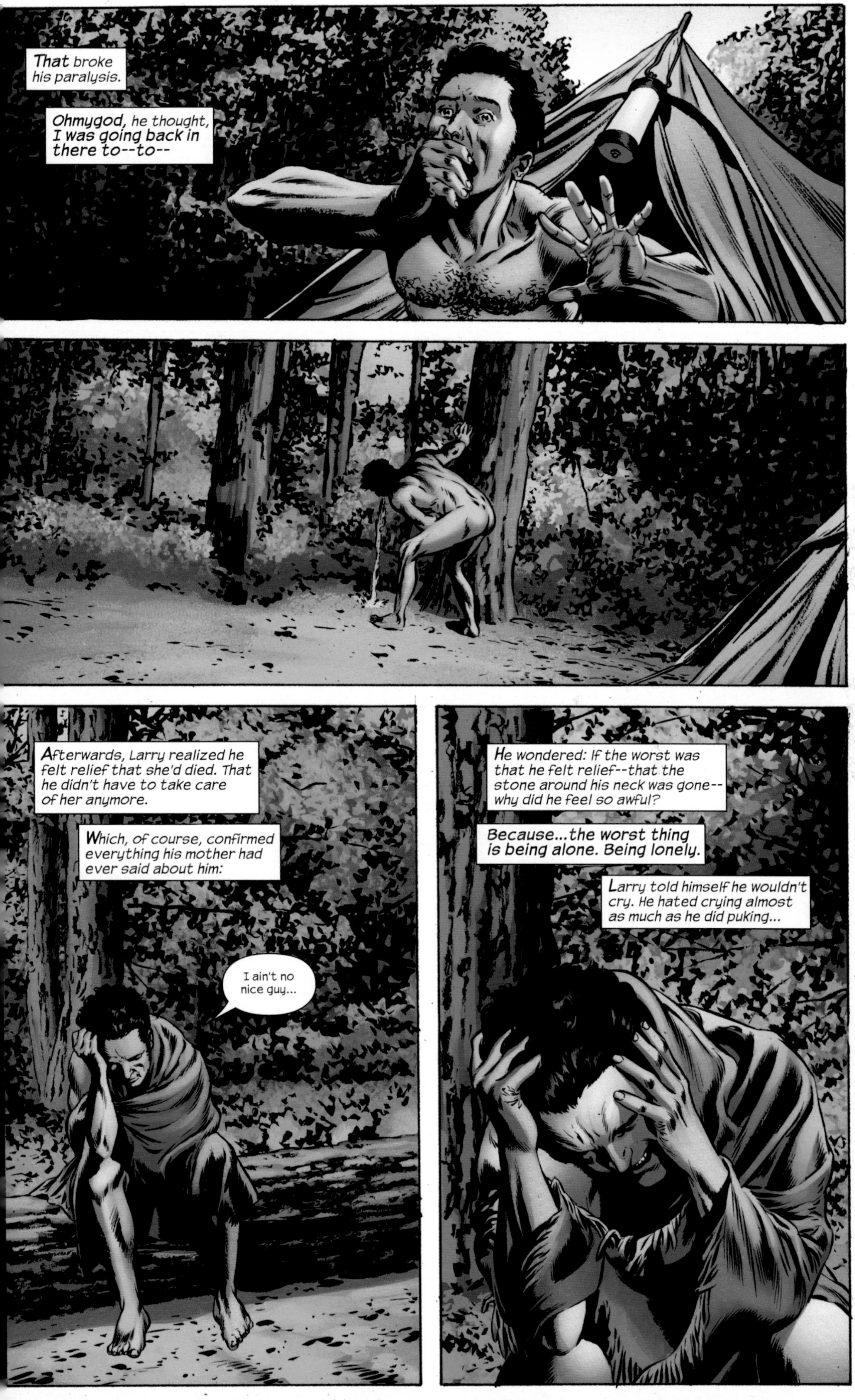
That broke his paralysis.
Ohmygod, he thought, I was going back in there to--to--
Afterwards, Larry realized he felt relief that she'd died. That he didn't have to take care of her anymore.
Which, of course, confirmed everything his mother had ever said about him:
I ain't no nice guy...
He wondered: If the worst was that he felt relief--that the stone around his neck was gone--why did he feel so awful?
Because...the worst thing is being alone. Being lonely.
Larry told himself he wouldn't cry. He hated crying almost as much as he did puking...

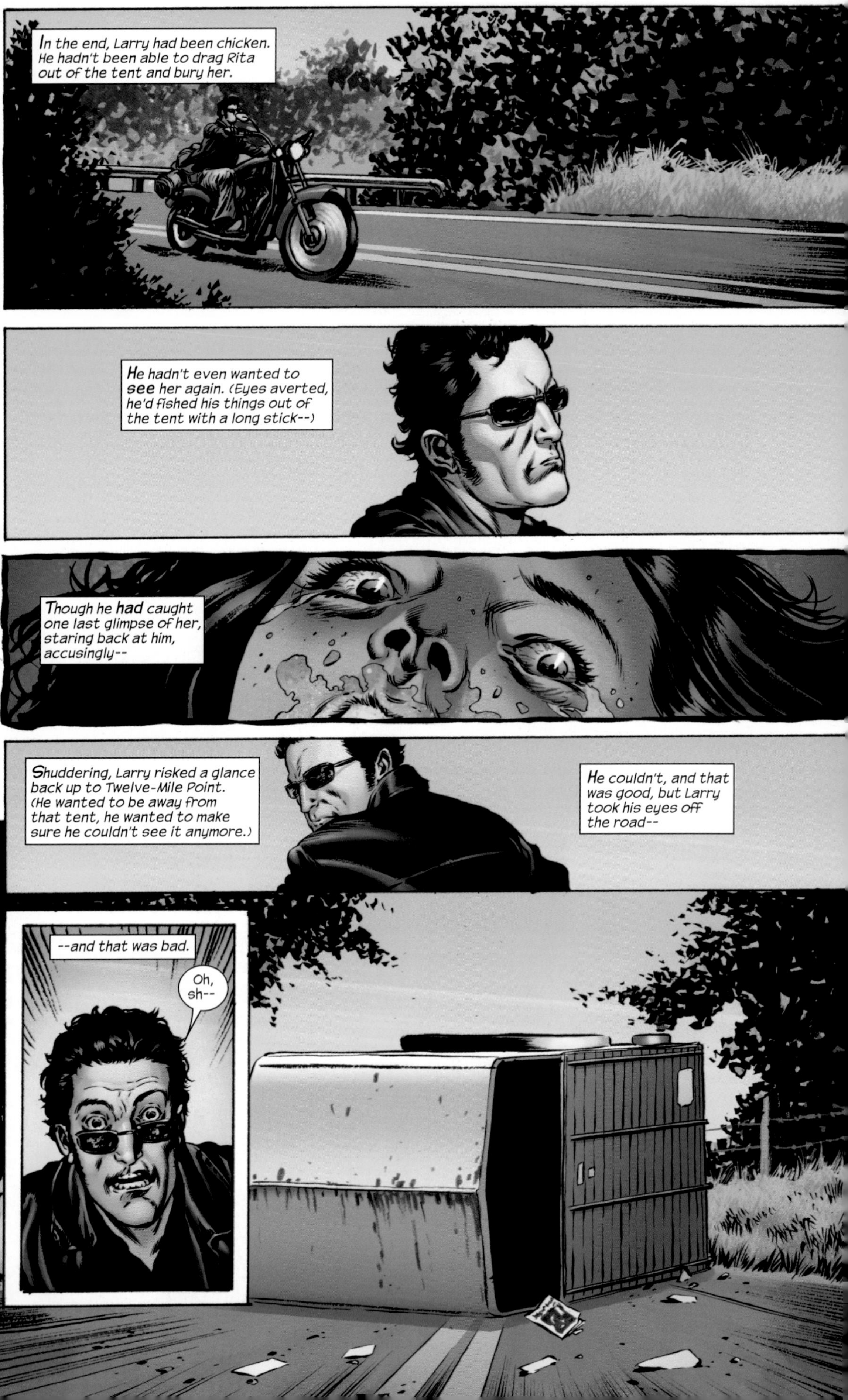
In the end, Larry had been chicken. He hadn't been able to drag Rita out of the tent and bury her.
He hadn't even wanted to **see** her again. (Eyes averted, he'd fished his things out of the tent with a long stick--)
Though he **had** caught one last glimpse of her, staring back at him, accusingly--
Shuddering, Larry risked a glance back up to Twelve-Mile Point. (He wanted to be away from that tent, he wanted to make sure he couldn't see it anymore.)
He couldn't, and that was good, but Larry took his eyes off the road--
--and that was bad.
Oh, sh--

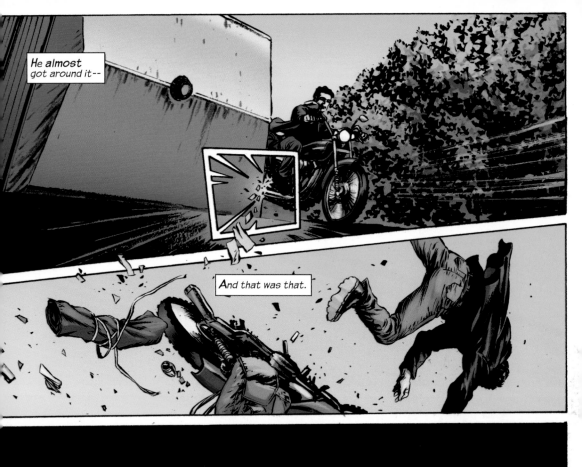

He almost got around it --

And that was that.

You all right?

Larry asked himself.

Yeah, I'm all right...

But, he could have fractured his skull and lain there in the hot sun until he died...

Or strangled to death on his own puke like a certain now-deceased friend of his...

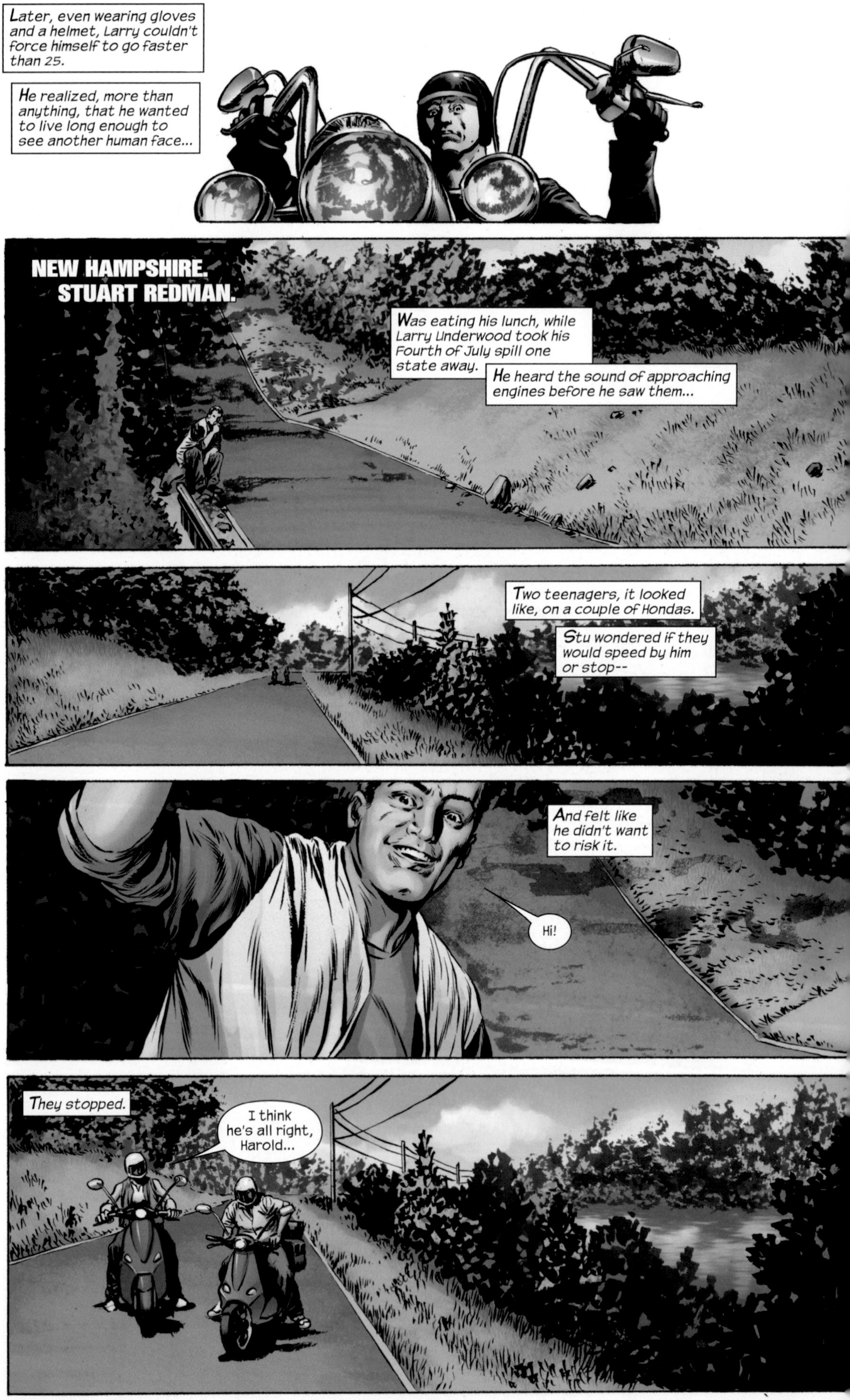
Later, even wearing gloves and a helmet, Larry couldn't force himself to go faster than 25.
He realized, more than anything, that he wanted to live long enough to see another human face...
NEW HAMPSHIRE.
STUART REDMAN.
Was eating his lunch, while Larry Underwood took his Fourth of July spill one state away.
He heard the sound of approaching engines before he saw them...
Two teenagers, it looked like, on a couple of Hondas.
Stu wondered if they would speed by him or stop--
And felt like he didn't want to risk it.
Hi!
They stopped.
I think he's all right, Harold...

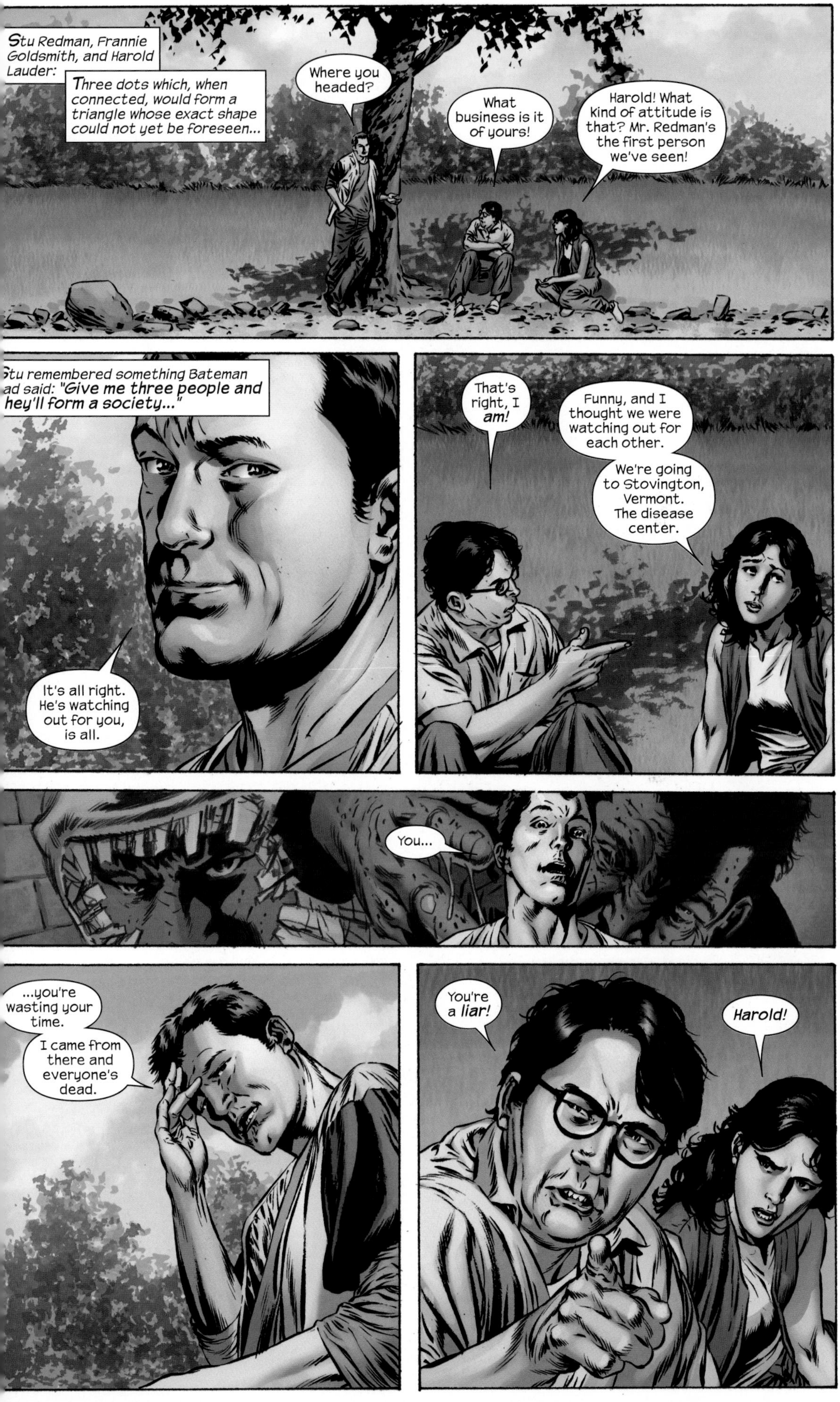
Stu Redman, Frannie Goldsmith, and Harold Lauder:
Three dots which, when connected, would form a triangle whose exact shape could not yet be foreseen...
Where you headed?
What business is it of yours!
Harold! What kind of attitude is that? Mr. Redman's the first person we've seen!
Stu remembered something Bateman had said: "Give me three people and they'll form a society..."
It's all right. He's watching out for you, is all.
That's right, I am!
Funny, and I thought we were watching out for each other.
We're going to Stovington, Vermont. The disease center.
You...
...you're wasting your time.
I came from there and everyone's dead.
You're a liar!
Harold!

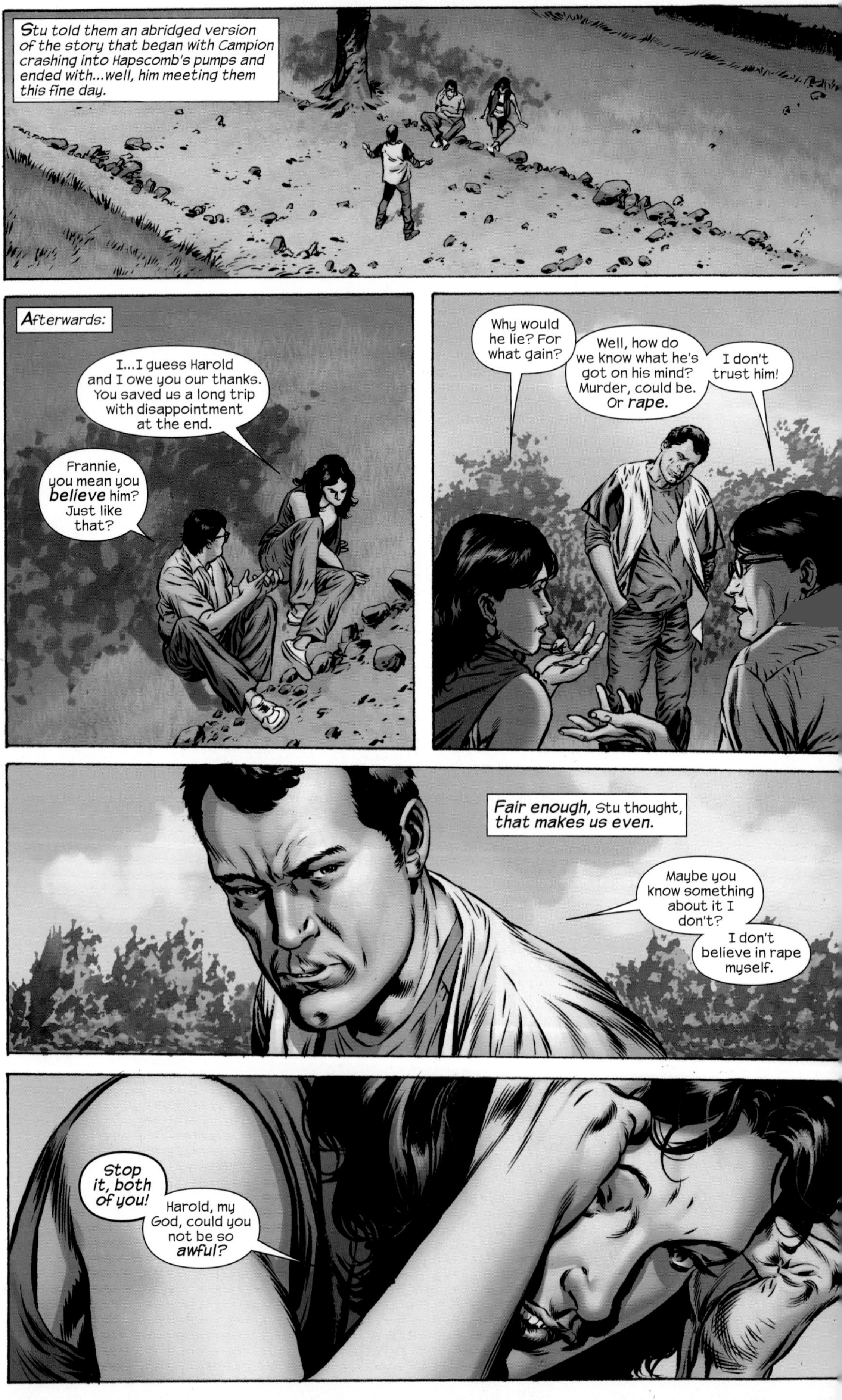
Stu told them an abridged version of the story that began with Campion crashing into Hapscomb's pumps and ended with...well, him meeting them this fine day.
Afterwards:
I...I guess Harold and I owe you our thanks. You saved us a long trip with disappointment at the end.
Frannie, you mean you believe him? Just like that?
Why would he lie? For what gain?
Well, how do we know what he's got on his mind? Murder, could be. Or rape.
I don't trust him!
Fair enough, Stu thought, that makes us even.
Maybe you know something about it I don't?
I don't believe in rape myself.
Stop it, both of you!
Harold, my God, could you not be so awful?

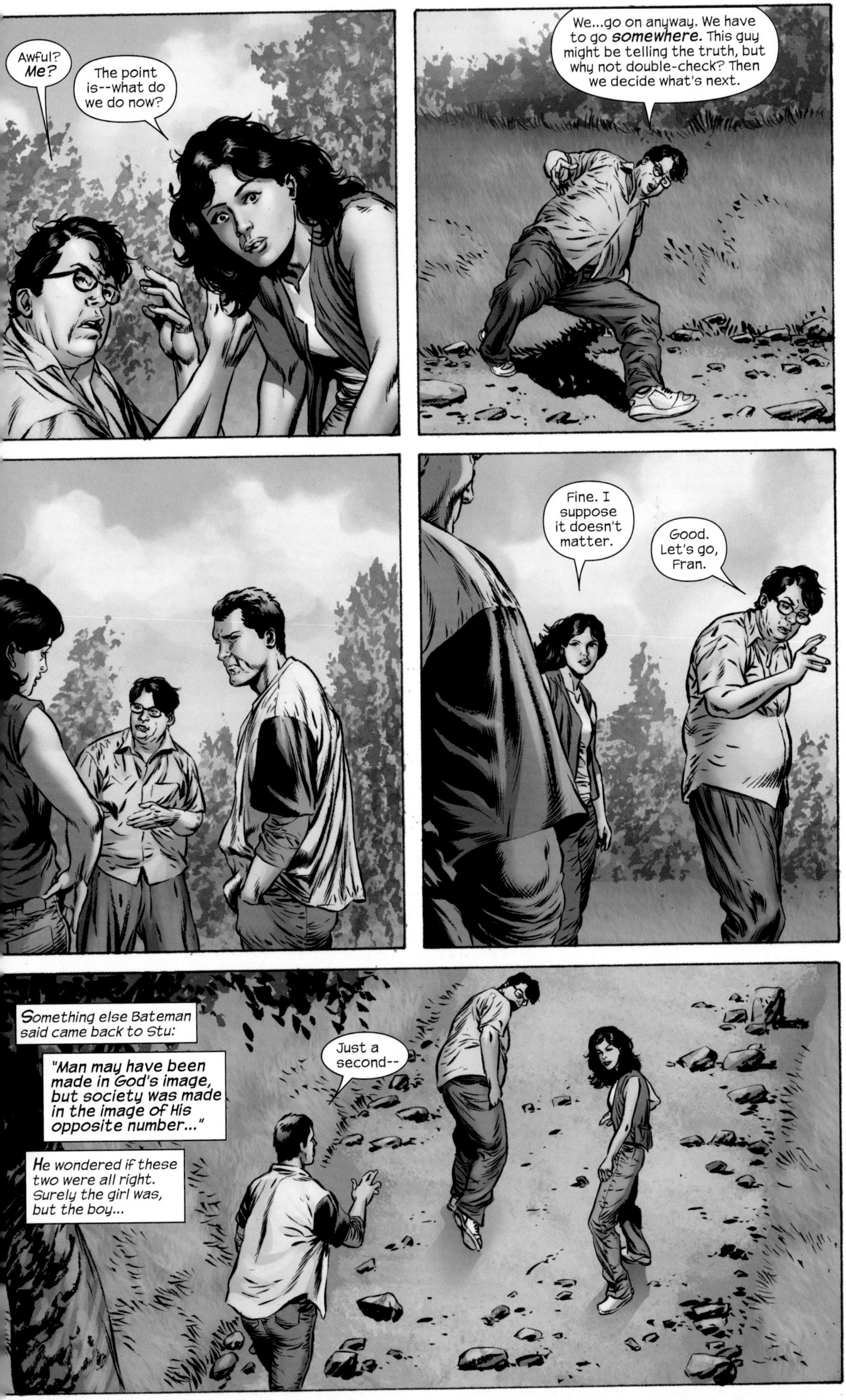

Awful? Me?
The point is--what do we do now?
We...go on anyway. We have to go somewhere. This guy might be telling the truth, but why not double-check? Then we decide what's next.
Fine. I suppose it doesn't matter.
Good. Let's go, Fran.
Something else Bateman said came back to Stu:
"Man may have been made in God's image, but society was made in the image of His opposite number..."
He wondered if these two were all right. Surely the girl was, but the boy...
Just a second--

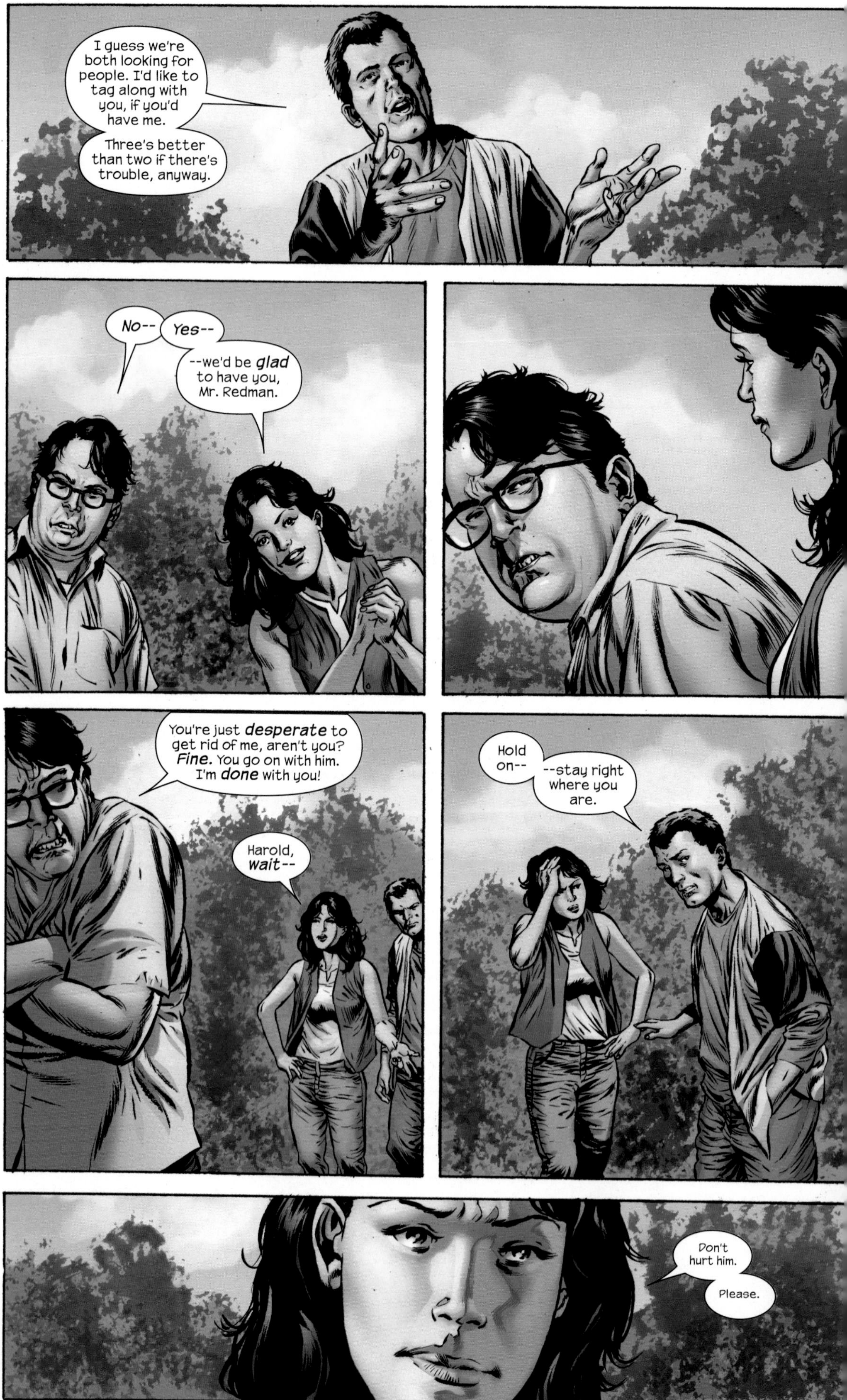
I guess we're both looking for people. I'd like to tag along with you, if you'd have me.
Three's better than two if there's trouble, anyway.
No--
Yes--
--we'd be glad to have you, Mr. Redman.
You're just desperate to get rid of me, aren't you? Fine. You go on with him. I'm done with you!
Harold, wait--
Hold on--
--stay right where you are.
Don't hurt him.
Please.

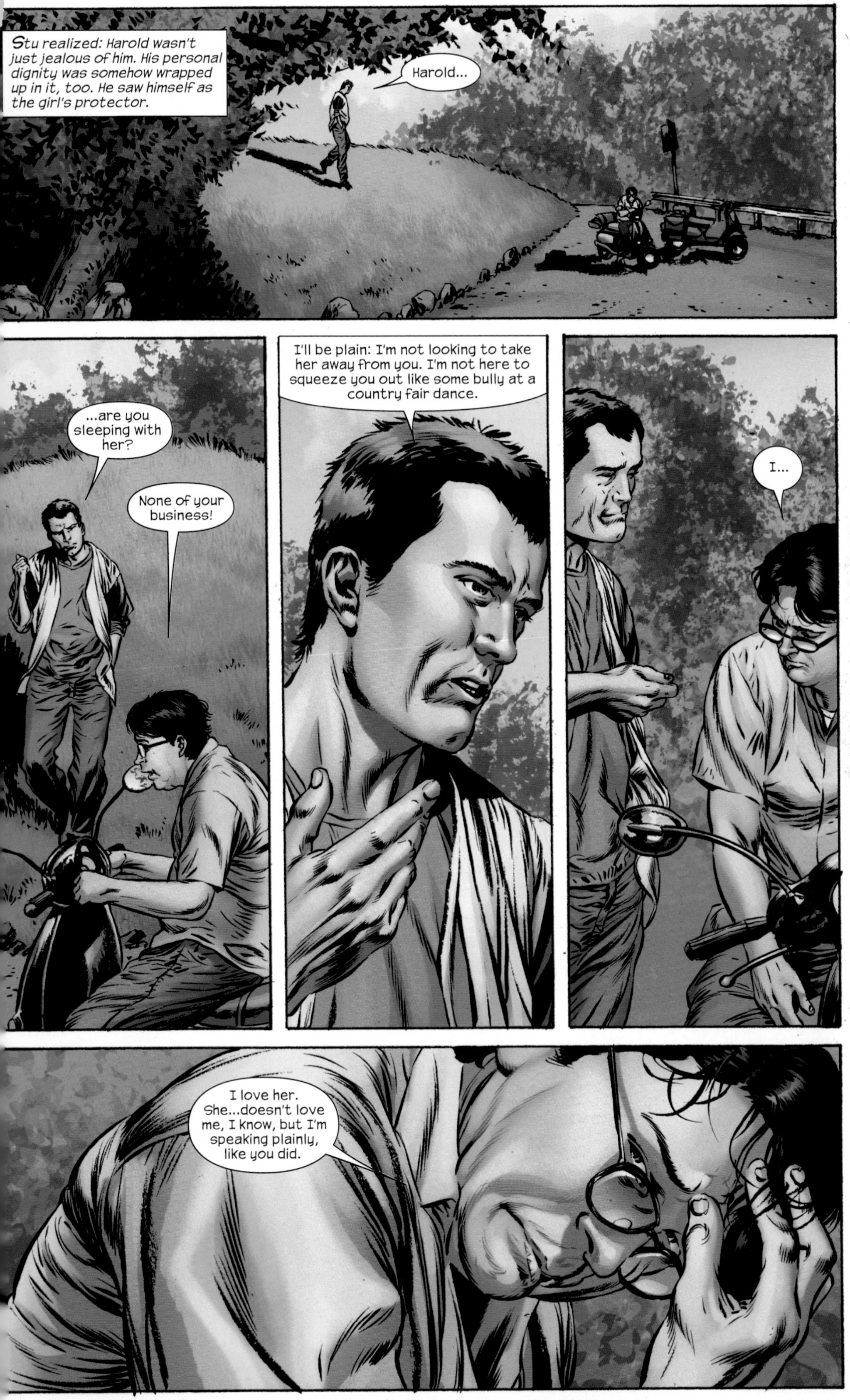
Stu realized: Harold wasn't just jealous of him. His personal dignity was somehow wrapped up in it, too. He saw himself as the girl's protector.
Harold...
...are you sleeping with her?
None of your business!
I'll be plain: I'm not looking to take her away from you. I'm not here to squeeze you out like some bully at a country fair dance.
I...
I love her. She...doesn't love me, I know, but I'm speaking plainly, like you did.

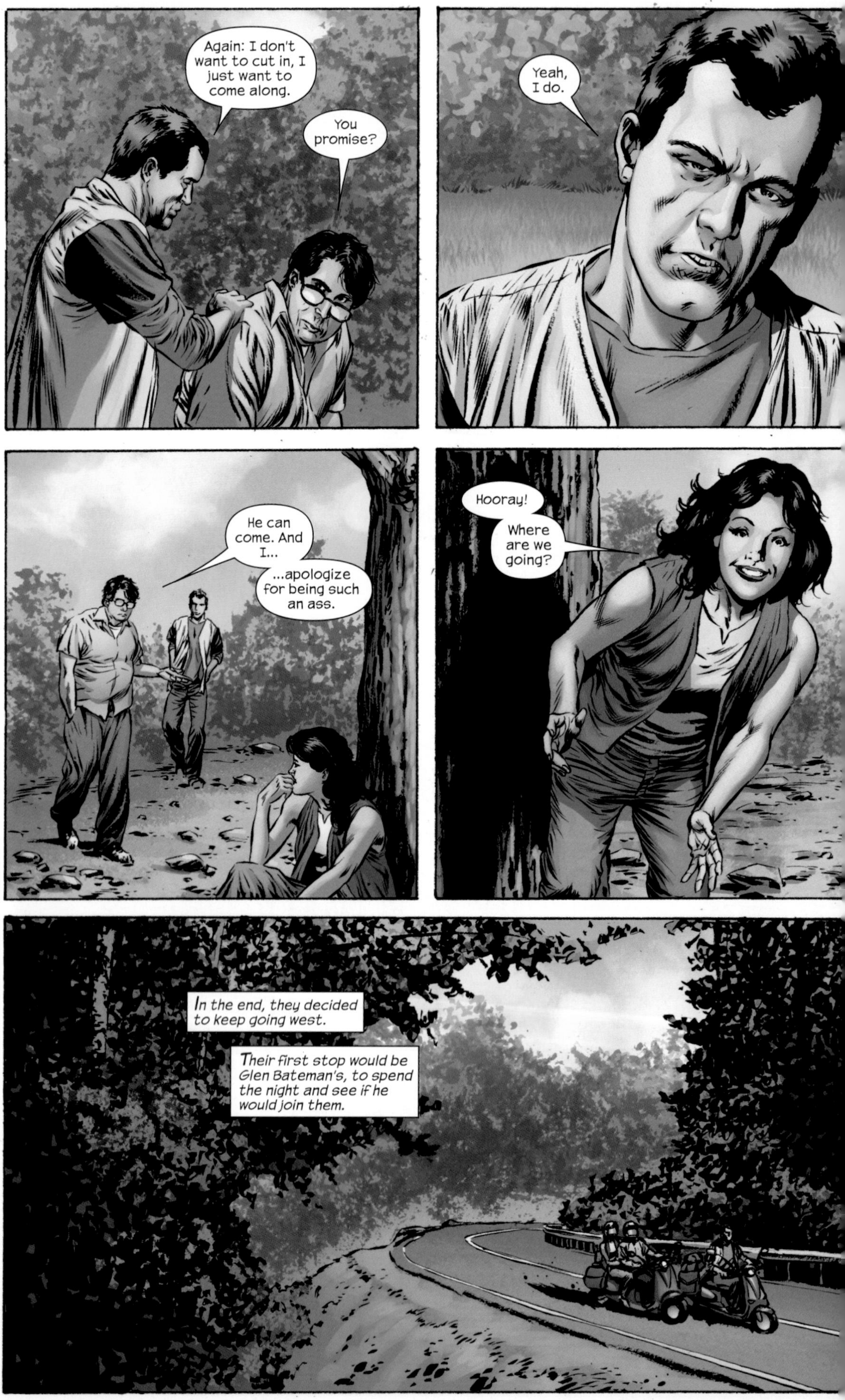
Again: I don't want to cut in, I just want to come along.
You promise?
Yeah, I do.
He can come. And I...
...apologize for being such an ass.
Hooray!
Where are we going?
In the end, they decided to keep going west.
Their first stop would be Glen Bateman's, to spend the night and see if he would join them.

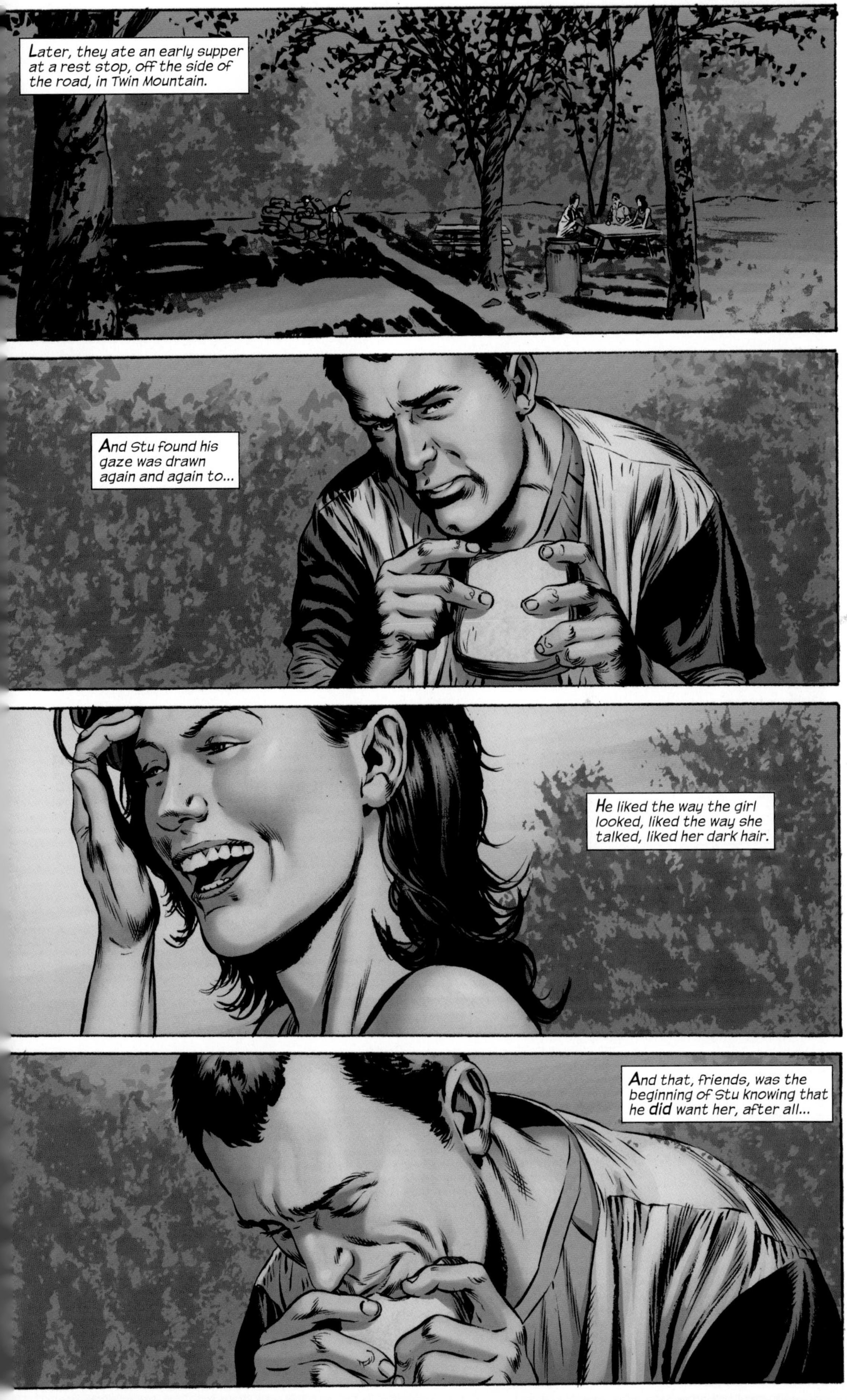
Later, they ate an early supper at a rest stop, off the side of the road, in Twin Mountain.
And Stu found his gaze was drawn again and again to...
He liked the way the girl looked, liked the way she talked, liked her dark hair.
And that, friends, was the beginning of Stu knowing that he **did** want her, after all...

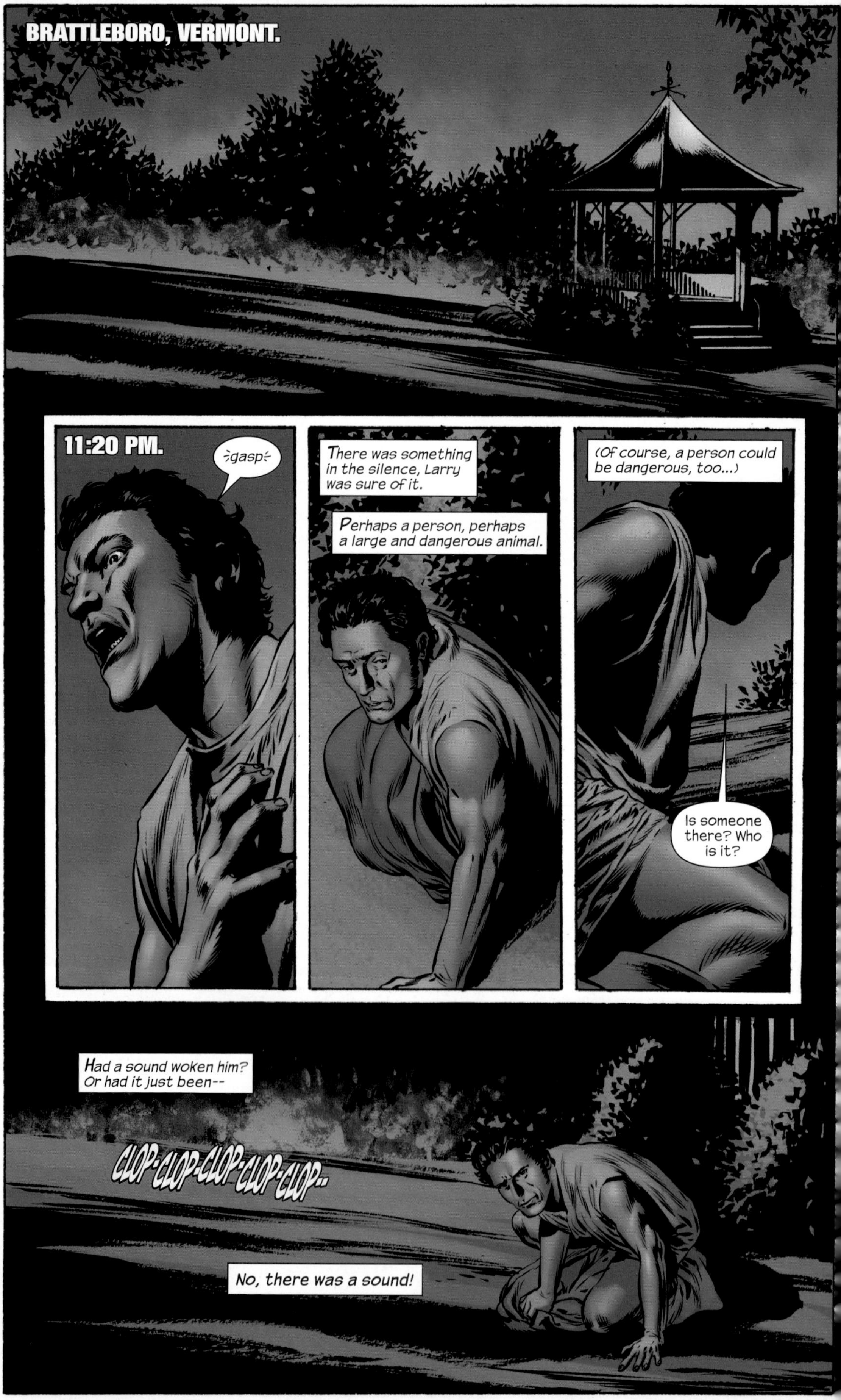
BRATTLEBORO, VERMONT.
11:20 PM.
gasp
There was something in the silence, Larry was sure of it.
Perhaps a person, perhaps a large and dangerous animal.
(Of course, a person could be dangerous, too...)
Is someone there? Who is it?
Had a sound woken him? Or had it just been--
CLOP-CLOP-CLOP-CLOP-CLOP--
No, there was a sound!

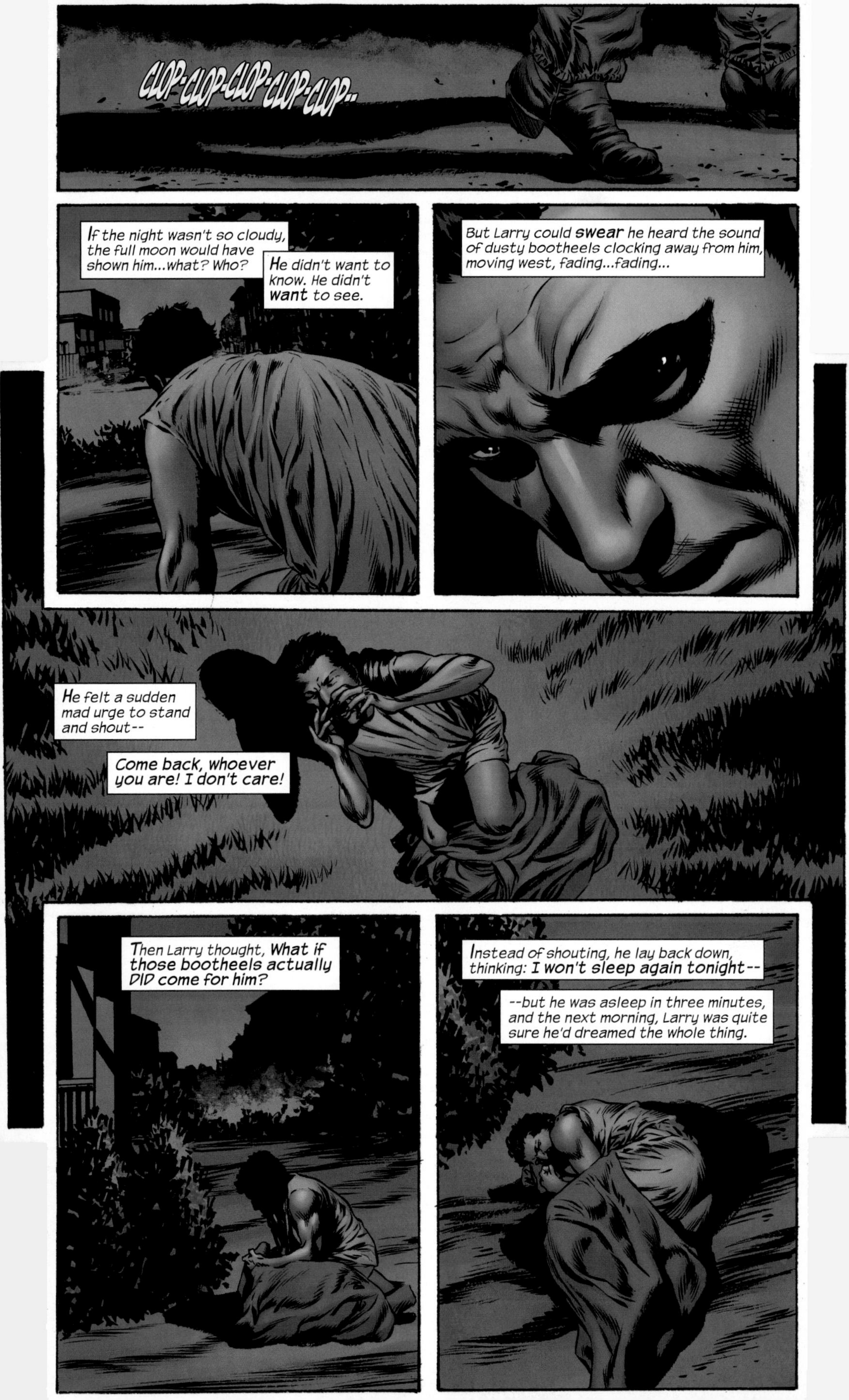

CLOP-CLOP-CLOP-CLOP-CLOP..
If the night wasn't so cloudy, the full moon would have shown him...what? Who?
He didn't want to know. He didn't want to see.
But Larry could swear he heard the sound of dusty bootheels clocking away from him, moving west, fading...fading...
He felt a sudden mad urge to stand and shout--
Come back, whoever you are! I don't care!
Then Larry thought, What if those bootheels actually DID come for him?
Instead of shouting, he lay back down, thinking: I won't sleep again tonight--
--but he was asleep in three minutes, and the next morning, Larry was quite sure he'd dreamed the whole thing.

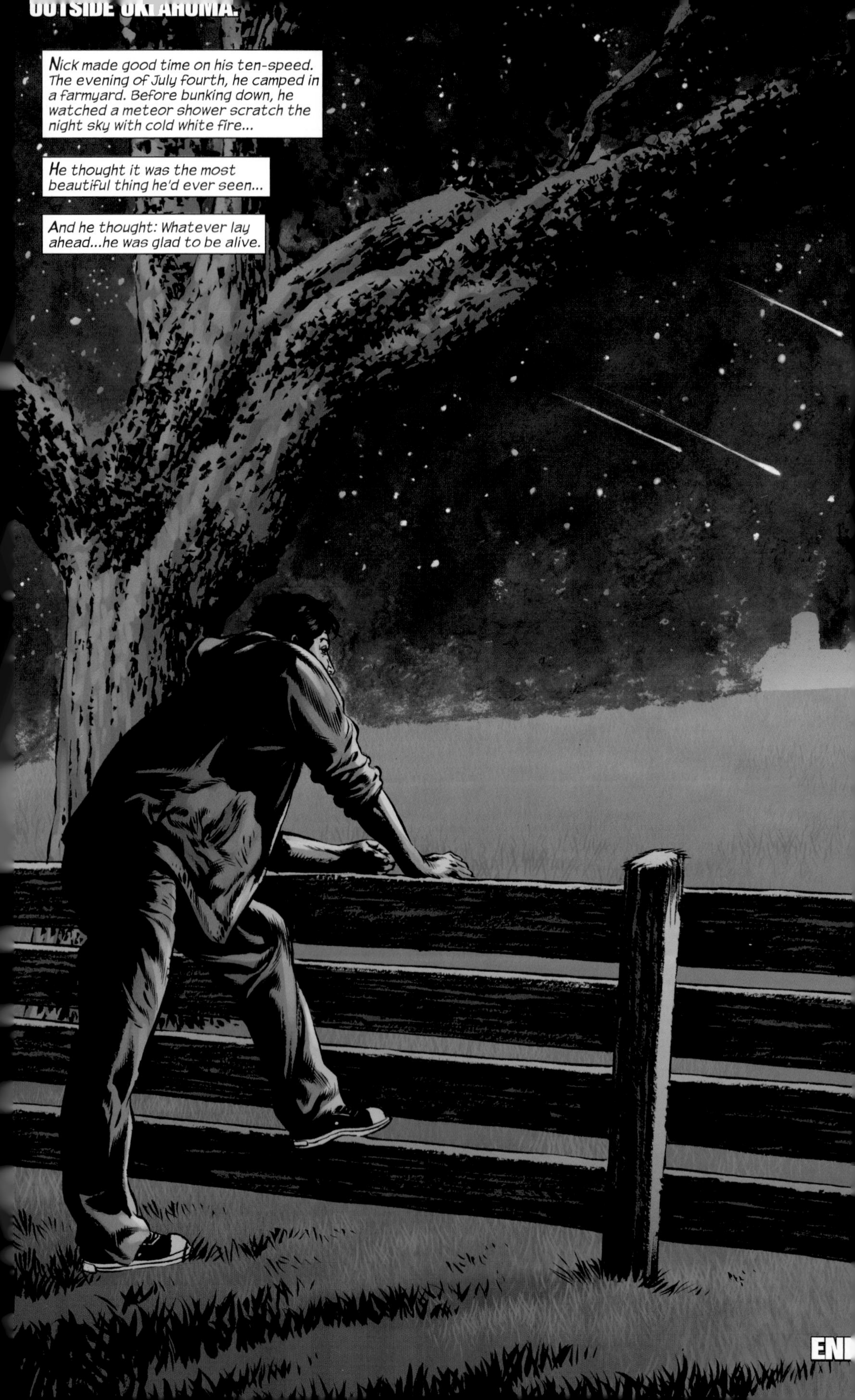
OUTSIDE OKLAHOMA.
Nick made good time on his ten-speed. The evening of July fourth, he camped in a farmyard. Before bunking down, he watched a meteor shower scratch the night sky with cold white fire...
He thought it was the most beautiful thing he'd ever seen...
And he thought: Whatever lay ahead...he was glad to be alive.

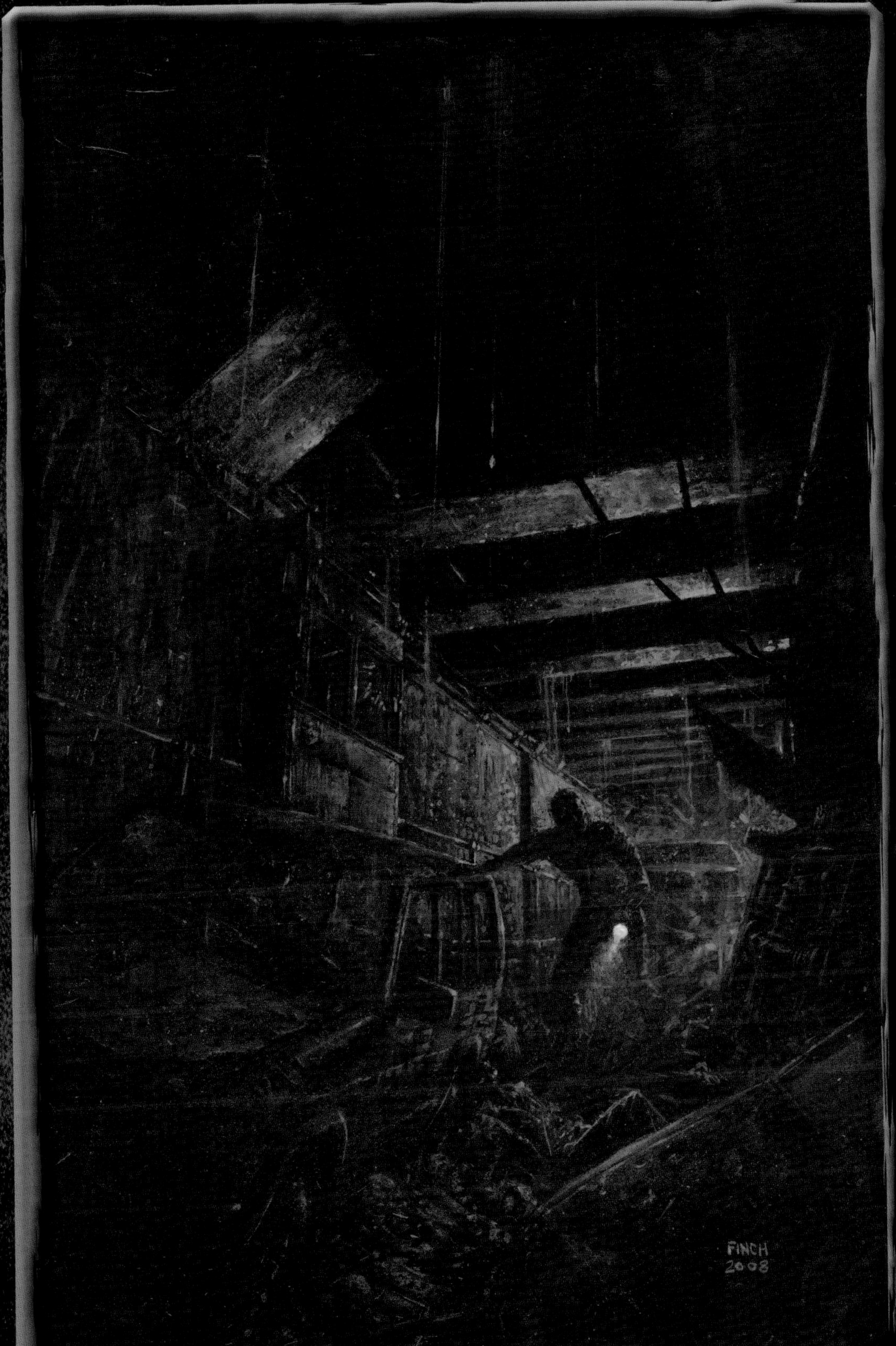
FINCH
2008

1 Lincoln Tunnel Variant
COVER BY DAVID FINCH

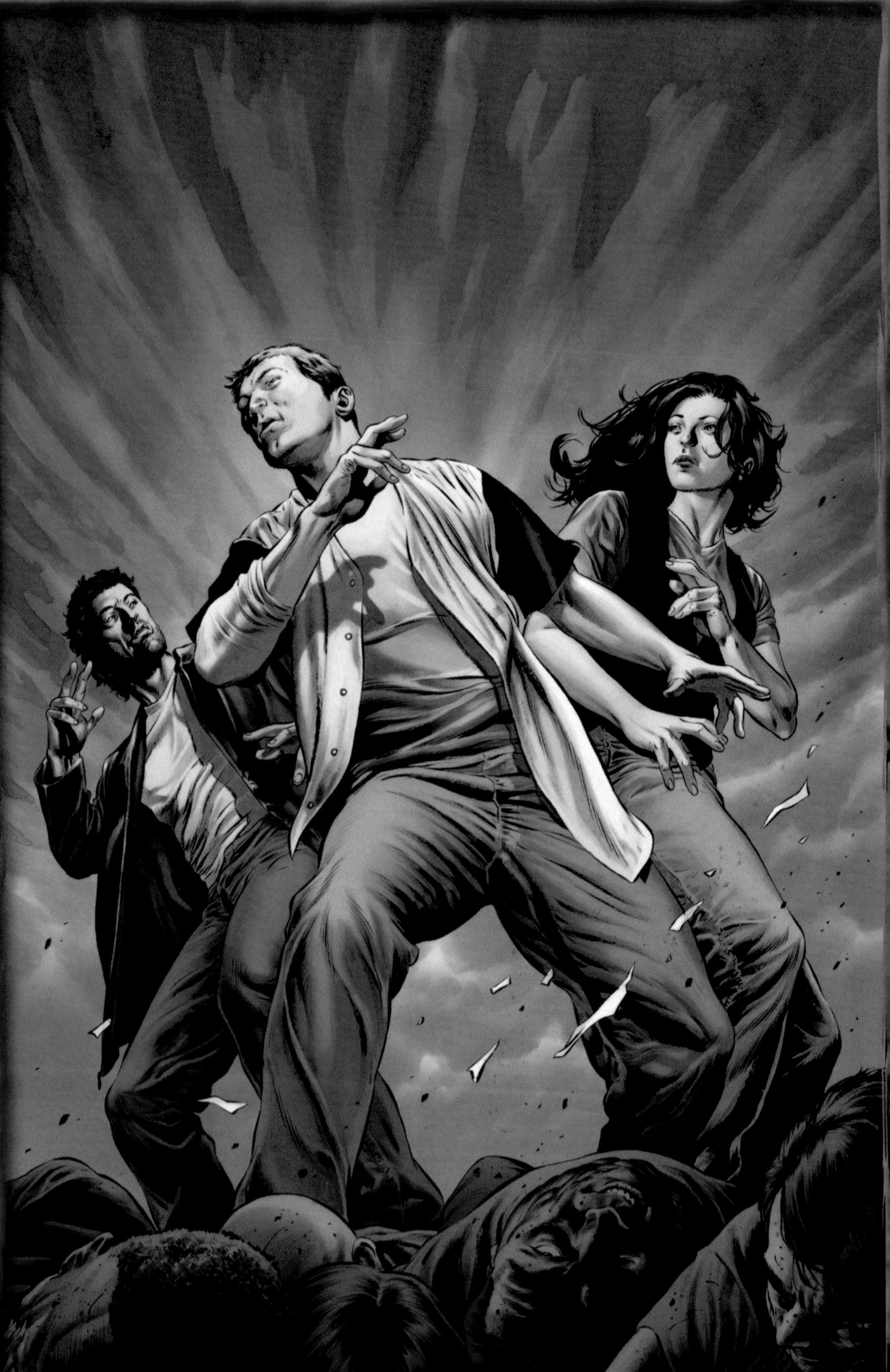

1

COVER BY MIKE PERKINS AND LAURA MARTIN

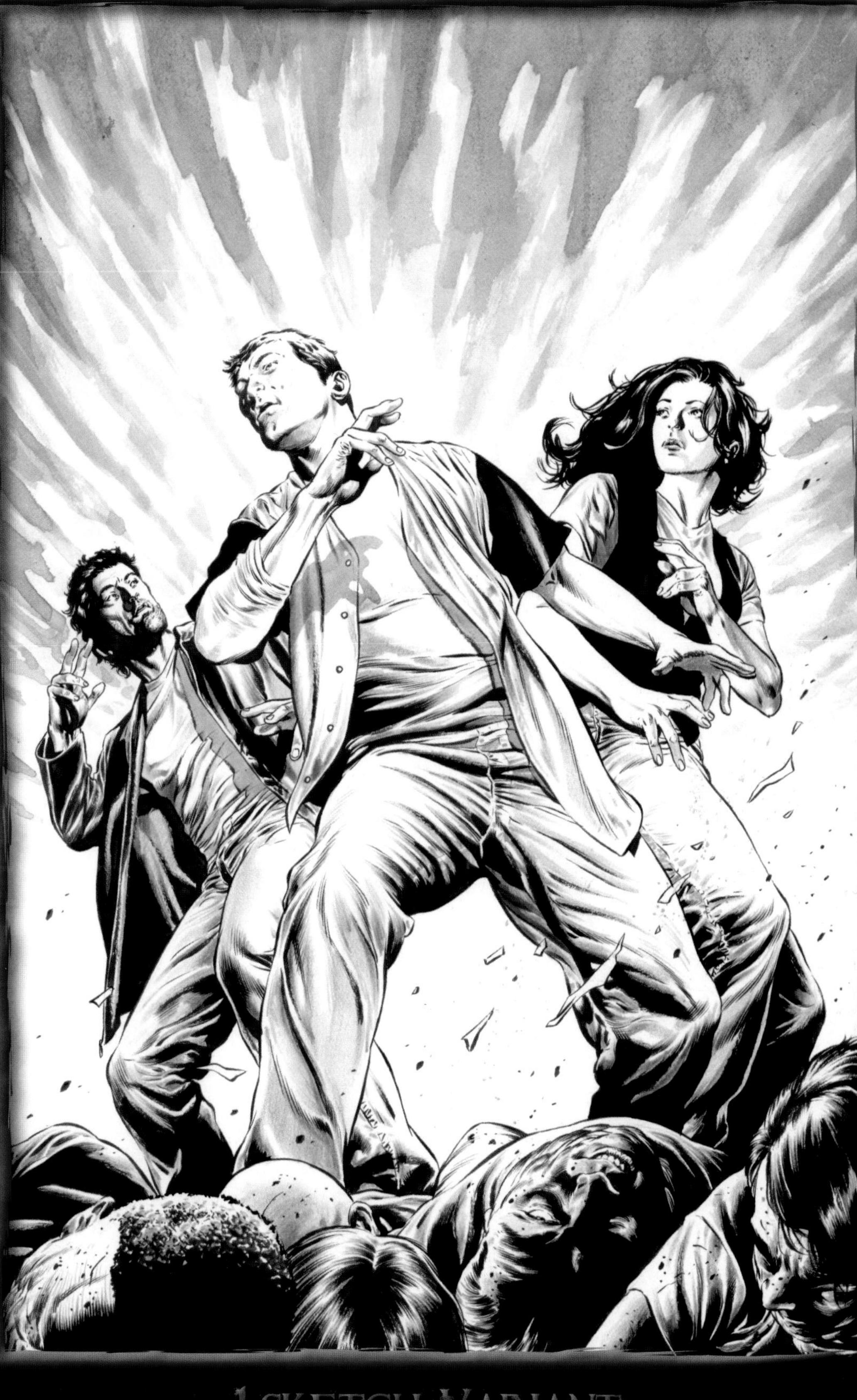

1 SKETCH VARIANT

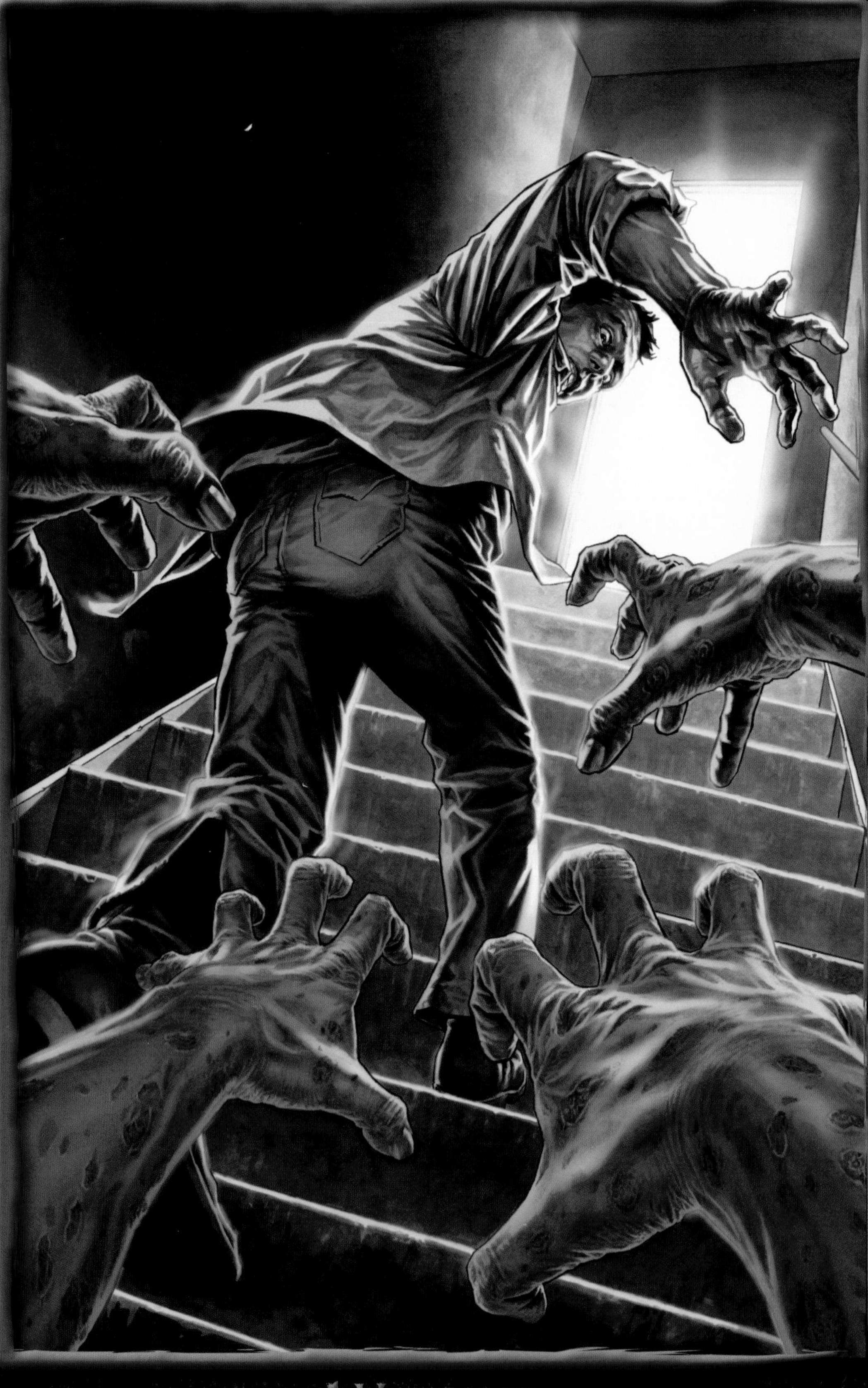

1 VARIANT

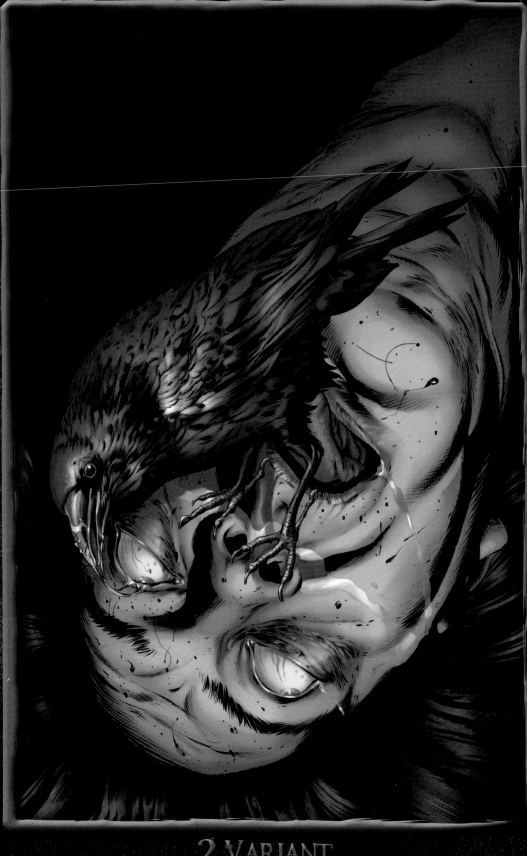

2 VARIANT
COVER BY MIKE PERKINS AND LAURA MARTIN

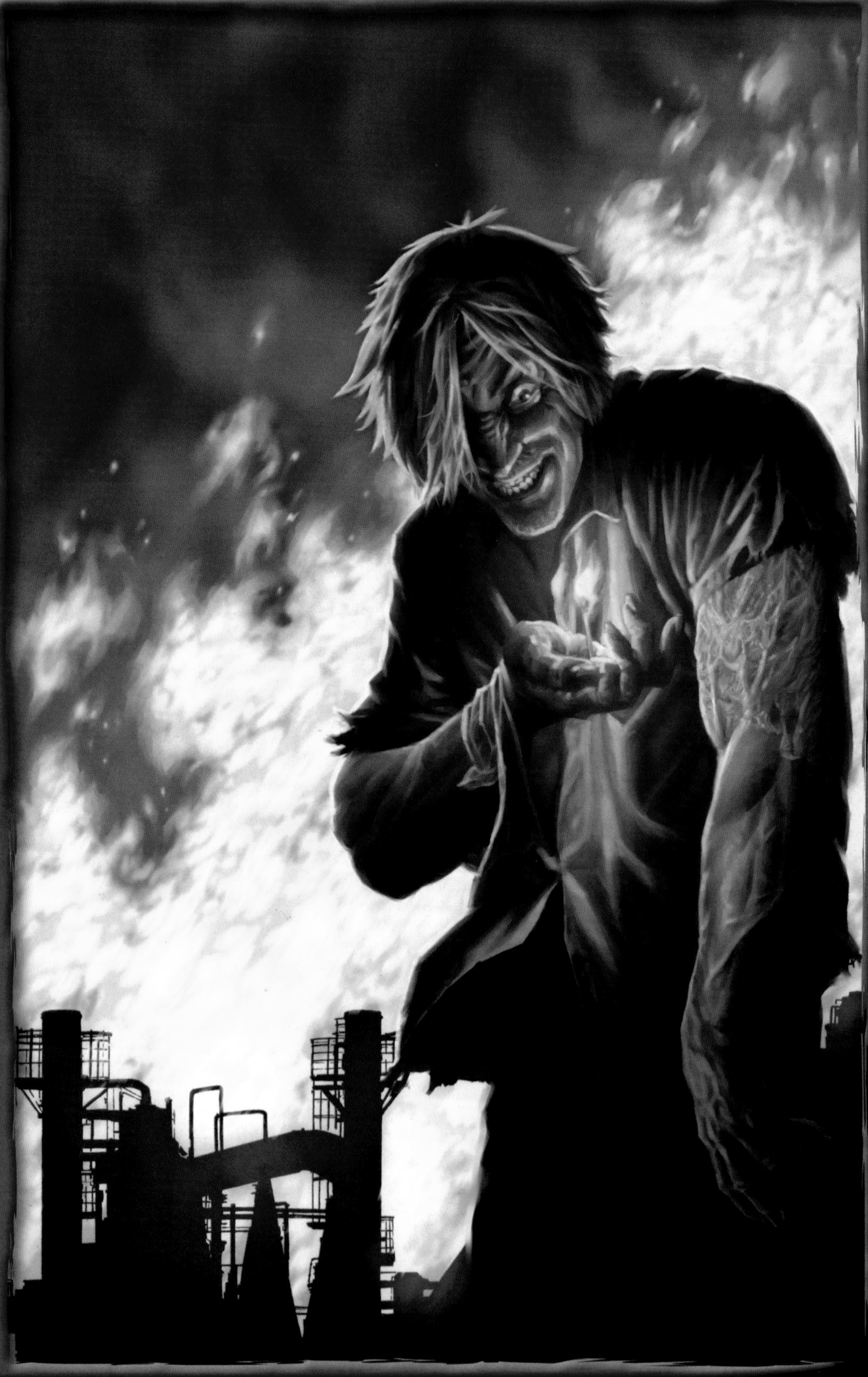

2

COVER BY LEE BERMEJO

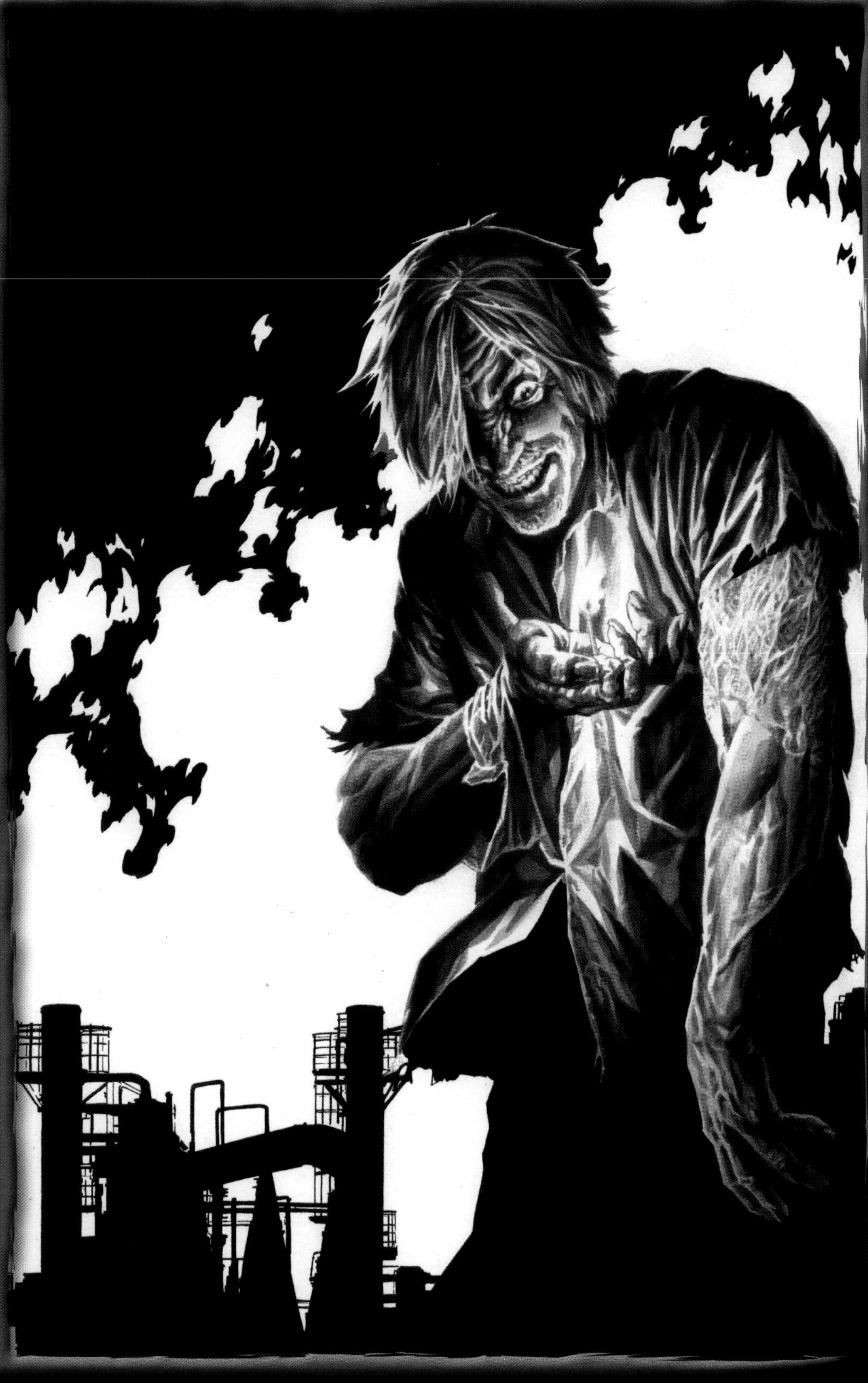

2 SKETCH VARIANT
COVER BY LEE BERMEJO

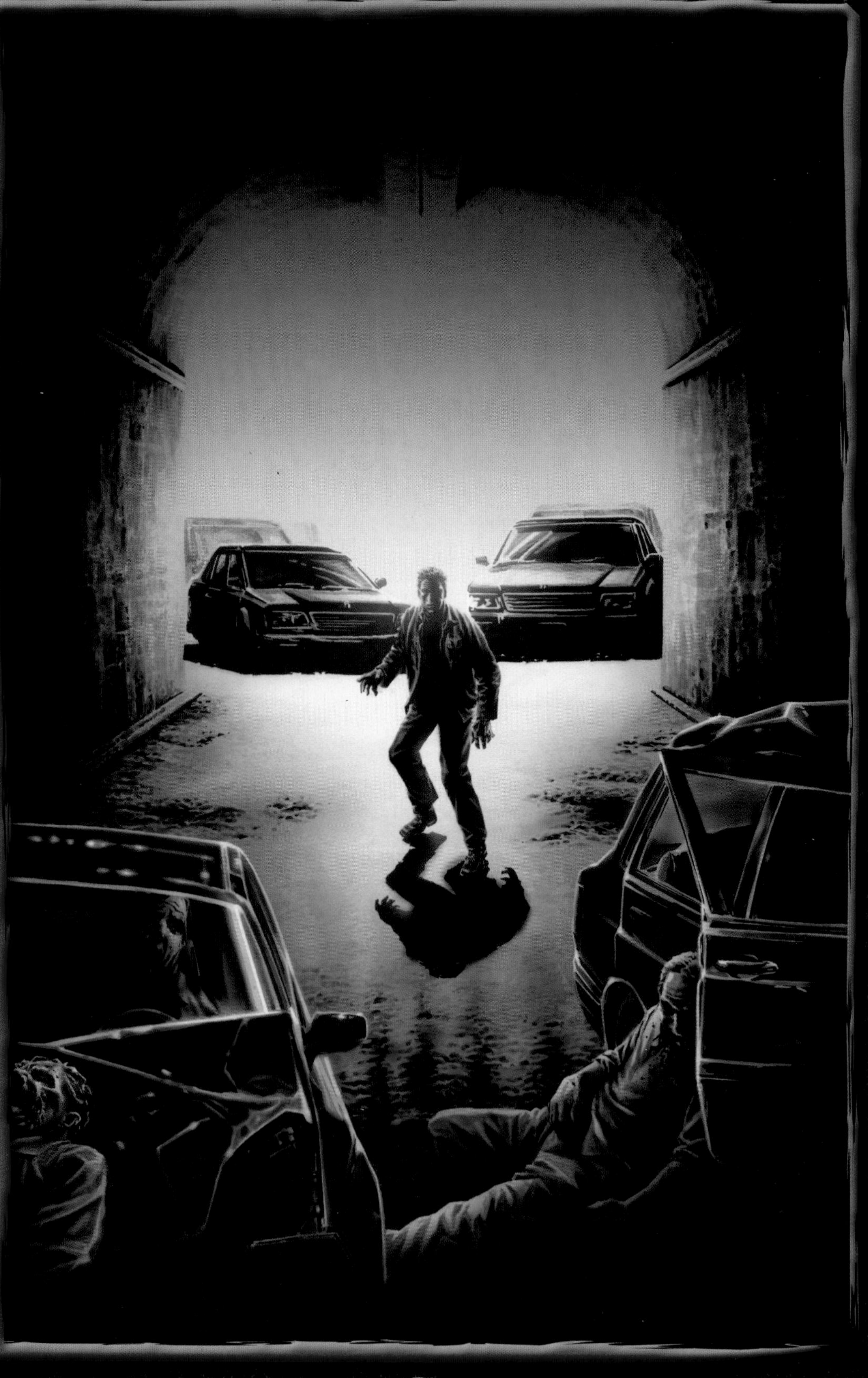

3

COVER BY LEE BERMEJO AND GRANT GOLEASH

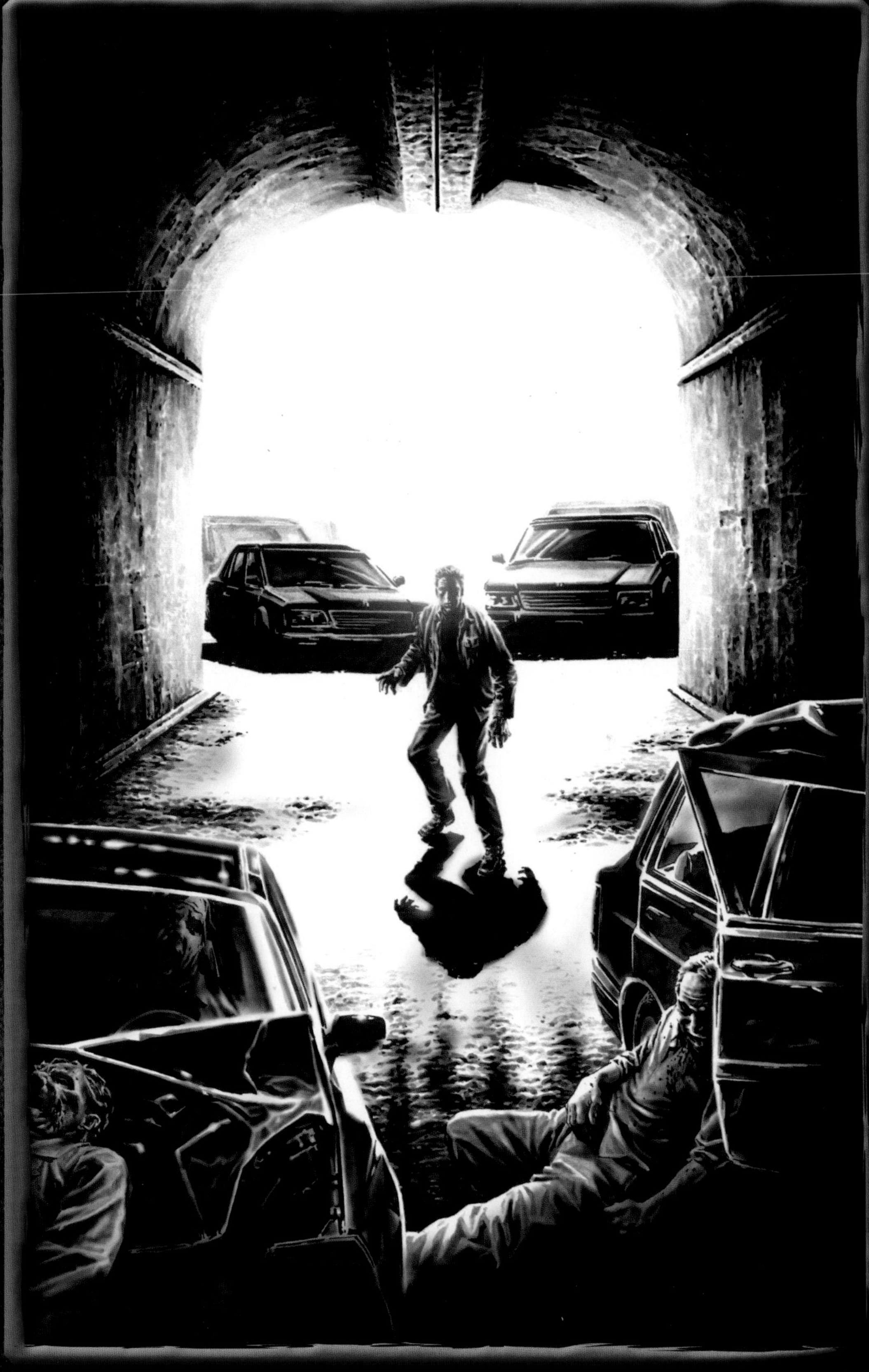

3 SKETCH VARIANT

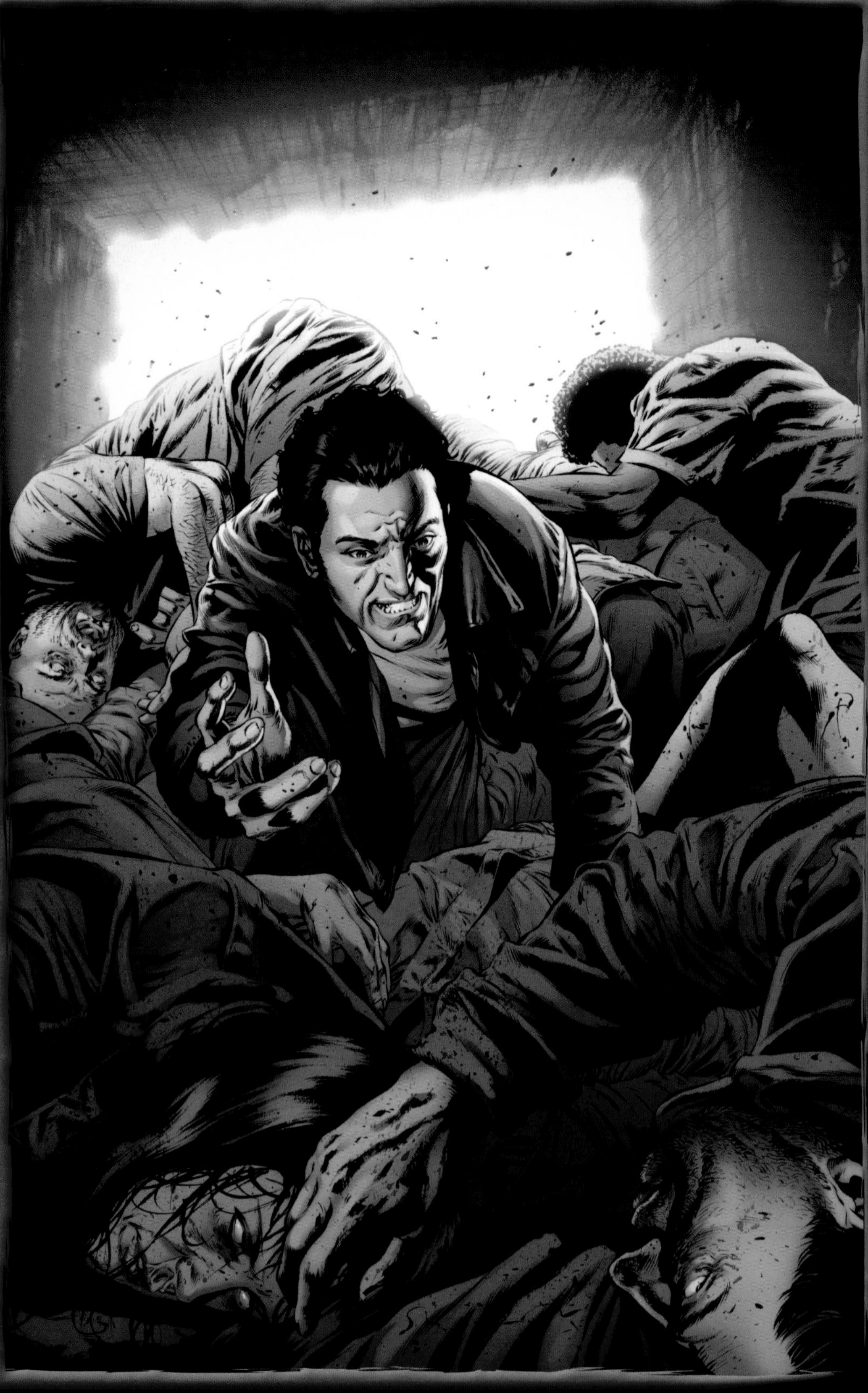

3 VARIANT
COVER BY MIKE PERKINS AND LAURA MARTIN

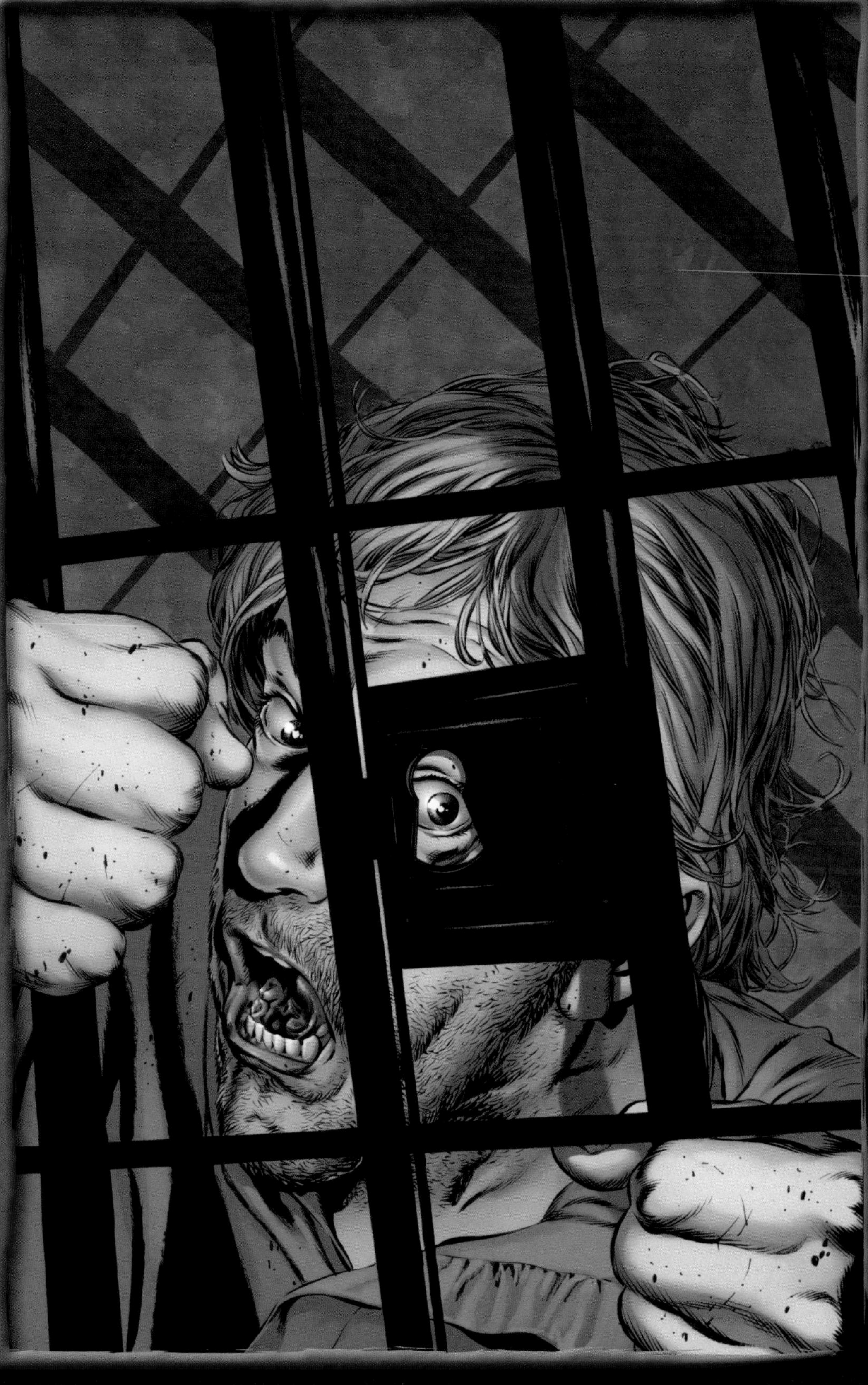

4 VARIANT

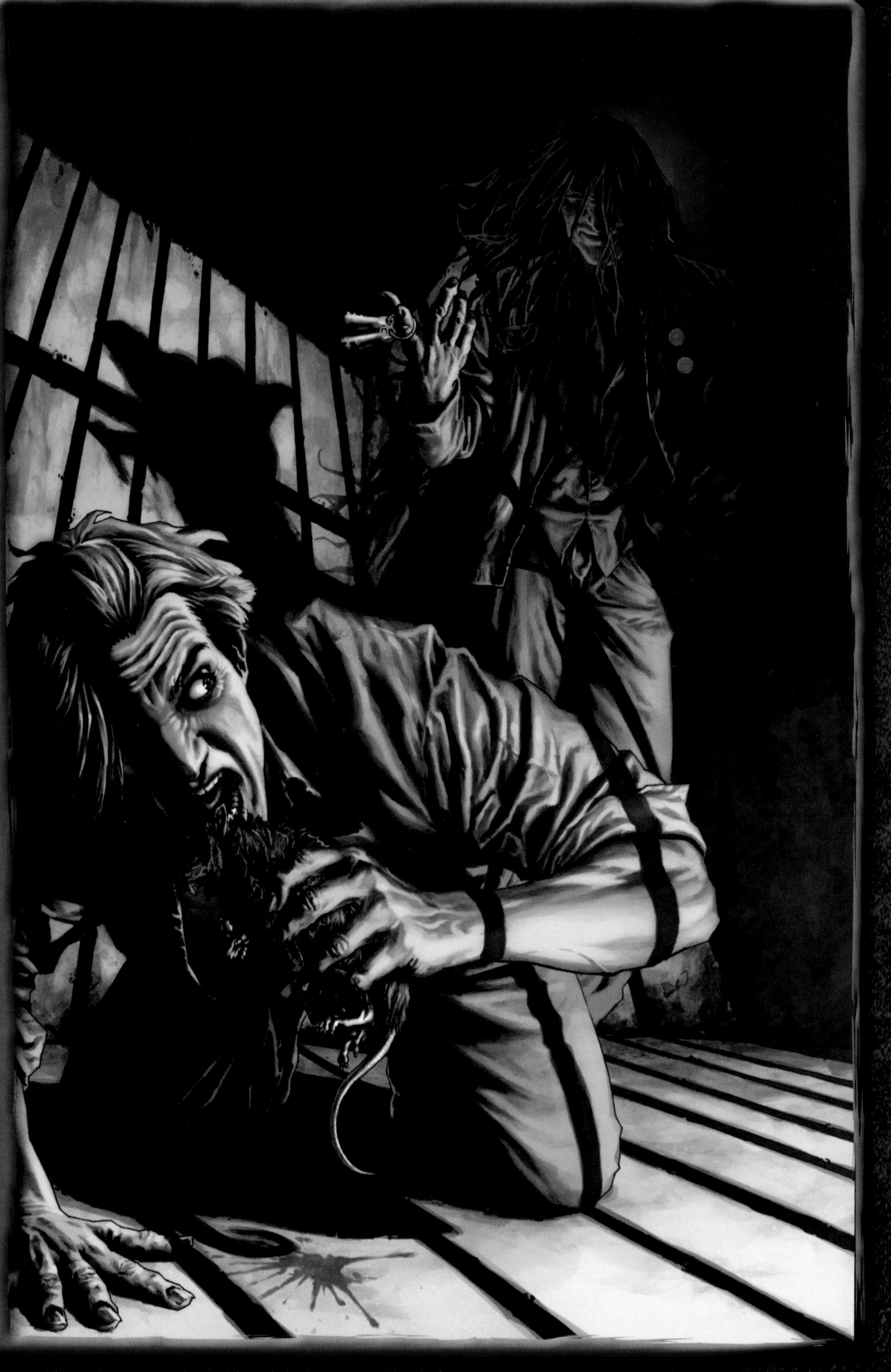

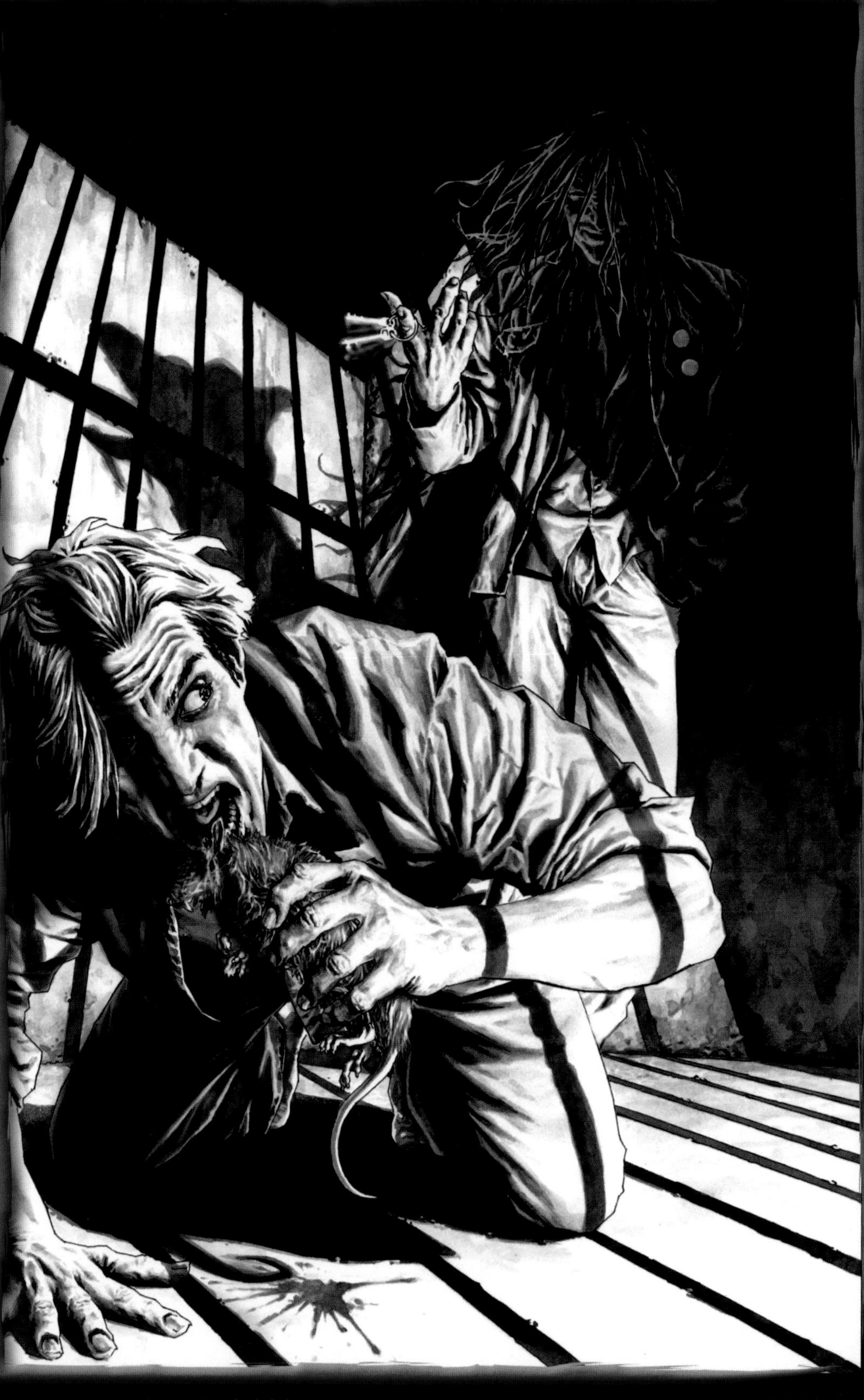

4 SKETCH VARIANT

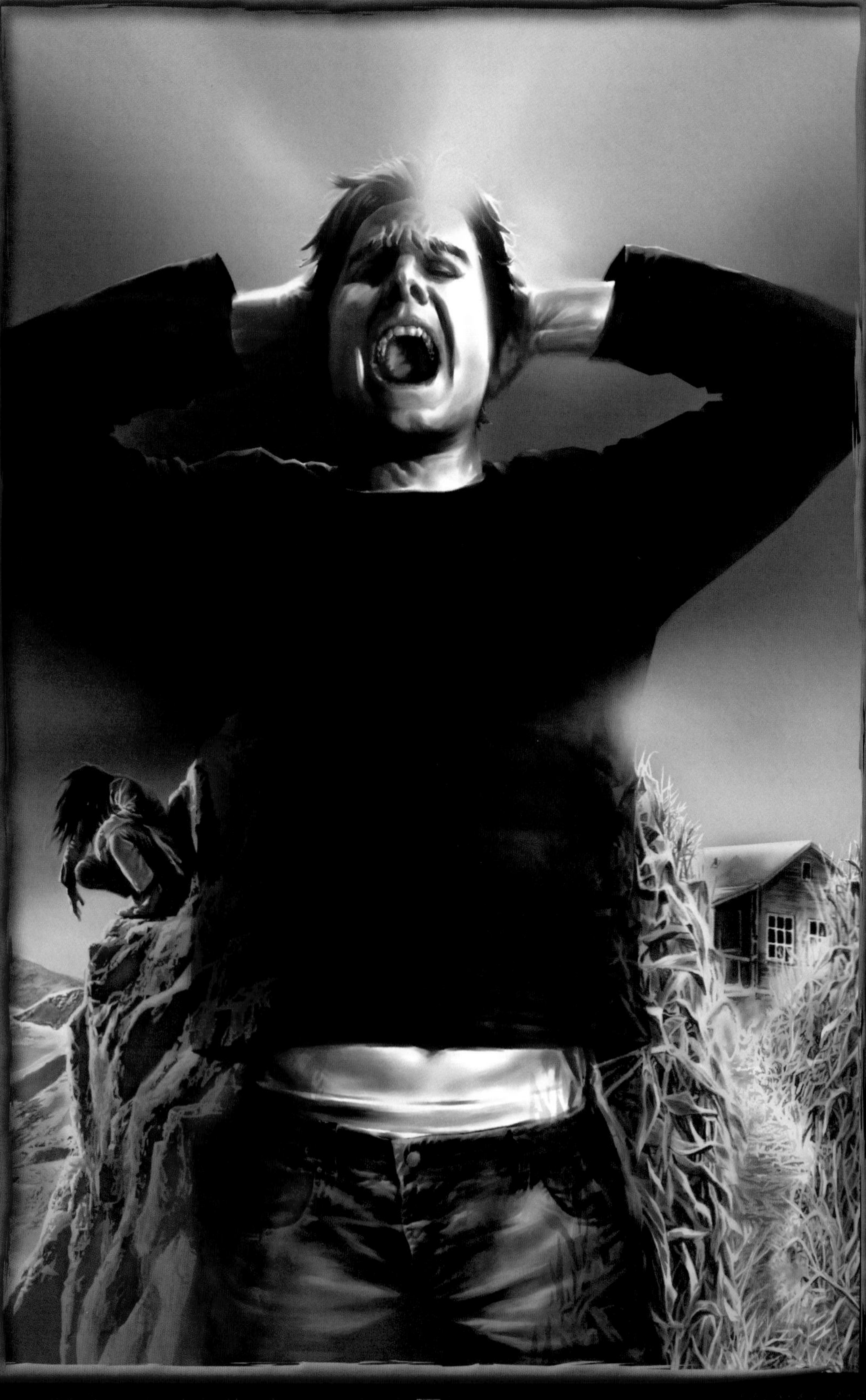

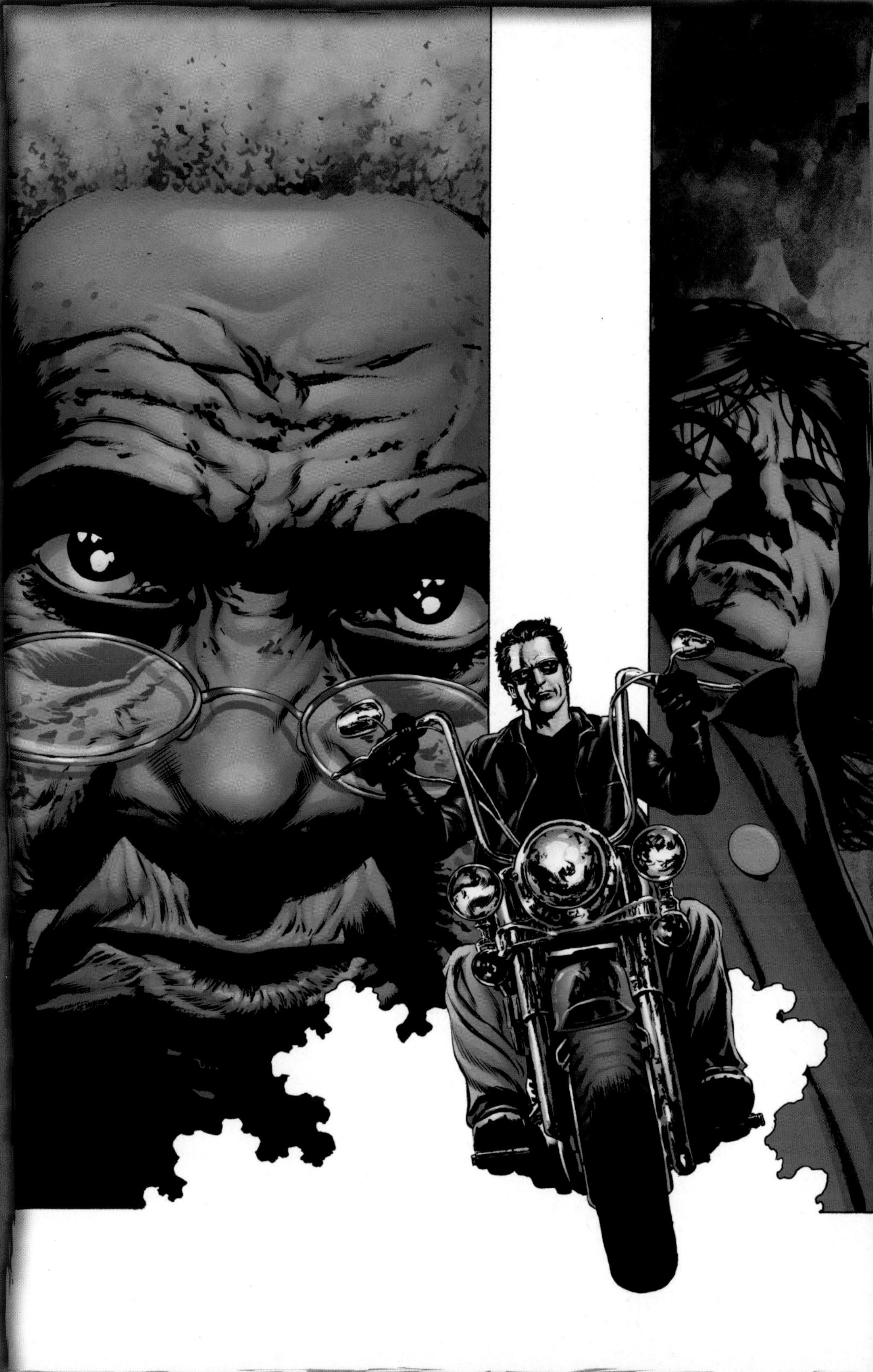

5 VARIANT

MIKE PERKINS ON INKING

When I'm approaching a page of comic book artwork I want it to be seen individually as a piece of illustration as well as a working part of an encompassing whole--this is one of the reasons I will add the gray tones to a page instead of leaving those decisions to the colorist.

For me, the gray tones on a page provide an added layer of depth, texture or atmosphere to a scene and, depending on what kind of mood I am trying to portray, my tools vary. I primarily add the gray tones utilizing three types of medium:

Gray ink wash (usually used for landscape depth or a gradual tone employing various shades of gray). This approach also provides a very smooth surface--a flat tonal area; the equivalent of a dead-line weight. I will also use the gray ink wash with other materials if I'm looking for a uniform texture.

If we take a look at the Central Park scenes with Larry and Rita, the majority of the trees in the background are illustrated, almost abstractly, by taking advantage of the texture of an organic sponge--dipped in the ink and then pressed repeatedly onto the artwork.

With the dream sequence involving Frannie and Flagg a similar process is used--but this time a harsher texture is appropriate--in this case an old terry-towel sock!

The final page of the issue needed a smoother texture for the night sky and for this I dipped a paper towel into the gray wash. The gradations are implemented one on top of the other by adding a little more black India ink between applications.

Along with the ink wash approach I will also use two differing gray pencils--one smoother in application than the other, depending on the texture needed. The smoother "Col-erase" pencil is ideal for skin tones as well as background elements and subtle shadows. The beefier "Prismacolor" pencil is the perfect tool for getting gritty with the artwork and I've used it a lot in the prison scenes.

In addition to these other tools, I will also avail myself of the vagaries of the brush and employ an inker's trick known as "drybrush." This is the process by which the vast majority of the ink is dried on the brush and then the brush is swept over the appropriate part of the panel in order to provide a variation in texture. It can offer a lot of diversification for an artist if approached with confidence.

THE FOLLOWING PAGES SHOWCASE THE ABOVE-MENTIONED
TECHNIQUES EMPLOYED BY PERKINS IN ILLUSTRATING THE STAND.

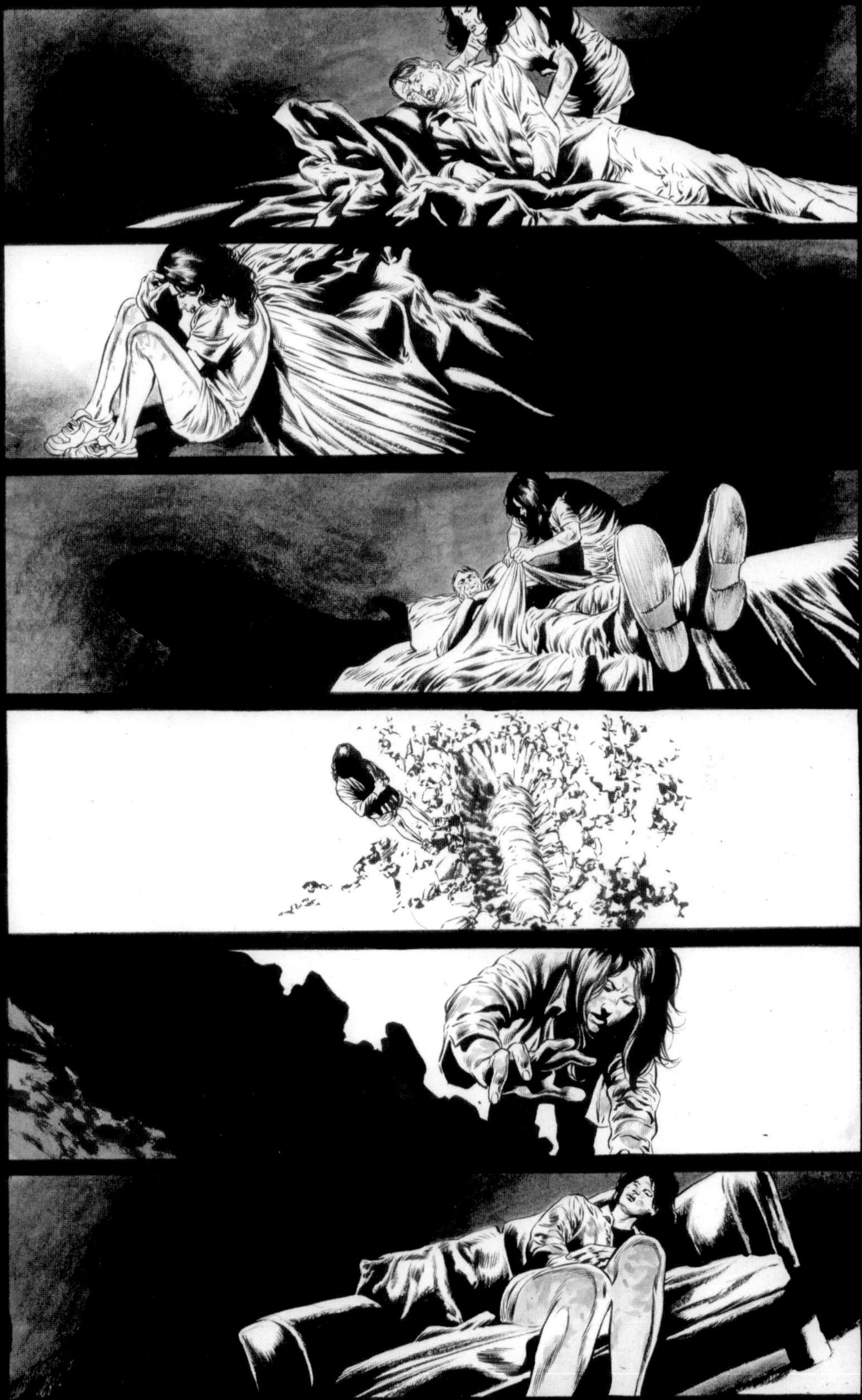

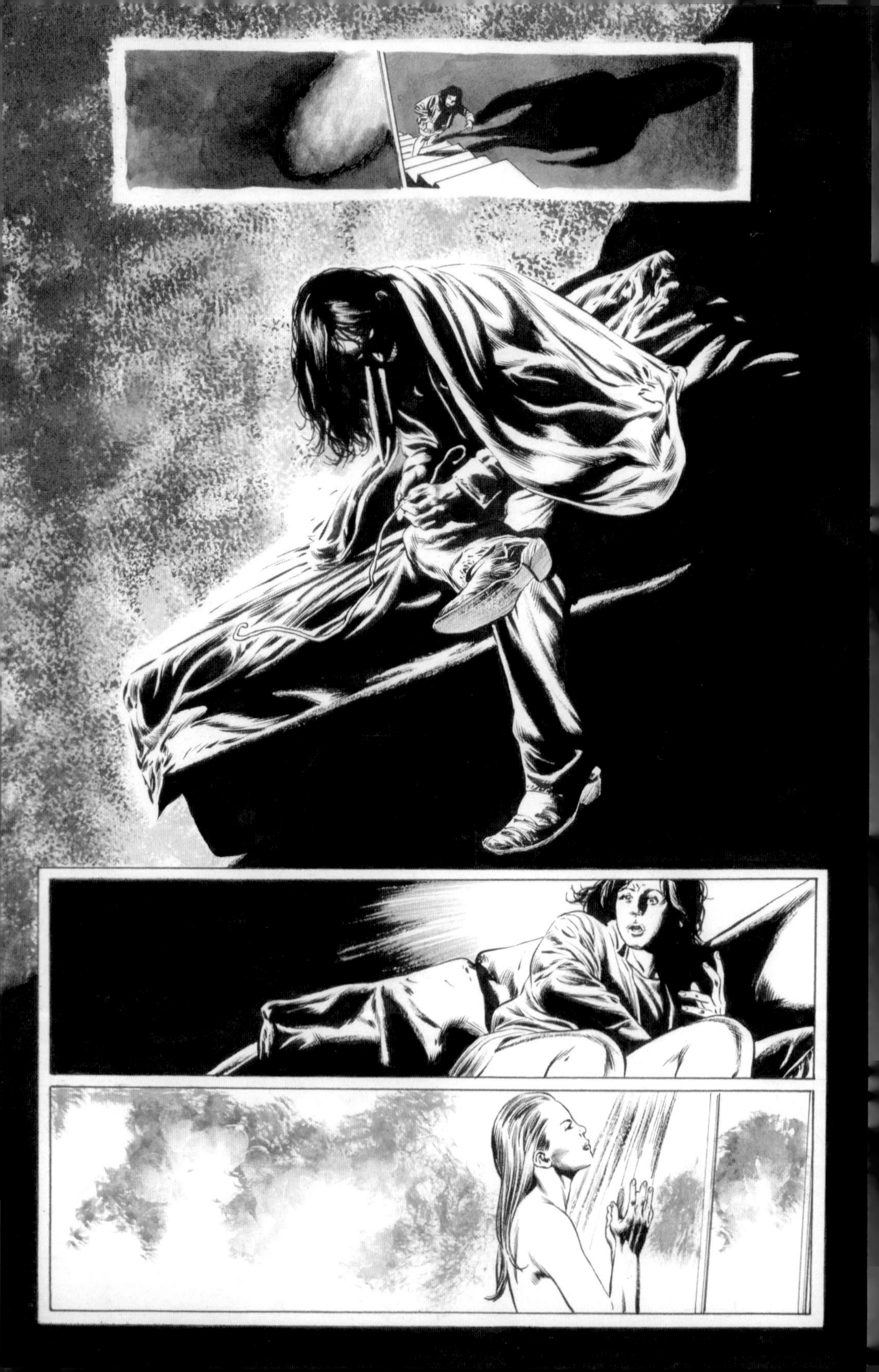

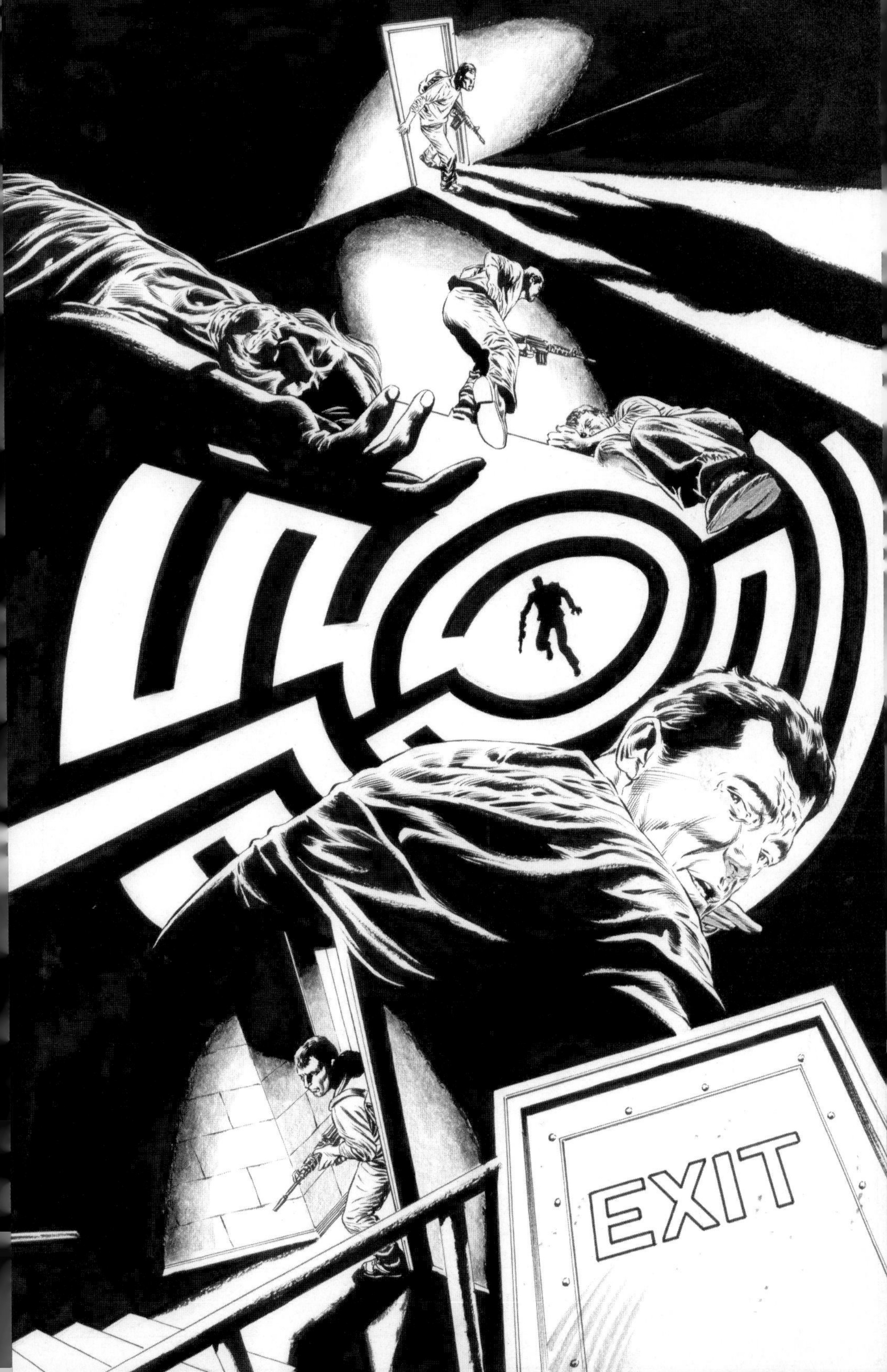
EXIT

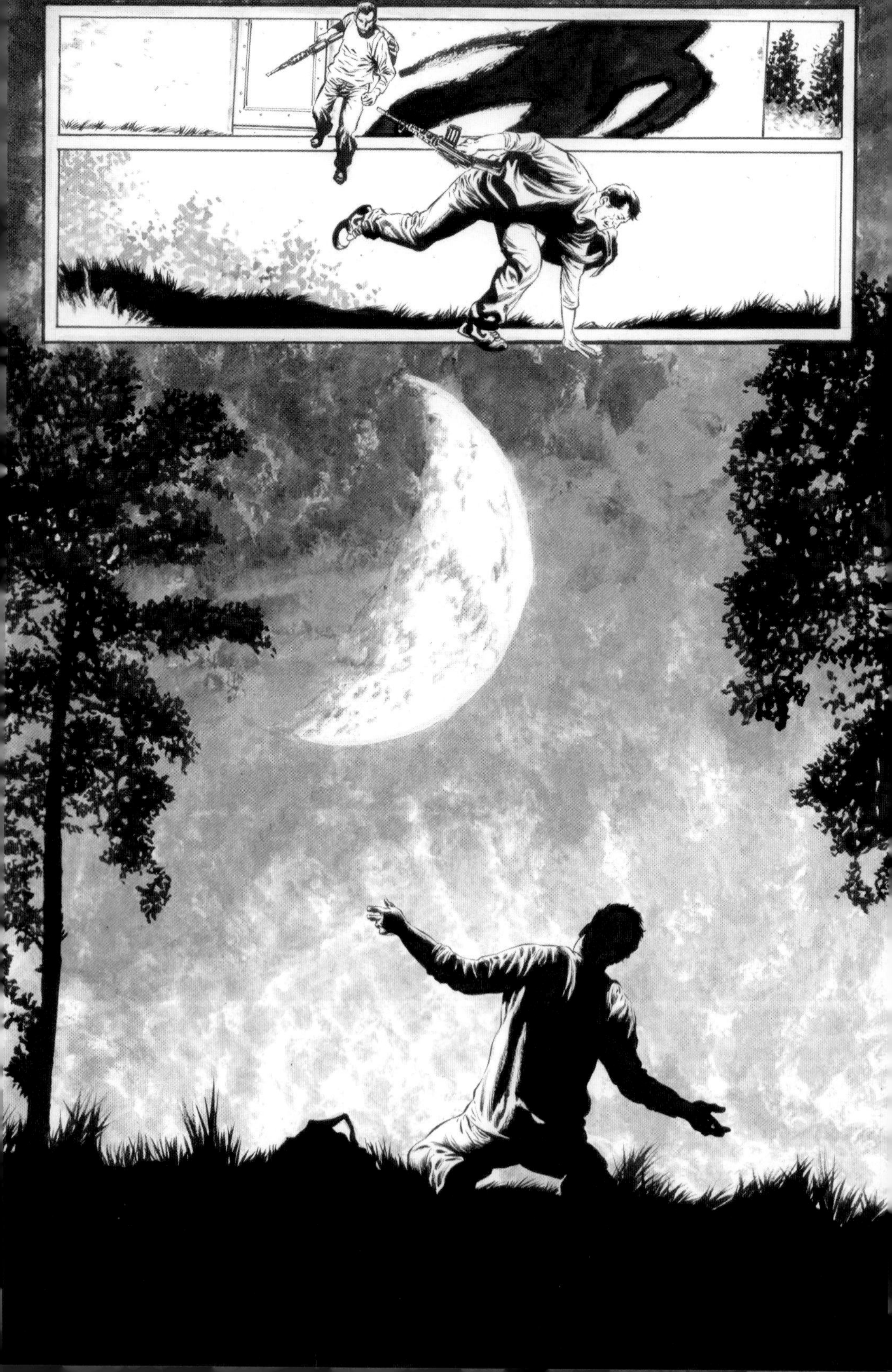

ESCAPE FROM NEW YORK

The Lincoln Tunnel scene and the walk through Manhattan beforehand are two of the most visceral scenes in the novel of The Stand. I knew I had to get these scenes spot-on with no guessing and assuming of settings ; this sequence had to be as realistic as possible and there was only ONE way to do that:

When I was in Manhattan for the New York ComicCon last year I made a point of re-tracing Larry's journey from Central Park, down Fifth Avenue, right on 39th Street and continuing on to the Lincoln Tunnel - making sure I took plenty of photographs along the way that I could use for exact reference. What made it even more poignant was when Bill Rosemann excitedly pointed out to me that Larry took his turn from Fifth Avenue right around the corner from the Marvel offices. I believe his words were " You see... it's destiny that Marvel is doing the adaptation of The Stand!!"

I believe this extra effort at authenticity has paid off - especially when you get the sense that this sequence is taking place in a real environment through the illustrations. Below are a few of the photographs alongside the resulting panel illustrations:

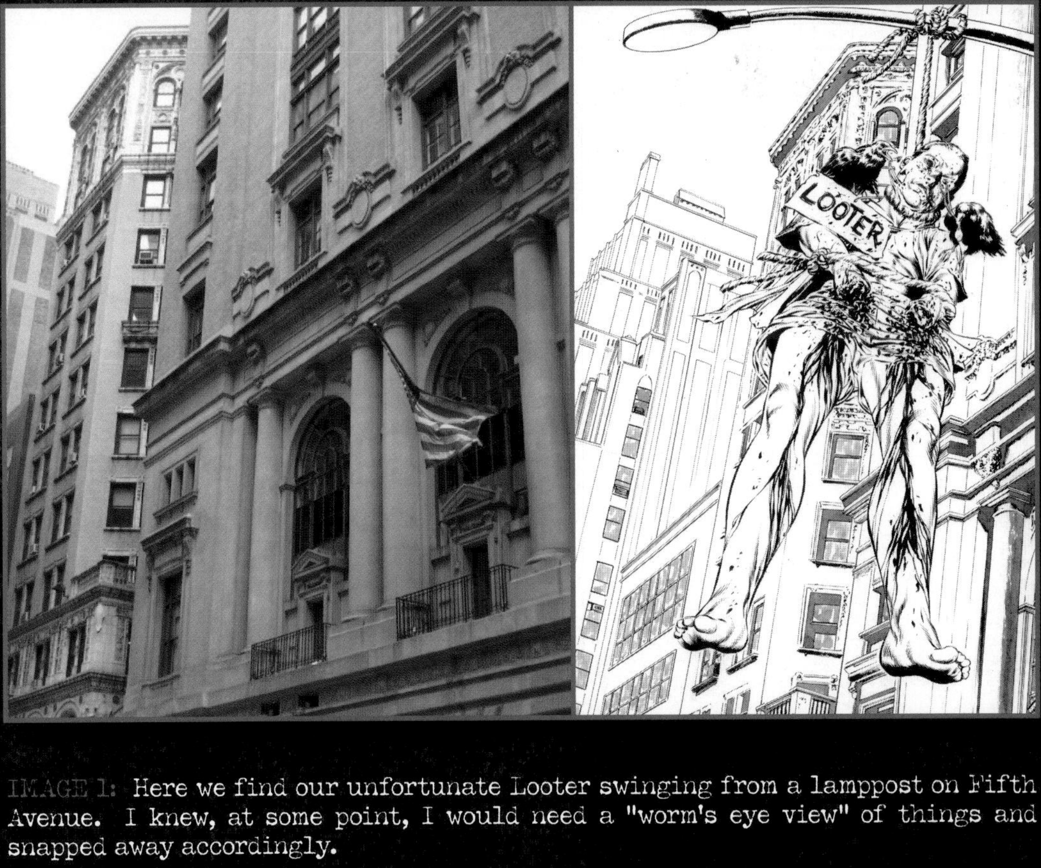
LOOTER

IMAGE 1: Here we find our unfortunate Looter swinging from a lamppost on Fifth Avenue. I knew, at some point, I would need a "worm's eye view" of things and snapped away accordingly.

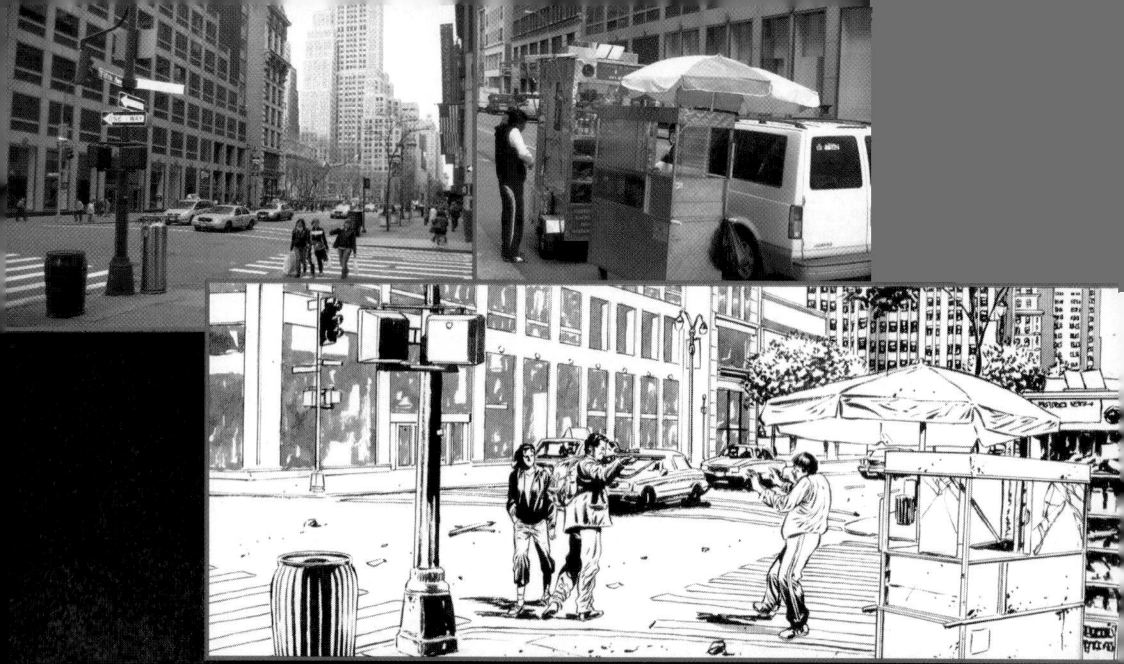

IMAGE 2: The point where Larry and Rita turn into 39th Street HAD to be exact - and yet I'v
attempted to set moments throughout the adaptation in the time frame of the unabridged versio
of the novel - at the beginning of the '90s (Thus, the disappearance of that eerie shiny caniste
thing by the crossing!). Admittedly, some of the shops and building work may not have been there
at the time but I guess I utilized the well-worn artistic license. Here I've combined two separate
elements from the photos: the street scene itself, and the ubiquitous New York hot dog stand.

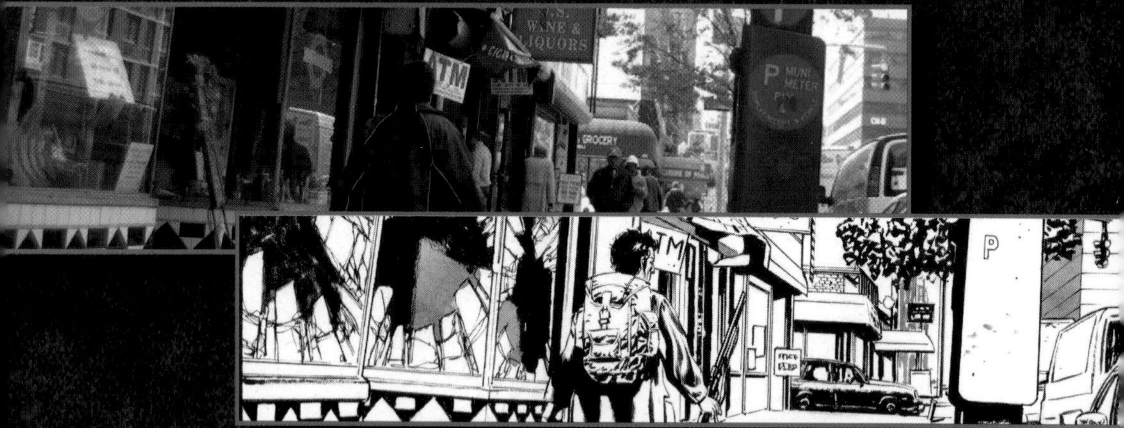

ATM
GROCERY
P
MUNI METER
ATM
P

IMAGES 3 and 4: New York street scenes can be notoriously hard to illustrate from memory. There
are too many elements in the real street environment for you to take in visually - this is where the
photo reference invariably helps (and simultaneously gives you more work in the long run!).

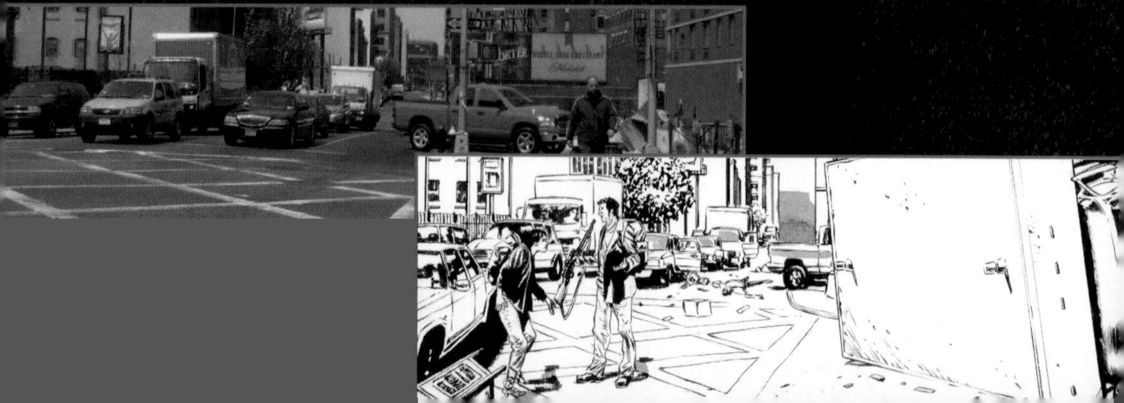

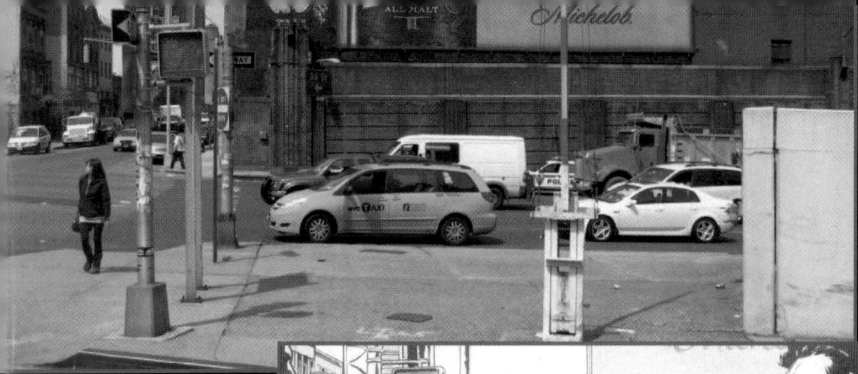
Michelob
ALL MALT

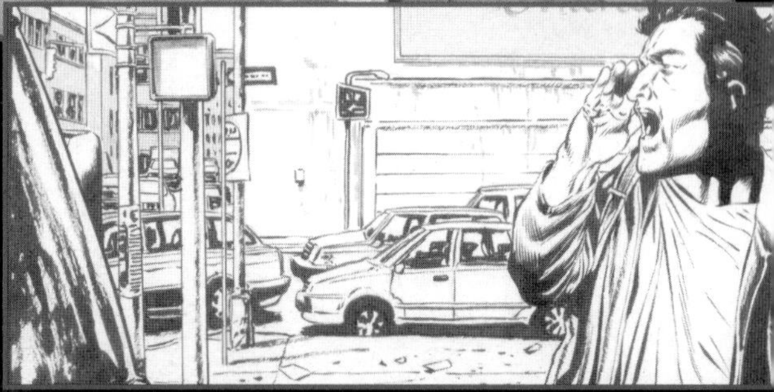

IMAGES 5 AND 6: I took many, many photos of the Lincoln Tunnel entrance
decay, grit and damage along the way). A lot of these images I used to por
of the variant covers for the first volume of The Stand - Captain Trips.
enough the need for me to get these settings exactly right and present
true vision of the events. I hope you feel it's worked out.

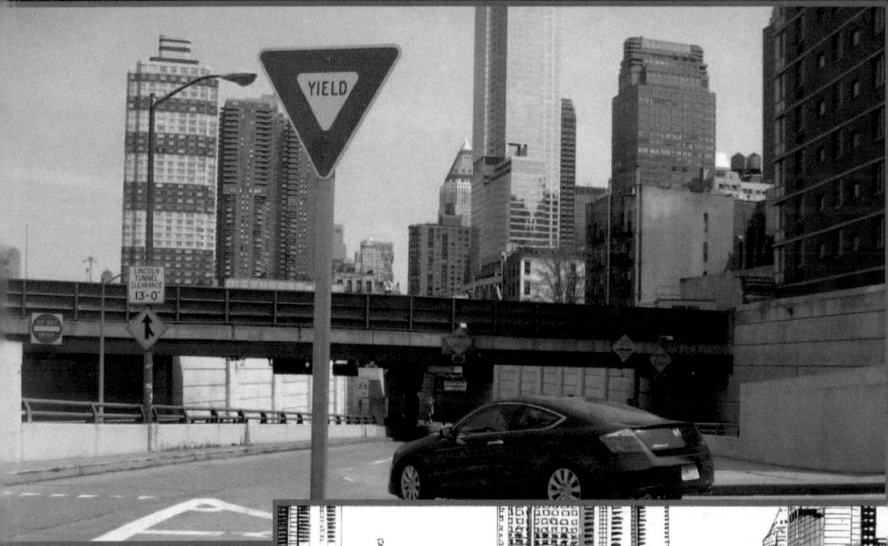
YIELD
LINCOLN TUNNEL CLEARANCE
13'-0"

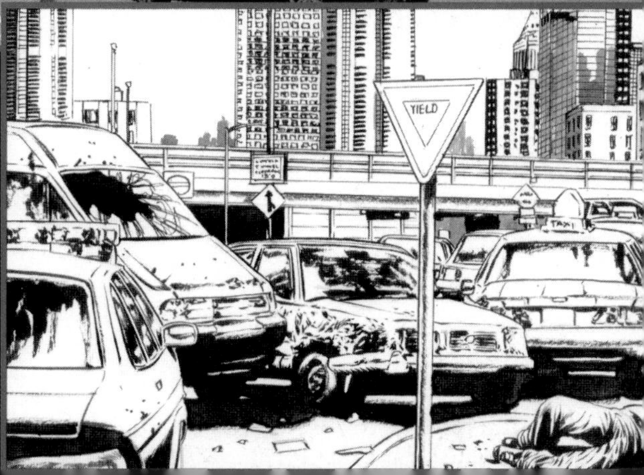
YIELD
TAXI

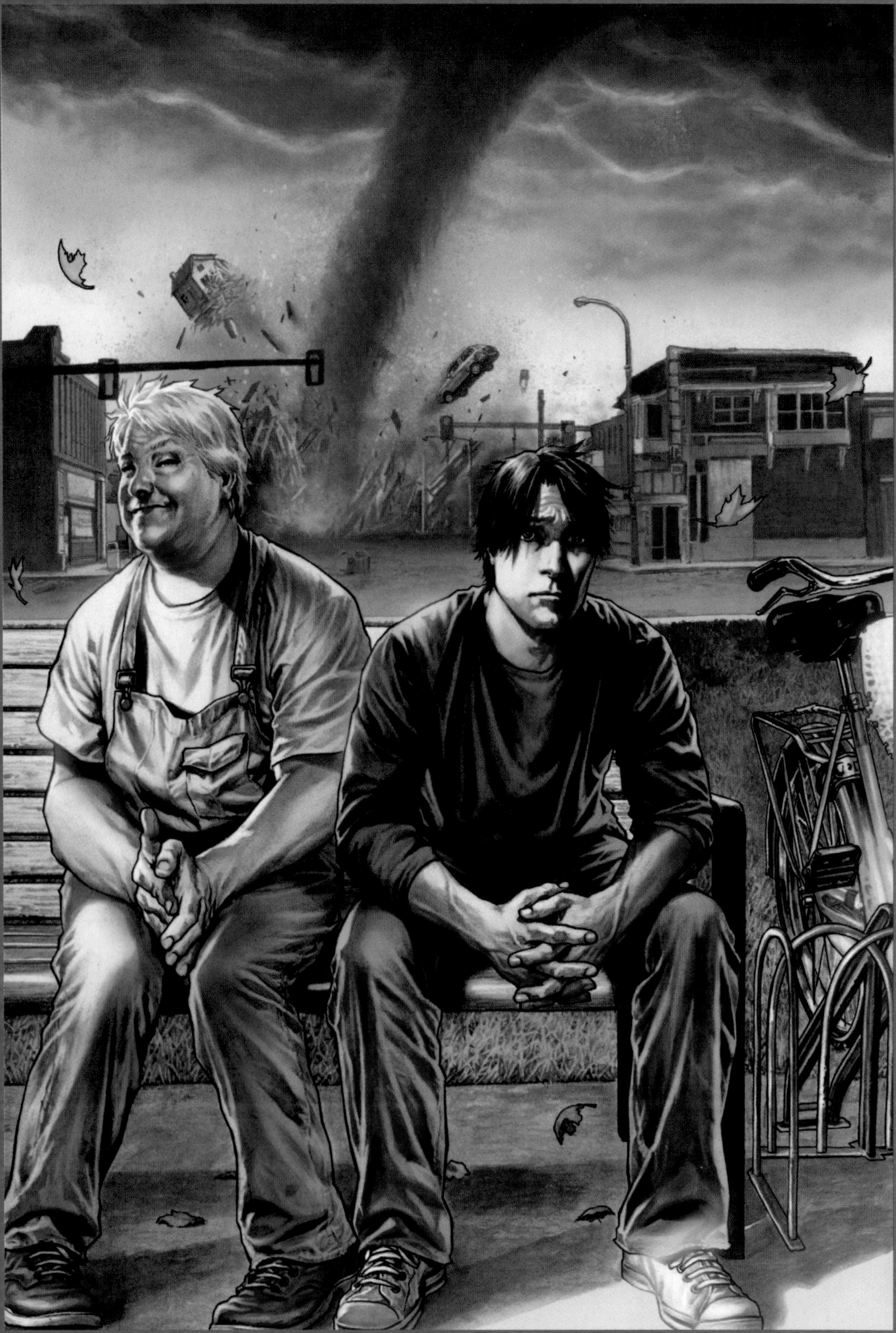